THE FLOATING
REPUBLIC

PEN & SWORD MILITARY CLASSICS

We hope you enjoy your Pen and Sword Military Classic. The series is designed to give readers quality military history at affordable prices. Pen and Sword Classics are available from all good bookshops. If you would like to keep in touch with further developments in the series, including information on the **Classics Club**, then please contact Pen and Sword at the address below.

Published Classics Titles

Forthcoming Titles

PEN AND SWORD BOOKS LTD

47 Church Street • Barnsley • South Yorkshire • S70 2AS

Tel: 01226 734555 • 734222

E-mail: enquiries@pen-and-sword.co.uk • **Website:** www.pen-and-sword.co.uk

THE FLOATING REPUBLIC

*An Account of the Mutinies at Spithead
and The Nore in 1797*

by

G. E. Manwaring

and

Bonamy Dobrée

PEN & SWORD MILITARY CLASSICS

First published in Great Britain in 1935 by Pelican Books.
Published in 2004, in this format, by
PEN & SWORD MILITARY CLASSICS
an imprint of
Pen & Sword Books Limited
47 Church Street
Barnsley
S. Yorkshire
S70 2AS

ISBN 1 84415 095 X

A CIP record for this book
is available from the British Library.

Printed and bound in Great Britain by
CPI UK

For a complete list of Pen & Sword titles please contact:
PEN & SWORD BOOKS LIMITED
47 Church Street, Barnsley, South Yorkshire, S70 2AS, England.
E-mail: enquiries@pen-and-sword.co.uk
Website: www.pen-and-sword.co.uk

"An attempt was made to give to the ships in mutiny
the name of 'The Floating Republic'."

*From the Report of "The Committee of
Secrecy", 1799.*

PREFACE

THE naval mutiny of 1797 is the most astonishing recorded in our, or perhaps any history; astonishing by its management rather than for its results, for other mutinies have been successful. Though a thoroughgoing and alarming mutiny, which shook the country from end to end since it occurred in the middle of a war, in one part at least it was ordered with rigid discipline, a respect for officers, and unswerving loyalty to the King. If throughout its course it was sensationally dramatic, marked by swift changes, halts, and rebounds, and in many ways mysterious, in its chief manifestation it never overstepped the bounds it had set itself in the beginning. Moreover, it was so rationally grounded that it not only achieved its immediate end, the betterment of the sailors' lot, but also began a new and lasting epoch in naval administration. Thus besides being a part of Naval History, it also forms a chapter in Social History, a queer, poignant, naked-nerved chapter, which even at the present day contains lessons that have never been properly learnt.

There are some admirable short sketches of this curious event in Mr. Tunstall's *Flights of Naval Genius*, in Stanhope's *Life of Pitt*, besides succinct pages in Brenton's *Naval History*, or Mr. Hannay's *Short History of the Royal Navy*, and in other places; and two full-length studies. The first is by William Johnson Neale, a distinguished lawyer who had once been a sailor, and who published his *History of the Mutiny at Spithead and the Nore* in 1842. His account is good, though too emotional, and full of small inaccuracies. The other is the invaluable piece of research by Professor Conrad Gill, *The Naval Mutinies of 1797*, published in 1913. This will always be a mine of information (though not altogether free from inaccuracies—for who can completely avoid those?); but when he wrote the *Spencer Papers* had not been published. As a further excuse for this new study we may say that the documents available to Mr. Gill in common with ourselves have been somewhat differently selected, that we have used some which he passed by, and that we have discovered many others which throw an entirely new light on certain incidents and characters. Our main difference, however, is one of standpoint. Mr. Gill seems to have had less sympathy with the sailors than we have, and thus we have arrived at conclusions different from his, conclusions which we feel may be of use in approaching certain aspects of our day.

We would like to acknowledge, with much gratitude, our indebtedness to the officials of the Public Record Office and of the London Library; to Mr. J. G. Bullocke, of the Royal Naval College, Greenwich; the Council of the Navy Records Society; the Trustees of the National Maritime Museum, Greenwich; the Rev. J. A. Goundry, of St. Mary Major, Exeter; Captain W. R. Chaplin, one of the Elder Brethren of Trinity House; Captain J. H. Godfrey, R.N.; and Mr. N. J. O'Conor; all of whom have put information at our disposal.

G. E. M.
B. D.

CONTENTS

PART I.—"THE BREEZE AT SPITHEAD"

PART II.—"THE FLOATING REPUBLIC"
THE NORE

CONTENTS

APPENDICES

PART ONE

THE BREEZE AT SPITHEAD

CHAPTER I

THE BOLT FROM THE BLUE

ENGLAND at the beginning of 1797 was weighed down by war-weariness. The spirits of men sagged, and everything that happened was either shot with stridency or muffled in a blanket of depression. At the beginning of the war, in 1793, France had been ringed round by the Allies—England, Spain, Holland and the Empire—and even some of the French had been on the English side; but the war had brought disillusion, alarms of defeat and universal republicanism, with the usual result of rasped nerves. The French had rallied to drive the English first from Toulon, and then out of the Mediterranean; Spain and Holland had knuckled under, and, worse still, had turned their coats and become allies of the French! As for the Empire, its outer province, Belgium, was now in the enemy's hands, and, in spite of the wealth poured into Vienna from the pockets of the English taxpayers, Austria was tottering. It was shaken from the West, and rattled at from the South by a brilliant young general, Napoleon Bonaparte, who in the first flush of his powers had overrun Italy, subdued the Papacy, conquered the kingdoms of Sardinia and Naples, and crumpled up several smaller states. There seemed, moreover, little point in going on with the war. Burke had alarmed everybody with his scare about the French Jacobin menace, "spreading the terror" he had called it; but seeing that the Jacobin régime in France had faded out, it would be better, surely, to treat with the Directorate, a reasonable set of people, rather than waste blood and treasure in opposing a menace which public opinion had been mobilised to fight, but which no longer existed. The General Election in the autumn of 1796 had expressed this view very clearly, and

3

shown that the temper was general; whereupon Pitt, who had never loved the war, had hurried Lord Malmesbury over to Paris to sketch out the preliminaries of a peace. Unluckily the negotiations had failed because the French bluntly refused to restore Belgium to its rightful owner, so the pall descended still more heavily over a country now being continually frightened by well-authenticated invasion scares.

The mass of the people, then, felt disheartened at the prospect of the ruinous and threatening war going on, with its crushing taxation, its fantastically high military expenditure, its attrition of foreign trade, not to mention its fears and sorrows. The French obviously meant mischief, and England had no ally left that she could rely on, no great army, and no general "but some old woman in a red riband," as a member of the Cabinet bitterly complained. True, there was the Navy, but it had not done much to rejoice at. Mediterranean affairs had been sadly bungled; and if Lord Howe had beaten the French on 1st June 1794, that was long ago, and the victory, feebly pressed, had in the end proved not very decisive; it was, in fact, what Nelson was to call contemptuously "a Howe victory." The Navy, it was felt, was not doing its job; it was neither keeping the French Fleet shut up, nor protecting the British shores from invasion. In December 1796, even, while Malmesbury was fruitlessly palavering in Paris, a large fleet with troops on board, enthusiastically directed by Hoche and that seditious Irish devil Wolfe Tone, had issued impudently out of Brest; and owing to a series of accidents, which might be called muddle, Lord Bridport, commanding the Channel Fleet, had not budged from Portsmouth in time to hustle it home. Most of it had reached Bantry Bay, where it was the winds of heaven, not the British Fleet, that had scattered it ingloriously. In February another small force of avowed banditti, bent on burning Liverpool or Bristol to cinders, had actually landed near Fishguard. Once more it was not the Navy that had dealt with them, but the local Fencibles, who had captured them easily, reinforced, it was derisively said, by a posse of women in red cloaks whom the bandits had mistaken for soldiers. It seemed that anything disagreeable in the way of invasion might happen, especially as the French evidently meant it to happen. All the time there were ominous rumours which kept the nerves jangling.

And what would the result be? Nobody could hopefully imagine a happy one. The most nervous people of all were the Governors and Council of the Bank of England, to whom things looked very black. The National Debt was huge (though the sum seems trifling to us now). Pitt, Chancellor of the Exchequer, owed them any amount of Treasury Bills, and though the Bank had clamoured for years to have them repaid, Pitt, in spite of promises, showed no signs of reducing them to any great extent; and now he was demanding another million and a half for Ireland, which was seething with rebellion, besides a huge subsidy to the Emperor. To cautious people there seemed only one thing to do—to hoard one's wealth; and such numbers of anxious rich old gentlemen hurried to the banks to carry off their money in bags that towards the end of February the distressed directors in Threadneedle Street came groaning to Pitt for succour: the drain on cash throughout the country was becoming disastrous, they moaned; they might have to close their doors! Pitt rose unhesitatingly to the occasion, and, suborning Council and King, suspended cash payments in specie, and placed the whole resources of the nation at the Bank's disposal. The City, after a momentary shock, reacted with its usual sense in knowing on which side its bread is buttered, and declared that it was ready to use Government-backed paper instead of gold to any amount. So confidence once more rode smiling, not now upon the Bank's solvency, but upon the broad shoulders of the nation's credit.

But there was still a good deal of uneasiness. The Bill for making these proceedings legal and for indemnifying the Bank was passed by Parliament, but not without opposition deep-toned with lugubrious prophesyings. Some members predicted disaster: English notes would go the way of French *assignats* and become waste paper; Sir William Pulteney declared that the Bank had forfeited its charter by refusing specie payments, and that at any rate its monopoly should be abrogated. The City found the suggestion scandalously unpatriotic. Fox and Sheridan declaimed thunderously in the Commons, Lansdowne cast a gloom over the House of Lords, where the Duke of Bedford rode his usual hurricane of invective. And if the Bank looked rosily at now being able to charge nearly 7 per cent. for lending the nation its own credit, more and more money being wanted, the holders of 3 per cents. were horrified to find their stock, as a consequence, steadily sinking. The price of food, of bread especially, was disturbingly high, and going higher—rises agreeable to profiteers, but bringing distress and even starvation to the masses, with an undercurrent of murmuring and disorder. Cries for peace became louder and more frequent than ever, and to the alarm of timorous Conservatives the radical Corresponding Society was swelling its ranks, and holding more open-air oratorical displays than ever; while, on the other hand, the suspension of Habeas Corpus brought sharply home to lovers of liberty that the forces of reaction were ready to pounce. It was a bleak, grey period, threatened with winds of adversity.

Only one gleam warmed that whole chilly winter, a dim ray which peeped out in the nick of time, a few days after the suspension of cash payments. Hearts beat more firmly at hearing that on 14th February Sir John Jervis' gallantry, twisted to usefulness by a lightning tactical stroke of Nelson's, had defeated the Spanish Navy off Cape St. Vincent. Some of the ships were captured, the rest allowed to stagger ignobly into port. It might have been a more dazzling victory; but such as it was, Pitt, desperate for something to show, snatched at the happy opportunity, and made the utmost of it. Jervis was created Earl St. Vincent and generously pensioned, while the great towns showered freedoms and gold boxes upon him; Nelson, recently promoted Admiral, was endowed with the riband of the Bath. All, it was given to suppose, would yet be well. What if the indefatigable Hoche was preparing another invasion at Brest? The British Navy was invincible: Britannia actually did rule the waves: the gallant British tars were the bulwark of the country. Everything else might be on the verge of collapse, but the Navy was strong, it was sound, it was brilliantly admiralled. The nation might wake or snore in comfort.

Then, without warning, the foundations of all security seemed to crash. The nation suddenly learnt that when, on 16th April, Lord Bridport had ordered the Channel Fleet to put to sea, the sailors had refused point-blank. It was like the crack of doom. The Navy in open mutiny! The Navy disloyal! With its right arm paralysed, the country was lost, its doors flapping open to its triumphant enemies! The situation, Lord Arden, a Civil Lord of the Admiralty, wrote as soberly as he could to the First Lord, Earl Spencer, "forms the most awful crisis that these kingdoms ever saw," [1] and the consternation was not confined to official circles. Patriots were in despair, merchants frenzied, the populace stunned. To everybody on land, in every class and every occupation, to every colour of opinion except the plain red, the event was "so seemingly unnatural, and even supposed to be so remote from possibility, that it is difficult to say whether surprise, grief or terror was the predominant feeling which it excited." [2] Any dreadful thing might happen now: the country was at war, and its chief, its only, safeguard had melted away overnight.

But if the nation had every right to be surprised, there was no excuse for the Admiralty. As early as 1795, Admiral Philip Patton had presented a report to Spencer—who showed it to some of the other ministers—stating that a general mutiny was possible, and showing why desertions were so common as to threaten the very existence of the sea force. This, from a responsible officer, should have awakened some premonition of trouble; but the august rulers of the state would not allow themselves to be made uneasy. There had, as every one knew, actually been mutinies: the dreadful one on the *Bounty* in 1789, out of which Captain Bligh had emerged so heroically; one, duly suppressed, on the *Culloden* in Lord Howe's fleet in 1794; and that on the *Windsor Castle* in the same year in the Mediterranean, which had ended in the removal of certain officers complained against. But these, surely, must be isolated instances, of no significance: there were scoundrels on every ship, and sometimes they might predominate. It was true that ships' crews sometimes addressed petitions to the Admiralty, but complaints are merely paper, they harm no one: the right to complain was only meant to serve as a healthy outlet for high-spirited men, and nobody dreamt of acting on them. And if the complaints voiced protests against the brutality of the officers, no doubt men did not like being flogged, but then what could officers do but flog when faced with the insubordinate prison-scum of which the crews were to some extent composed? Nevertheless the constant if thin stream of piteous letters which trickled in to the Admiralty should have warned the mandarins that something was getting the sailors on the raw. For instance, in 1793, two sets of prayers arose from the *Winchelsea* at Spithead:

Draft us on board any of His Majesty's ships. As we don't wish to go to sea in the *Winchelsea* . . . our usage was more like Turks than of British seamen. . . .

We are nockt about so that we do not no what to do. **Every man in**

8

her would sooner be sot at like a taregaite by muskettree than remain any longer in her.

On 28th July the hard-bit men of the *Amphitrite* declared that flogging was their portion, and that "when we complain we are threatened to be flogged or beat round the quarter-deck"; those of the *Weazle* sloop wrote, on 16th August 1795, that their lieutenant, who frequently came on board drunk, amused himself "by making us strip and ceasing [seizing] us up to the riggin and beating us with the end o rope till we almost expire," and added that they had "put up with his cruel usage a long time without having an opportunity of informing your Lordships." The unfortunate sailors placed unjustified and childlike confidence in the imagination of the Lords of the Admiralty, who, if civilian, probably had no conception of the horrors of life on a man-of-war, and, if naval, took it all as part of the order of nature. At any rate they one and all turned a stolid ear to such cries of distress, even to the one uttered on 19th August 1795 by the ship's company of the *Nassau*, which began: "the ill-usage we have on board this ship forced us to fly to your Lordships the same as a child to its father. It is almost impossible for us to put it down in [*sic*] paper as cruel as it really is with flogging and abusing above humanity," and went on to point out that such treatment hardly encouraged them to "Face the Enemy with a cheerful Heart."

Heartrending documents, written by illiterate men who had not the education to state their case lucidly or even well, certainly not the literary skill to give even a shadowy picture of what they had to endure (it was impossible for them to put it down as cruel as it really was), sporadically loaded the Admiralty post-bag, as that from the *Shannon*, Sheerness, 16th June 1796. The poor devils of that ship complained of

the ill-treatment which we have and do receve from the tiriant of a Captain [whom they referred to as "Captain Fraizere"] from time to time, which is more than the spirits and harts of true English Man can cleaverly bear, for we are born free but now we are slaves. . . . We hope your Lordships will be so kind to us and grant us a new commander or a new ship for the Captin is one of the most barbarous and one of the most unhuman officers that ever a sect of unfortunate men eaver had the disagreeable misfortune of being with, which treatment and bad usages is anufe to make the sparites of Englishmen to rise and steer the ship into and enimies port.

That was strong enough, and other letters appeared, in numbers sufficient to show that the protest was general and that a storm was brewing, as from the *Blanche*, from the *Reunion*, with reports about captains or lieutenants who would mercilessly belabour their men, throw their clothes overboard, cut their one comfort—their grog—or, last ignominy, shear off the queues or love-locks which the sailors cherished as part of their self-respect.[3] The Lords of the Admiralty, however, oblivious of being the only protection injured seamen had against the tyranny of the captains, and others, who strutted the decks, irascible, unjust, and bolt-laden godlets, ignored these poignant appeals. They were unmoved by the fact that the sailors literally did turn to them "the same as a child to its father." Why need they bother? For even if the men complained, they nearly always protested their loyalty at the same time. After all, life in the Navy had always been harsh; discipline must be kept; the King's business must be carried on, especially in war-time. No doubt complaints would crop up now and then, but so long as the sailors went on fighting, that was all that really mattered.

At the end of 1796, however, warnings of a different kind shadowed the horizon. It began to appear that besides being driven out of themselves by the brutality of some of the officers on certain ships, the men throughout the service felt that they were being unfairly treated in the matter of pay and victuals. They addressed several petitions to the Lords of

the Admiralty,[4] who quashed them, not even showing them
to Spencer. Yet he did have an inkling of what was going on,
and a respectful admonition sent him by Captain Pakenham,
on 11th December, was, we might think, one which would
rouse any intelligent and humane man, as Spencer undoubtedly was. Pakenham, after speaking about the memorial being addressed to the Admiralty by the captains for an
increase in their own pay, went on to say that there was a
strong feeling among some of the officers that the people
whose pay really ought to be increased were the men. That
of lieutenants had lately been added to, now the captains
were putting forward similar demands, and the men, who
knew they were under-valued, who realised that they would
be four times better off on shore, would suppose that every
rank had "their own immediate advantage for its object, and
to have lost sight in that pursuit of every attention to the
underpaid condition of the thoroughbred seaman." Since
the pay of soldiers had been raised some two years earlier,
Pakenham continued boldly, no doubt the seamen also would
apply for a rise unless something was done for them: "and
that is the consequence I would take the liberty of warning
your Lordship of. It seems to me too probable to give
foundation for any doubt."[5] This admirable and honourable
letter shows that the men's feeling was known and sympathised with by many of the officers; but what it also shows
is that the sentiments of the men were strong, even angry,
and, to the minds of some of their commanders, justifiably
so.

But Spencer, punctilious gentleman and conscientious
civil servant though he was, evidently did not realise that it
must have been some very uncommon motive, or unusual
pressure of thought, that prompted Pakenham to write a
letter raising such a point, single-handed, with his highest
superior. And though, as the sequel showed, he could be
imaginative and active enough when he saw the occasion

demanded these virtues, at this moment he allowed his humane self to be overlaid by his political self. Besides, he had not at this time the remotest idea of how the sailors lived. The Sea Lords, who had not shown him the complaints, "kept him in a state of repressive ignorance."[6] So he did not think of the seamen, but of what the Chancellor of the Exchequer would say if he suggested that expenditure should be increased, how Parliament would rage and fume, and the country cry out. It was unthinkable that he should do anything about it. What honourable First Lord could hold up his face after such a betrayal of his estimates? How could he persuade all these people that more pay was not only fair but expedient, not to say necessary? Perhaps it is the difficulty of ever persuading anybody to do anything that accounts for what seems to the layman the infuriating dilatoriness, the everlasting shilly-shally of politicians, for the "too late" accusation so often hurled at them, usually with justice. No doubt on this occasion Spencer, seeing appalling Parliamentary troubles ahead of him if he tried to alter things, took what must have seemed the easiest line—to lie low. So much at least one gathers from his prompt answer to Pakenham, an answer which seems all the more astonishing seeing that he prefaced it by thanking Pakenham for giving him information of which he "should have been very sorry not to have been possessed on a subject of so much importance." And then, instead of making use of this important information, Spencer poured out a resistless spate of politicians' phrases: ". . . utter impossibility . . . expense . . . in some points of view . . . at a more suitable season . . . public discussion infallibly productive of much mischief . . . absolute impracticability. . . .":

> . . . Though undoubtedly [this subject is] one which we cannot but wish for a proper opportunity of giving some relief upon, it is, however, so very dangerous to be stirred that I trust every one will see the propriety of not allowing it to be agitated on any account whatever.[7]

In fact, if the snake could not be killed it must be scotched. But there are times when to temporise, to wait and see, to expect the opportunity, is extremely perilous, and costs more in the end than immediate action or concession. In the light of later events there is much in the letter which is ironic— such phrases as "productive of much mischief," and "absolute impracticability," when the mischief actually produced from doing nothing was far greater than ever entered Spencer's mind, and the "absolute impracticability" resolved itself into the simplest thing in the world. If the question was dangerous to be stirred, it was far more dangerous to let it lie, as Spencer was soon to find out.

CHAPTER II

THE FERMENT WORKS

BETWEEN the decks of the ships, in air thick with the eternal stench of bilge-water and rotting boards, the men came together in discreet twos and threes, or, crouched in the gun-berths, evaded the eyes of the "narks," or informers. They were sore, they felt themselves despised, their moderate complaints had been met with the contempt of silence. Fur cap nodded with shiny tarpaulin hat or gaudy turban-kerchief over the mess-table, the gleam of a gold ear-ring might be caught bobbing by a chequered shirt in the gloomy recesses of the orlop-deck when the smoky candle flickered. Old salts, tough as whipcord, at last expressed in rum-husky whispers their suspicion that though they were serving their country well, the country in return was treating them as though they had less than the sentiments of beasts: they had been patient and dumb as oxen, but now they were beginning to feel a sense of intolerable wrong.

There was no escape; they were prisoners. Many of them had been kidnapped, torn forcibly, sometimes with knocking on the head, not only from seamen's taverns or wharf-side brothels, but from their wives and families amid riots and tumults of impotent would-be rescuers. Worse still, perhaps, they had been seized as they entered home waters after a voyage abroad of two or three years (an instance of nine is quoted),[8] pounced on when in sight of their homes—often without the pay due to them—and shipped on to warships for an indefinite period, without prospect of release until the end of the war, whenever that might be, and without hope of a holiday—since men allowed on shore seldom came back. Any who had joined from a love of romance repented it bitterly after a week. Cooped up in a fœtid atmosphere, often for days together when the weather was foul, and drenched with salt water as well; huddled with the dregs of the gaols, or men who had been shipped as boys, probably for some trivial offence, and had never known a different life; pestered with thieves from whom their small belongings were not safe; never free from the fiendish bullying of officers high or petty, they lived a life without hope. There was no leisure, no leave, no books, to qualify their miserable existence: * there was nothing to make a man feel himself a human being. The life was "brutalising, cruel, and horrible";[9] and with it all, apart from the dangers of the sea, the men who lived in these disgusting conditions, and fed on the most outrageous food, were expected to show spirit in a fight, in which ghastly wounds were hastily botched up in dim light by inexperienced surgeons (who sometimes borrowed the carpenter's tools), and during which badly maimed men were simply thrown overboard.

There must have been many mutterings among the heads that lay so close in the hammocks, jammed together, "fourteen inches to a man"; but men will stand an amazing amount of degradation so long as they see nothing better, while their conditions appear to be a part of things as they are, unalterable, fixed for ever. But once they catch a glimpse of something different, and believe it attainable, a spark is lighted which it is extremely dangerous to try to put out. The match was ready, for within the last two years the ranks of the Navy had been invaded by a new element—by men who would not live in this state of brutish acquiescence, who knew there really was something better. They had flocked in on account of the need of an enormously increased personnel caused by the war,† and by the frequent desertions,

* In 1812 a shocked Admiralty provided libraries, and the seaman's life was rendered gayer by the availability of such books as the *Old Chaplain's Farewell Letter*, *The Whole Duty of Man*, and *Advice after Sickness*. Hutchinson, 43.

† In 1792 the muster was 16,000; in 1794, 85,000; by 1802 the figure had risen to 135,000.

especially to the American merchant service—a need so huge that, even leaving out of account losses in battle, all the efforts of the press-gangs, even when they unlawfully captured landsmen, were not enough to man the Fleets. In March 1795 an Act was passed for raising a number of men in each county roughly proportional to the population; and in April another Act was passed requiring each port to supply a "quota" of men.* These recruits were, mostly, better educated than the normal run of seamen. They were not the sweepings of the dock-sides or prisons, or ignorant men who had known nothing but the sea; they were sometimes even men who had failed in some profession—schoolmastering, the law, or business—and had probably run into debt; they were tempted by the bounties offered by the mayors and sheriffs—which might be as much as £70—and it was these men who, when the authorities had emptied the prisons, got rid of seditious elements, and all undesirables generally, came to swell the ranks of the service. Realising the beastliness of the conditions of life at sea, they kicked, and began to light a gleam of hope in those who had never thought of kicking. Busily, circumspectly, on upper deck and lower, from the forecastle hands to the cockpit servants, at greasing the guns or manning the fore-tops, they blew gently but steadily on the tiny, timid flames, urging the men to ask for at least the common decencies of treatment, without which a man is more wretched than a brute.

Whoever it was that organised the seamen must have been a man of ability amounting to genius. But no ringleader ever appeared; it was as though the Fleet spoke with one voice, spontaneously. Yet means of constant communication were entirely lacking. Letters could occasionally be sent from one ship to another, but the only time the men on different ships could talk to each other was when Sunday visiting was allowed. On fine afternoons in port boat-loads of "liberty

* *E.g.* Newcastle, 1240; Bristol, 666; London, 5704.

men" would row busily from ship to ship, to be regaled by their hosts with the rum saved from the dinner ration; and it is probable that on these visiting days, under cover of noisy greetings and sailors' yarns, of showing the ship, and perhaps of privy gambling, the whispering went on, the organisation was woven. Without authority to give orders, with uncertain and intermittent communication, whoever the guiding spirit was, he managed to weld into a solid mass as motley and tough a lot of people as a leader ever had to handle. There were old tars, young sailors, sturdy loyalists, seditious malcontents from Ireland or elsewhere, pressed men, volunteers, gaol-birds, men of no education, and quota-men of more than a little; there were escaping debtors and honest men; there were men you could trust mingled with thieves and cardsharpers whom to trust with a chew of tobacco would be folly; and to increase the difficulty there were 10 per cent. of foreigners.

Not only did the leader get this strange medley to act in concert, but he managed them so as to allow him to frame their demands with consummate skill. In the early petitions one point was put forward, and one point only, a perfectly reasonable one, which everybody would be able to appreciate, one which involved no idea of personal wrongs or of other people's shortcomings, but was on the face of it perfectly fair. It was the point of pay, and this was all that the Admiralty was asked to consider in the humble petitions sent separately from every ship. They were put in the most respectful, loyal language,* and both common humanity and common-sense policy would suggest that at least some sort of acknowledgment should be made. But from first to last the Admiralty, with the exception of Spencer himself, behaved with an astounding lack of wisdom, sometimes approaching idiocy; the petitions therefore were met with complete

---

* They seem to have been in substance the same as that to Howe, given on p. 23.

silence, as though the men who sent them were beneath notice.

Apart from the way the men lived, a consideration of how much they got, and what they were expected to do with their money, makes the ignoring of the petitions seem outrageous. The Able Seaman was rewarded with 24s. a lunar month, the Ordinary Seaman with 19s. From these sums so much was subtracted for one thing and another that either was lucky if he touched 10s.[10] A universal deduction was for the Chatham Chest, a kind of pension fund; but the pension, if he was lucky enough to get one when disabled, only amounted to a niggardly £7 a year, in contrast with the £13 received by the seaman's Chelsea brother. If at any time he was in the sick bay, even for wounds or on account of disabilities incurred in the service, he was allowed no pay at all. Out of what was left he had to buy his slops (seamen's clothing and bedding), often at extortionate prices owing to the rapacity of the pursers, who would absorb quite two months' pay for an outfit; to get extra food to supplement the sometimes inedible ration; and, if married, to support wife and family. He was better off in the merchant service. And when it is realised that the pay was often anything up to two years in arrear, sometimes considerably more,* that it was issued in full only when a ship was paid off, and always in tickets convertible into cash at the port of commission alone, it is not surprising that the sailor, tempted by the wares of Jews and bum-boat women who flocked hungrily round the ships in port, was ready to dispose of what tickets he had at a fantastic discount. If he was transferred or "lent" to another ship, the purser would often neglect to hand him his ticket, and pocket the thing himself. If a sea-

---

* "At the time of the Nore mutiny it was authoritatively stated that there were ships then in the Fleet which had not been paid off for eight, ten, twelve, and, in one instance, even fifteen years." Hutchinson, 44. But he gives no authority.

man posted his ticket home, his wife had to traipse to the port of commission, sometimes to be sent empty away because of a Q (query) written on the ticket, so that she also often disposed of it to agents at a discount of half a crown in the pound. It is therefore readily understandable that most of the seamen's families starved, or were supported by a grudging parish. No wonder the first petitions were for more pay.

For a month or two the expectant sailors waited in vain for some sort of sign. When none came they began to grow restive; the more indignant spirits clamoured for action, and there was talk of refusing to sail when next ordered to do so.[11] But either the organisation was not ready, or more probably the cautious leaders, in full control, decided that they would put themselves still more in the right by leaving no legal stone unturned. They skilfully organised a fresh set of petitions, to be addressed this time to Lord Howe.

They had faith in Richard, Earl Howe, or "Black Dick," as he was affectionately called. They had the admiration for him men always have for a successful leader, and those who had been with him in the Battle of the First of June plumed themselves on having been his comrades in arms. They loved him, for his harsh, dark features would sometimes soften into the most charming smile; he was notoriously "the sailor's friend," and after an action would always go down to the cockpit to sit and chat with the wounded: he had even been known to give men leave, and had hinted, if rather vaguely, after the Glorious First, that he would try to get their pay increased.[12] If he could not do something, who could? He was the nation's sea hero; he had been First Lord, he was still nominally in command of the Channel Fleet, for though too old to go to sea, especially in winter, he was too inspiring a figure to be allowed to retire. He, surely, would take up the tale of the sailors' wrongs, and after he had spoken they would be redressed.

Drafts of the petition to be presented were sent, by what means can only be guessed, from the *Queen Charlotte*, Howe's old flagship, which appears to have been the headquarters of the movement. They went under cover of private letters, the one to the *Minotaur*, for instance, being addressed to an A.B. of twenty-two, who had joined from Sunderland about six months before,[13] and was of the type, evidently, on which the organisation was built up. He received definite instructions:

MESSMATE,

If your ship's company approve of the enclosed petition, you are requested to get a fair copy, and let us know on what day it will be convenient for you to send it, that they may go by the one post, as it will be the means of insuring success by showing it to [be] the general wish of the Fleet. Let it be directed to Lord Howe, without any signature at bottom, only the ship's name and day of the month. Therefore wishing it success,

We are yours, etc., etc.,

THE CHARLOTTES.

Send the copy to your acquaintance, and every other ship with these directions. Direct for any man on board of us with whom you are acquainted. We think Tuesday 7th [March] will be a proper day, as there will be sufficient time to collect the sense of the Fleet.[14]

The petition was carefully scrutinised in secret conclaves by each ship, at least one of which felt it knew better than the Charlottes, who soon received the following shrewd criticism from the *London*:

26 *February* 1797.

MESSMATES,

I duly received your letter yesterday, and have shewn it to several and all agree in returning you their hearty thanks for your kind intentions. The resolutions is generous, the intention noble. In short it is worthy of the conquerors of the Glorious First of June. I beg leave, however, to mention one thing which you have forgot. You intreat his Lordship to intercede [with] the Board of Admiralty for augmentation of pay. But that is not under their jurisdiction to do; it is a national affair, and must be addressed to the hon. House of Commons. It is from them alone that we can expect redress. They are the purse bearers of the nation. Let them be petitioned, and I make no doubt but their generosity. One thing more you might have added, there has been no alteration in the pay of the Navy since the reign of King Charles the Second when at that time every thing was so reasonable that even double the money now is hardly equivalent to purchase any of the necessaries of life. You will, if you please, reflect on these reasons, and if you approve, not otherwise, please to adopt them. I have no more to add but to assure you of our hearty concurrence to your petition as you may depend. Shall be forwarded to you in due time according to your request with every other assistance in our power to grant consistent with reason, peace, and good fellowship. Proceed in your endeavours. Proceed in caution, peace and good behaviour. Let no disorder or tumult influence your proceedings, and I have not the least doubt but your late glorious commander will step forth in behalf of his fellow-conquerors.

Please to send word what ship you would wish us to acquaint with it and it shall be done. I shall now conclude with wishing you all all manner happiness, and believe me to remain

Yours most affectionately,

"London." [15]

That letter is not quite so scholarly as the one from the flagship, but the pen which wrote it was directed by an able mind, quick to take up points, and a calm head which saw that disorder or tumult either in discussion or action would be fatal, a head which realised the importance of legitimate action up to the last possible moment. The Charlottes, though they had thought more clearly in one respect, were impressed, and answered:

Yours we duly received and acknowledge the justness of your remarks, and are thankful for the hints they contain, but our reason for addressing the Lords of the Admiralty in preference to the House of Commons was this, the Board of Admiralty are all professional men and might take umbrage at not having the compliment paid them first. If they adopt the prayers of our petition they will soon pass motion in consequence, and bring it before the House with all the ministerial party to back it, and thereby take the merit to themselves. If through their means it should miscarry we still have the House of Commons open to us with all force of opportunities on our sides, whichever way it is we have not the least doubt, but by unity amongst ourselves and a steady peaceable perseverance to carry our point.

With regard to your second point we think it noble and extremely applicable to our purpose, we have therefore adopted it in the best manner we are able. Therefore wishing unity with perseverance with success to our endeavours

Remaining yours, the

CHARLOTTES.[16]

The leaders were determined to have right on their side all through; they would take no step which might be misinterpreted; they would take care not to huff the Admiralty, and would allow no mutinous act to spoil their chances. Their grammar might be questionable, their pompous dignity in writing to each other may seem comic, but they had clear, responsible minds and determined hearts. In the event, their plan for sending all the letters in one batch was foiled by the Fleet putting to sea earlier than they expected; but some of the missives went off together in February, and some by the Fleet packet after the ships were away, on 3rd March. The petitions went to London.

Lord Howe was at Bath, recuperating from a bad attack of gout. When these letters were forwarded to him he probably looked at them in irritation: he was in no mood to be bothered with letters, obviously not personal ones, which came from the Fleet. His job was done; he had handed over to that fellow Bridport, who was always being tiresome, and whom he disliked. He had practically retired, as a man of seventy-one might well do. It was only because Spencer, and Pitt, and finally the King, had told him that his retiring just then would make a bad impression, that he had stayed on at all. Heroes, they had implied, were needed in times of despondency. He was old, he felt old: even on the Glorious First of June he had had to be supported in his chair on deck to direct the action. He tore open one of these preposterous-looking letters and read:

To the Right Honourable Richard, Earl Howe, Admiral of the Fleet and General of Marines.

The humble petitioners on board His Majesty's Ship *Queen Charlotte* [monstrous, his own ship!] on behalf of themselves and their Brethren on Board of the Fleet at Spithead. [On behalf of the Fleet! This looked like some illegal combination.] Most humbly sheweth that your petitioners most humbly intreat [the rogues had learnt the jargon somehow!] that your Lordship would be pleased to take the hardships of which they complain into consideration and lay them before the Lords Commissioners of the Admiralty, not doubting in the least from your Lordship's interference in their behalf they will obtain a speedy redress.

It is now upwards of two years since your petitioners observed with pleasure the augmentation which had been made to pay of the Army and Militia, and the provision that took place with respect to their wives and families, of such soldiers as were serving on board, naturally expecting that they should in their turn experience the same munificence, but alas no notice has been taken of them, nor the smallest provision made for their wives and families except what they themselves sent out of their pay to prevent them being burdensome to the parish.

That your petitioners humbly presume that their loyalty to their Sovereign is as conspicuous and their courage as unquestionable as any other description of men in His Majesty's service as their enemies can testify, and as your Lordship can witness who so often led them to victory and glory and by whose manly exertions the British Flag rides triumphant in every quarter of the Globe.

And your petitioners humbly conceive that at the time when their wages were settled in the reign of Charles the Second* it was intended as a comfortable support both for themselves and families, but at present by the considerable rise in the necessaries of life, which is now almost double; and an advance of 30 per cent. on slops, your Lordship will plainly see that the intentions of the legislature is counteracted by the before mentioned causes and therefore most humbly pray for relief.

Your petitioners relying on your goodness and benevolence humbly implores that my Lords Commissioners of the Admiralty will comply with the prayers of this petition, and grant such addition will be made in their pay as in their Lordships' wisdom they shall think meet.

And your petitioners will in duty bound ever pray.

28th Feb. 1797.[17]

* As a matter of fact under the Commonwealth. From 1st Jan. 1652-3 the wages of A.B.'s were raised from 19*s.* to 24*s.* a month. Ordinary Seamen continued at 19*s.* C.S.P. Dom., 1652-3, p. 43.

One letter of the sort was annoying enough—at his age a man should be allowed a little respite to take the waters in peace—but they kept on coming in. There were eleven of them altogether. As he read them, it occurred to him that they were all curiously alike in phrasing. He looked at them more carefully. Ah! that was it. Although at first sight they seemed to be written by different people, they were all really written by the same man disguising his handwriting (he was wrong there). The petitions were therefore a single petition, from a single discontented wretch of a fellow, probably one of your "state-the-case" men who thought he had been wrongfully pressed, and not from the whole Fleet. He was sure his brave fellows were both happy and sound. However, to make sure, he wrote and suggested to Lord Hugh Seymour, a Lord of the Admiralty, that he might ask a few questions when he was down at Portsmouth as to whether anyone had noticed any discontent in the Fleet. Seymour—who made cursory enquiries when the Fleet was at sea!—answered that no one had heard of anything being wrong.[18] "So I was right," Howe thought, sighed with relief as he hobbled across the pump-room on his crutches, and put the affair out of his mind.

One thing only was left to do: to get rid of the petitions. He was still, perhaps, a trifle uneasy about them. So when he went up to London, on 22nd March, he handed them over to Seymour, who showed them to Spencer. The First Lord was shocked, horrified. Here was this deplorable question of increased pay, which meant, naturally, swollen estimates, cropping up again! At the next Board meeting he dealt with the matter: everybody thought it was clearly "impossible to do anything officially on the subject without running the risk of unpleasant consequences by a public agitation of so delicate a topic," and so "it was judged advisable by the Board to take no notice of the circumstance."[19] Again the note of irony sounds in our ears in the politicians' phrases.

"Unpleasant consequences" seem trifling compared with a mutiny of the whole Fleet; and as for "public agitation," the whole country was to discuss the question. Spencer's awareness was asleep; that the sailors had a legitimate grievance and were feeling bitterly about it does not seem to have penetrated his consciousness even yet, although this was his second warning. "It is a stain on the memory of a truly good-hearted man, that the First Lord had nothing better to say than that money would be needed to satisfy the men; that an application to Parliament for more money in those times of heavy taxation and financial stringency would be troublesome; that to ventilate the causes of discontent in the Fleet might start bad mischief; and that in short the best course was to say nothing, do nothing, and hope that nothing would happen." [20] To reassure him in this last blessed hope, Seymour had reported that all things at Portsmouth suggested the profoundest calm. How should they not have? The organisers of the petitions had been far too wary to let any whispers get abroad, and the men before sailing had taken care to behave with the most disarming docility. Yet Spencer was more to blame than Howe; he was young, he was imaginative; and Howe, after all, though he has been upbraided for not insisting on a searching investigation, had done all that could be expected of a war-worn veteran. He had cogitated (a little), he had made enquiries, and had handed the documents over to the proper authority. If he had acted with more vigour . . . but then history is made up of ifs, and in a few days the game passed to other hands.

CHAPTER III

THE CRITICAL POINT

ON 30th March the Fleet once more rode placidly at anchor at Spithead. The graceful lines of the ships swung gently on the tide, the occasional sunlight cheerfully reflecting the paint—black from the water to the lower gun-deck, then bright with various yellows, sweeping up to the vivid red or blue of the poops above the quarter-deck guns—a gallant, heartening sight to those on land. Every now and then gleams of gold, or scarlet, or pale blue flashed from the forecastles, while the Admirals' flags or Captains' pennants fluttered from their appropriate topgallant mastheads. Boats, with their crews gaily tricked out in any uniform that struck their captain's fancy, rowed busily as active ants over the wind-dappled water between ship and ship, while the bum-boats swarmed rapaciously out from the shore. All was peacefully everyday, innocent of omens; and Admiral Lord Bridport went on leave until the 10th of April.

Yet the ships were humming with men bitterly disappointed at finding that their petitions to Howe, the cry of man to man, had not evoked the faintest sign of response. You cannot, obviously, send a reply to anonymous letters, but what they had hoped for was some statement in orders, or some sign of activity in Parliament. Had Howe, the sailors' friend, done nothing? They were deeply filled with the sense that Black Dick, of all people, had deserted them, had forgotten the men who had made him a hero:

> [We] flattered ourselves [they were to write] with the hopes that his
> Lordship would have been an advocate for us, as we have repeatedly, under
> his command, made the British flag triumph over that of our enemies:—
> but, to our great surprise, find ourselves unprotected by him, who has

seen so many instances of our intrepidity, in carrying the British flag into every part of the seas with victory and success.[21]

So the busy traffic in reasonable plotting began again, by secret letters, or whispered word of mouth on visiting days. The men would wait a little longer, patiently, but while they waited they would organise, prepare the next step. Since both Howe and the Admiralty had either thrown their petitions into the wastepaper-basket, or silently filed them, they would address "the Right Honourable and the Honourable Citizens and Burgesses in Parliament assembled," very respectfully indeed, as from loyal and zealous men; adding a plea which should bring shame to the heart of any Member inclined to obduracy:

> We, your petitioners, therefore humbly implore, that you will take these matters into consideration, and with your accustomed goodness and liberality, comply with the prayer of your petitioners, and we are in duty bound ever to pray, &c.[22]

And, to show that they were all the while prepared to go through the proper channels, they would once more assail the deaf ears of the Admiralty; but to make sure that this time at least their grievances would not be smothered under the feather-beds of officialdom, they would send copies to Charles James Fox, fat, debauched, a gambler, but a fiery defender of libertarian ideas, and leader of the opposition. He would certainly not let slip a chance of sticking a barb into Pitt by showing up the horrible injustice of naval administration.

But, as the unregarded seamen had learnt from acid experience, petitions, poor slips of paper, do no good by themselves; so on the day the letters went off, it would be made plain to everybody, by some drastic action, that they meant to be heard. To be certain that any move would be effective, the leaders had to be perfectly sure that everybody—veteran, quota-man, and boy—would be with them in this. So all the while the routine business of organising went on, there went on with it a constant screwing up of dubious men to sticking-point, and a bringing in of ships that had not conformed, such as the *Defence*, which had sent no petition to Howe, and until the 15th April was an uncertain factor. When she had agreed to come in, the crew received a letter of congratulation from the *Royal Sovereign*, and instructions such as had, no doubt, been sent to the other ships:

> *Royal Sovereign*,
> SPITHEAD,
> 15*th April* 1797.

FRIENDS,

I am happy to hear of your honourables courage towards redress. We are carrying on the business with the greatest expedition. We flatter ourselves with the hopes that we shall obtain our wishes, for they had better go to war with the whole Globe, then with their own subjects. We mean the day the petitions go to London to take charge of the ships until we have a proper answer from government. The signal will be first made by the *Queen Charlotte*. The first signal is the Union Jack at the main with two guns fired: this is for taking charge. . . . The second signal is a red flag at the mizzen topmast head, and two guns: this is to send a speaker from every ship. The petitions is to be ready to go on Monday if possible. You must send them and your letters to Mr. Pink, the Bear and Ragged Staff, as that is our post office. Direct one petition to Evan Nepean, Secretary to the Admiralty. The other to Honourable Charles James Fox, South Street, Grosvenor Square.

Success to the proceedings.[23]

How far the men were prepared to go can be darkly read into the words omitted in the above, which state that the first signal was "for taking charge, and sending the officers and women out of every ship." *

But events moved more swiftly than the slow-maturing plans, and even before the 15th something had happened to make the men of the *Defence* decide one way or the other.

---

* Men's wives—perhaps a courtesy title—were allowed to stay on board when the ship was in port.

On the evening of the 12th, by some undiscovered chance, perhaps through the mysterious Mr. Pink, Captain Patton of the Transport Office heard what was in the wind.[24] He promptly hurried off to tell the Port-Admiral, Sir Peter Parker, and then hastily rowed out through the darkness to the *Royal George* to give the tidings to Lord Bridport.[25] Bridport was at once alert, and the next morning dashed off a note to Spencer, which he sent up in all haste by a trustworthy hand:

> *Royal George,*
> SPITHEAD,
> 13*th April* 1797.

> MY LORD,
>
> I am sorry to inform your Lordship that a circumstance reached me yesterday which gave me much concern. It has been stated to me that representations have been made by the crews of the Channel Fleet to Lord Howe and the Admiralty for an increase of pay. If this should be the case it would be very desirable for me to know what steps have been taken in consequence thereof. I am particularly anxious to receive such instructions as your Lordship and the Board may think expedient with as little delay as possible as I yesterday heard that some disagreeable combinations were forming among the ships at Spithead on this subject. Captain Glynn will deliver this with the utmost expedition to your Lordship. He is not acquainted with the contents.
>
> PS.—It is reported to me that this subject proceeded from the *Queen Charlotte*.[26]

Spencer, evidently a little flurried, yet still hopelessly blind to the importance of the petitions, and in his funk of Parliament obstinately resisting any idea of urgency, wrote back, under the protection of the magic words, "Secret and Confidential":

> Some time ago Lord Howe transmitted to Lord Hugh Seymour several letters (in number eleven) purporting to come from the crews of the ships mentioned in the enclosed list. The letters were all in nearly the same words, and had much the appearance of being copied by the same person, though they are written in different hands. Lord Howe of course took no other notice of them, and as it appeared impossible to do anything officially . . .

And the rest we already know.[27] He considerately enclosed the eleven pleading letters written to Howe.

Bridport was thunderstruck at this communication. Patton had told him vaguely that there had been petitions, but he had not had the least shadow of an idea that things were going on in this way, and to this extent. Was it not obvious to the most complete muddle-head that all this was serious? that the whole Fleet was behind these petitions? that it was solid, and determined to get what it wanted? That old dodderer Howe! It was, naturally, on *his* flagship that the trouble would begin—as he had, with a spice of malice, suggested to Spencer. It was notoriously a turbulent, ill-disciplined ship.[28] He, Bridport, was in a difficult enough position as it was, with all the responsibility of command without the place, since Howe was still nominally Admiral. If it had not been for that gouty, be-bandaged figure at Bath, the petitions would have come to him, and he would have known what was fermenting. And if Spencer could not see how serious the business was, the only thing to do was to drive this aspect well home. He controlled the Hood blood that boiled in his veins, to compose a reproof which hardly veiled his indignation, though phrased in terms of the greatest suavity. He wrote to Nepean on the 15th:

Herewith I return you eleven anonymous letters, transmitted to me by this morning's post from the Admiralty. You will also receive a petition delivered to me by Vice-Admiral Colpoys from H.M.S. *London*; and one from the crew of H.M.S. *Royal George* bearing my flag, to which I have pledged myself that an answer will be given, as I consider the latter to be the sense of the Fleet, from the best information I have received. I have very much to lament that some answer had not been given to the various letters transmitted to Earl Howe and the Admiralty, which would in my humble opinion have prevented the disappointment and ill-humour which at present prevails in the ships under my orders. I therefore conclude their Lordships will not direct the squadron to proceed to sea before some answer is given to these petitions, as I am afraid it could not be put in execution, without the appearance of serious consequences, which the complexion of the Fleet manifestly indicates. I have not time to enter farther into the particulars of this painful subject, being anxious to save this night's post, to which I hope to receive an answer by express, if their Lordships shall deem it necessary.

You will also herewith receive a petition which has this moment been transmitted to me from the *Queen Charlotte*, whose people have taken the lead in this business.[29]

If only he had known sooner! Those fools in London! he probably thought savagely, as he paced his deck that cold grey afternoon,[30] and saw the clusters of eager men talking over eventualities; for now the crews knew that some rumour or other had got about, and there was no more need of, or use in, secrecy. Sir Peter Parker, as directed by the Admiralty, had told the captains to sleep on board (he had already himself thought of this brilliant measure!), and warned all officers to be ready to repress the least sign of disorder with a firm hand, thus giving the whole of that day an unmistakable sense of strain. Boats plied from one ship to another in the chilly north-west breeze, carrying messages, orders, petitions, and again petitions. Yet the men, rigidly self-controlled, showed not the least sign of mutiny; they obeyed all orders. No handle was to be offered the authorities for stern repressive acts. If only, Bridport thought, the Admiralty would take his advice, and not commit the supreme folly of ordering the Fleet to sea.

But on the Friday, Sir Peter Parker had, a little belatedly, written to the Admiralty a fairly accurate account of the sailors' plans, adding that "their Lordships, knowing whether any petitions have been received by them . . . will be able to determine what degree of credit should be given to the information [from Patton] I have received on the subject"[31]—an illuminating comment on the thoroughness of Lord Hugh Seymour's researches! Their Lordships knew only too well that a good deal of credit might be given to the report, and Bridport's letter of the Saturday not **having** come to hand, arrived at the easy conclusion that there were a lot of mutinous dogs on board, and that the sooner they were sent off to sea the better. They could do no harm there, and, what was more, could not send in bothering petitions, which, however humbly worded, showed a subversive spirit at work somewhere. In fact, they completely misunderstood the state of the seamen's minds, nor did it occur to theirs that the seamen in combination could exercise a strangle-hold upon the Fleet.

It was Easter Sunday, a bright, sunny day, with a south-west wind scudding a few black clouds along like ominous watchers for a possible tragedy, when Bridport received orders to prepare for immediate sailing, and at once to send Admiral Gardner's squadron to St. Helens, the usual start-ing-place for a cruise. If Bridport was dismayed at having to give the order, which blew to smithereens all his hopes of avoiding "serious consequences," the men, too, unprepared for such a sudden crisis, felt the ground cut from under their feet. The order to Gardner's squadron (Bridport withheld the general order) upset all the leaders' plans. Any action would have to be impulsive. Would it be possible at that stage to make a gesture that was firm, without overstepping the bounds into riot, to declare, as we should say, a strike, rather than disintegrate into chaotic mutiny? And would the men stand firm?

Tautly expectant from the second the flags fluttered out their message, the crews watched Gardner's ship, the *Royal Sovereign*. No move to obey the order was made; all that could be seen were the gesticulating figures of the officers haranguing the crew, using every means of persuasion and argument, and probably threats, to get the men to weigh anchor. On the spur of the moment, the sailors of the *Queen Charlotte* manned the fore-shrouds and gave three ringing cheers, echoed ship by ship throughout the eager lines.[32] The mutiny had begun! This was the signal! No flag, either tricolour or red, was hoisted, no gun fired. With lightning presence of mind the leaders in the *Queen Charlotte* put off in a boat—their example being followed at once by those in the *Royal George*—and toured the Fleet, visiting every ship, telling them to send two Delegates to the *Queen Charlotte* that evening. As they went, each ship in turn sent a boat of its own to follow in regular order, so while divine service went on, "parties of seamen rowed in public procession through the Fleet in a line of boats."[33] There was no stopping this unofficial gala, though on the *London*, Admiral Colpoys, made of stout, but perhaps not very wise, stuff, boldly tried to prevent the emissaries boarding him. By God, the rebels should not soil *his* decks with their dirty feet! He called out the marines. But Bridport, foreseeing disastrously explosive bloodshed, sent him a message not to resist.[34]

The Admiral commanding then did the sensible thing, which perhaps only one man in a hundred would have been sensible enough to do. He ordered each captain to muster his men and ask them to state their grievances. In the meantime he wrote a rapid message to the Admiralty, telling them frankly that to use what their Lordships called "vigorous and effectual measures for getting the better of the crews . . . or securing the ringleaders" would be worse than absurd.[35] There was nothing to be done, in fact, but to comply "in some measure with the prayer of the petitions," which he hoped would be done; for on the *Royal George* and *Queen Charlotte*, at any rate, there was "no objection to go to sea, provided an answer is given to their petitions." Rear-Admiral Sir Charles Morice Pole took the letter post-haste to London, and told the Admiralty exactly what had happened.

It was time, Bridport no doubt felt, for the Admiralty to begin to realise the situation, for that afternoon he had got from them, in answer to his letter of the day before, an order of such startling ineptitude, that even he, who had already suffered from Admiralty supineness, was staggered. Not only was he once more ordered to put to sea at once—that did not matter, since it was impossible to do—but he was told to communicate to the men a message conceived in the best style of Parliamentary evasiveness, as though their Lordships had been a Minister in the House answering a question he fully intended to burke. Even in his edited version the sailors heard:

> I am to acquaint the crews of His Majesty's Ships under my command, that I have transmitted their petitions to the Lords Commissioners of the Admiralty, and I am authorised by them that their petitions will be taken into serious and immediate consideration as their importance requires.[36]

"Could departmental vacuity go further?"[37] Bridport probably thought not, and tried to better things by an appeal.

> And the Commander-in-Chief trusts this answer will be satisfactory, and that the different ships' companies will immediately return to duty, as the service of the country requires their proceeding to sea.

The bluff did not act: Bridport can hardly have hoped that it would, knowing that his personal influence was not very great;[38] and the men were made profoundly suspicious by the phrase, "serious consideration," which seemed to them, not unnaturally, to mean precisely that their case was not being considered with any great attention.

That evening two Delegates from every one of the sixteen line-of-battle ships in the Fleet gathered together in Howe's great state-cabin on the *Queen Charlotte*. Seated round the table, under the dubious light of the swinging oil lamps and the purser's dips, which lit up now the bronzed face of some weather-beaten tar, now the pale features of a young and perhaps fanatical revolutionary, the new commanders of the Fleet deliberated in council. If one of them was leader, which cannot be proved, it was probably Valentine Joyce of the *Royal George*, twenty-six years old, nearly the youngest man there, but a sound, experienced, authoritative sailor, or he would not have been Quarter Master's Mate. His chief coadjutor, it was widely believed, was Evans, "a lawyer of abilities, but [in the opinion of a certain Mr. Thomas] of most villainous principles," [39] who had been disqualified for malpractices. At any rate he had earned the confidence of the seamen—quite capable of seeing through a rogue—for he was elected a Delegate, though since he went under an assumed name as an ordinary seaman, [40] he has not yet been traced. At all events this mysterious person was not Joyce's companion from his ship, for an A.B. called John Morrice, an Aberdonian of thirty-three, and most likely tough, was the other nominee from the *Royal George*. Of much the same age, but of petty officer rank as Yeoman of Sheets, was John Huddlestone of the *Queen Charlotte*. The *Royal Sovereign* preferred to put their confidence in two younger men, A.B.'s, both aged twenty-seven or so, from Piltown and from York. The *London* was more aristocratic in its choice, being represented by a petty officer, William Riely (or Riley, sometimes printed Ruly), a Quarter Master—ranking with a Bo'sun's Mate—who hailed from Westminster, and a young spark of twenty-four from Greenock, a Gunner's Mate, who, though of lower rank and four years younger than Riely, signed before him on petitions. The *Pompée* went higher still, and had the Quarter Master to represent it. None of the men seems to have been long on his present ship, and they appear to have come from all over the country, with only a small sprinkling of Irishmen, such as Patrick Glynn of the *Queen Charlotte*, A.B., and Patrick Dugan of the *Glory*, once a Midshipman and now Quarter Master's Mate, with perhaps one or two more whose names do not betray their Irish origin, such as William Anderson of the *Duke*, also once a Midshipman, now Quarter Master. The Delegates, then,

were trustworthy seamen, not, as is usually supposed, sedition-mongers from Dublin, nor landsmen unable to adapt
themselves to the service, who might be expected to dislike
unfamiliar conditions; though they may have been quota
men who saw how disgraceful those conditions were. Nor
were they mainly men greedy for more pay, for, as we have
seen, many of them were not to be affected by the rises in
pay demanded. Some were young men, perhaps too eager
for change of any kind, one or two may have been revolutionaries, but most were hardy men, no longer youthful,
many of them in responsible positions, and all of them,
apparently, competent. Not one of them was a mere Ordinary
Seaman, only thirteen were even mere A.B.'s; five of them
were seasoned Midshipmen of mature age who had worked
their way up, many were of petty officer rank. This was no
rabble of discontented scum, knowing nothing of the sea,
but men whom their companions had learned to trust, the
flower of all that was not quarter-deck.[41]

The extraordinary thing about the deliberators was that
these men did not heat each other up into forming a council
of offensive war, but coolly remained a committee to establish
means of keeping order among their rebel selves—a supremely able tactical measure. If any revolutionary tendencies
poked up their heads, they were crushed: for, as the men had
told Fox, "[we] are not actuated by any spirit of sedition or
disaffection whatsoever; on the contrary, it is indigence and
extreme penury alone that is the cause of our complaint." [42]
It was to that aspect that they were determined to keep the
issue narrowed. They therefore drew up an exemplary set of
rules, most of which ended with the warning that any man
neglecting them would be rigorously dealt with—paradoxi-
cally unmutinous rules, as: "The greatest attention to be
paid to the orders of the officers. Any person failing in
respect due to them, or neglecting their duty, shall be
severely punished." Watches were to be kept with all the

usual strictness; any man attempting to bring liquor on board, or found drunk, would receive no mercy; though women might come on board, none must be allowed to go back again, as a safeguard against tattle ashore and leakage of news, to prevent which even "liberty" from ship to ship was strictly forbidden, as well as letters to the land, which might contain alarmingly inflammatory stuff. It was naturally ordered that "no ship shall lift an anchor to proceed from this port until the desire of the Fleet is satisfied." To maintain the spirit, and to show the others that all was well, every ship was to give three cheers at eight o'clock in the morning, and again at sunset.[43]

These men were sure of their backing: they knew, sitting in unaccustomed state in the great cabin, that they had the whole Fleet behind them. All petty squabbles had been sunk. The foretop men with their pride of skill forgot their superiority over the duller after-guard; both felt their fraternity with the mass of despised "waisters"—the scavengers, pumpers, sewer-men and pigsty keepers, mostly landsmen, who lived in the waist of the ship. The marines, usually a race apart, were embraced as fellow-sufferers, and even the unfortunate boys, whom everybody kicked and cuffed when they came within reach, were regarded as part of the great community. General discontent, due to increasing hardships and a sense of wrong had made them one. "Scarcely a dissenting voice was heard in any ship, from the Quarter Masters, Boatswain's Mates, etc.: [petty officers] to the most contemptible sweeper."[44] Yet an oath cements feelings, and was very seriously regarded by the sailors; so the Delegates decided that every man in the Fleet should swear "by his Maker that the cause we have undertaken be persevered in till accomplished." In case of disturbance on any ship—there may always be counter-revolts—a red flag, signifying "battle," was to be hoisted on the fore-topgallant masthead, or, at night, two lights, one above the other. On seeing that signal, a boat with the Delegates would repair immediately to the scene of trouble.[45]

There was nothing more the Delegates could do that evening: the next move lay with the Admiralty. The men, most likely, rested calmly, but the repose of the officers was less easy through that night of uncertain waiting. Sir Alan Gardner reported to Bridport that Captain Bedford had "overheard below that it is at present determined by the men of the Fleet to wait until Tuesday for an answer to their petitions, and in case it does not arrive by that day's post that a signal with a Union and two guns is to be made on board the *Queen Charlotte*, when the whole of the officers are to be secured and sent on shore." [46] Anything might happen, and they were helpless. What would, what could, the Admiralty do?

CHAPTER IV

DELICATE NEGOTIATIONS

ON Easter Monday the Fleet awoke under a new command, that of the Delegates, or "General Assembly": that was exciting, but if any boisterous or seditious spirits hoped that this would make any change in their lives, they were quickly disillusioned. Except for the cheers at eight o'clock and at sunset, the normal routine, dull and harassing, went rigidly on, under the usual officers, to whom the greatest respect was shown. No violence, not even rudeness, was hinted to any, though some were politely told that boats would be waiting for them at a certain time to take them and their belongings ashore. They went, but the others were not allowed out of their ships, except on official business. Discipline was to be maintained; and to show that they meant this, the leaders caused yard-ropes to be rove at every fore-yard arm, grim symbols of capital punishment, not to put fear into the hearts of the officers, but to state plainly to the men that they meant to be obeyed, and that this business was in no way a revolution. This point of view was rammed home by the declaration that if the French issued from Brest, the Channel Fleet would instantly out and at them. During the next few days the few delinquents learnt the lesson: a man on the *Pompée*, for instance, who brought a pint of spirits on board, was tied up to the gangway and duly flogged with the "cat" to the tune of twelve lashes; for lesser offenders, the sailors devised the more amusing punishment of ducking overboard, a discipline the regulations were innocent of, but which proved effective.*
Full honours were shown the Delegates whenever they came

* Any account of the mutiny. It is possible that each ship appointed a forecastle captain, but this is doubtful.

39

on board, and on returning to their own ships they were treated with all the solemnity reserved for captains. The side-boys, dressed in white, rigged the side-ropes to the gangway, the men fell in on the quarter-deck, the marine sentry stiffened himself to attention, the Boatswain "piped the side" in a tremendous blast on his whistle, and all the men uncovered. The only thing lacking to the ceremony was the dignified row of officers and Midshipmen lined up on the quarter-deck.

The new authority was absolute, not only of the Delegates within each ship, but of Headquarters, the *Queen Charlotte*, over the rest of the Fleet. The crew of the *Royal William* (the Port-Admiral's ship, which sent no Delegates), who omitted to join in the ritual cheering, were warned that any further carelessness in this matter would mean their being fired into:[47] any ship which seemed recalcitrant was brought to anchor between two staunch ones, and threatened with instant sinking if it misbehaved. And not only was the Assembly all-powerful in the matter of discipline, it directed naval policy as well. It decided that only the large ships should bear the weight of the seamen's interests; frigates and sloops were forbidden to interfere in the business, they had other jobs to carry out,[48] and it was seen that they did carry them out. Thus when on the 17th the *Romney* and the *Venus*, detailed for convoy duty to Newfoundland, refused to unmoor, the crews wanting to stay to join the fun and see the game played out, they quickly received, if not peremptory orders, a "desire and earnest wish" from the *Queen Charlotte* not to play the fool, but to sail as told, which, on the 20th, they did.[49] The Delegates were unanimous that trade must not suffer; they were not fighting the country, but the Admiralty; they knew that they must get and keep the sympathy of the country, of the great trading middle-classes, without which no attempt at redress of grievances has ever been possible in England; it was for this reason that they published their petition to Parliament on the 18th. To have realised the importance of the trading class was an illumination in the Delegates amounting almost to genius, an illumination not shared by their successors at the Nore. It is not surprising that the men had confidence in their leaders, and awaited developments with cheerfulness, under bright blue skies flecked with white.

Sir Charles Pole, hurrying as fast as he could, arrived in London at midnight on the 16th. He at once roused up Nepean, and stayed closeted with him and Spencer till half-past two in the morning. The Earl at last saw that he could not exorcise the evil by doing nothing, and proceeded to act with energy. He was still under forty, and, if the crowds that flocked to admire his tall dark person cutting figures on the ice of the Serpentine are any indication, physically active. Calm, gentle, dignified, distinguished by his grace, his learning, and his humanity, he was of the best type of *grand seigneur*, who added to his other obligations that of being a trustee of the British Museum. Member of the inner circle of the Whig aristocracy, he looked upon himself as born to serve the State; and if he was merely a representative Englishman of the governing class, with plenty of sound sense and a kindly nature, he made up for any lack of genius by the activity and enthusiasm with which he pursued his duties; he never left unanswered a letter from the meanest individual, and manifested his virtues by a rigorous punctuality.[50] At this crisis everything urged him to activity. As soon as possible he hastened off to see Pitt, on whom everything depended; then Dundas (afterwards Lord Melville), Secretary of War and—rather negligently—Treasurer of the Navy. The results of his cogitations and his interviews startled the outer world. Since, as he phrased it in his note to the King, the comic imps seeming to guide his pen, "representations . . . on the very delicate subject of an increase in pay [had been] brought forward and enforced in an unpleasant manner," he would himself go down to Portsmouth and grapple with the mutineers. So at five o'clock that evening, Spencer and Lord Arden, accompanied by Rear-Admiral Young and the second Secretary, Marsden (noted for his Oriental scholarship), bundled into carriages or coaches, and set off with a great cracking of whips down the turnpike road.

They arrived at Portsmouth at noon on the 18th, and travel-stained and travel-shaken, without pausing for a moment, settled down at the Fountain Inn to bring order into the Navy. They summoned Bridport and other officers to a Board, so as to hear what was going on, and then issued a project to the men, to be sent through Bridport, for they would not meet the men themselves. In this document, unfortunately, they ignored both the real situation and the desires of the sailors. It was a mean, chaffering project, which they entrusted to the three Admirals, Gardner, Colpoys and Pole, to take to the Assembly on the *Queen Charlotte*, where the Delegates told them that an answer would be returned at ten o'clock the next morning. But the next morning the Lords Commissioners waited in vain, filled with anxiety, till eleven, till twelve, till one, when a note came from Gardner to say that the answer would not be ready till four.

All that morning, and all that afternoon, as during the evening before till far into the night, irritated men sitting in Howe's state cabin debated in every accent known to the three kingdoms the piffling proposal made them. It seemed to brush aside the petition they had sent through Bridport, signed, since they no longer feared to be made examples of at the yard-arm, a petition extremely moderate in sentiment, respectful in language, and perfectly clear.[51] They had stated, as before, that their wages were too low, and all that Spencer offered them was four, three, and two shillings a month extra for A.B.'s, ordinary seamen, and "landsmen," respectively! "Landsman," moreover, was a hitherto unheard-of rating, and had, in fact, been proposed by the Board in the hope of splitting the ranks of the formidably united petitioners. It was a move that seemed worth trying. The men had asked that their provisions should be up to weight and of better quality: this was ignored. They had asked that when in port they might have vegetables, and fresh meat instead of flour: this was ignored. They had prayed that the sick on board should be better looked after, and that the necessaries meant for them should not be embezzled: no notice was taken. They had pleaded that "we may in some wise have grant and opportunity to taste the sweets of liberty on shore": not a word was mentioned about this. They had asked that the wounded should continue to receive pay, and this was granted with the addition that disabled men should either be pensioned or housed at Greenwich. They had also suggested, fruitlessly, that grievances of individual ships (complaints about officers) should be listened to, and, if possible, redressed; and they had concluded:

> It is also unanimously agreed by the fleet, that from this day no grievances shall be received, in order to convince the nation at large, that we know when to cease to ask, as well as to begin; and that we ask nothing but what is moderate, and may be granted without detriment to the nation, or injury to the service.

All they had got in reply to this very reasonable document was a "project" that convinced them they were being trifled with. Very well, so their tempers crystallised after many weary hours of discussion, the authorities would see. The fact that the First Lord had come down might be a symptom of goodwill, but it might also be one of fear: for their part, they had the power of the Fleet behind them, including the marines: even the sick at Haslar had tied handkerchiefs together to make flags, which they hung out as a signal of encouragement. They would stick to their point, publish their appeal to Parliament, and while still being perfectly respectful, would stand by their guns. They would make Spencer understand that they were determined.

There was probably so little that Spencer did understand, least of all the tenacity of temper born of the depth of grievance, which lay behind the so moderately worded requests. And after all, unless he knew, what could he really understand of the plea that a pound on board ship should weigh sixteen ounces? and that the food should be better? For what the sailor was given to eat was more fit for animal than for human needs, and indeed the oatmeal gruel—burgoo or skillagolee—usually went to the pigs if there were any on board. The meat, two pound of salt beef, when not salt horse, and one pound of salt pork on two days of the week each, was sometimes years old, shrunk hard as wood (carved into boxes it took a very pleasant polish), and was largely bone and gristle, or inedible fat; the biscuits, often weevily, were sometimes so old that they "presented a mixture of rottenness and acari [mites]": [52] the hard centre usually went overboard; the foul cheese was lively with long red worms, the butter was rancid, and mostly used for greasing. A meal almost invariably meant indigestion, and such was the rarity of vegetables that scurvy, loathsome and dreaded, was common. Nobody ever drank the water undisguised if he could possibly help it. Drawn from rivers, it was stored in wooden casks, which had sometimes contained oil, and by the time it was issued to the men it was slimy, and full of green grassy stuff. The men drank swipes till it went sour, and after that a poor kind of wine, sometimes literally vinegar, and—rum. Rum was the one generous ration: half a pint a day (diluted), served in two portions, was the only light in life to gladden the sailor's heart. He could collect it, or swap other things for it, and for a short time dream himself out of hell. But the punishment for drunkenness was the "cat," and it seems "curiously hard that men so eager to get drunk should have been so carefully encouraged to drink, and so brutally punished for drinking the drink allowed to them." [53]

Even the nasty, indigestible and unhealthy fare was given in short measure, apart from the fact that the shrunken meat yielded so small a proportion of edible stuff. For when the purser issued a pound of food, he weighed out only fourteen ounces, because he was allowed money on what were callously called "savings"; in fact, the whole system encouraged him to cheat. Indeed, many pursers derived their chief income from illegal pickings, and it is not astonishing that they were often "rapacious sharks," embezzlers, diluters of wine, and thieves of money from living and dead. Fourteen ounces to the pound had become so much a matter of usage, that when the sailors protested against it, they were not crying out against a fancied evil, but against a recognised practice. The same might also be said as to the sick men's necessaries, so partial were the doctors to chicken.

What must have seemed the most heartless of all the Board's shortcomings was the silent passing over of the plea for leave. It was true that once men got ashore they seldom returned, but that was because they knew that once back they would not step on land again for a very long time. They were, virtually, prisoners in their ships; some of them had not seen their homes for years—anything from two to twelve. The Delegates asked only for leave when convenient, and even suggested that limits should be drawn round the ports beyond which it should be a punishable offence to go. After the question of pay, which affected their families, the humane granting of a little leave was the thing the sailors most ardently desired.

Thus it is not surprising that the answer the Board ultimately did get at half-past four on the 19th, when they were sitting at dinner, was not that meek subjection they seemed to think they had a right to expect. The Delegates first objected to the distinction between seamen and landsmen, and then stated what their demands for pay actually were: a shilling a day for A.B.'s, "and that of petty officers and the ordinary in the usual proportions," and that the marines should also have their pay advanced while serving on board: they asked for the Greenwich pensions to be raised from £7 to £10, repeated their remarks on the food question, and added that "until the grievances before stated are redressed, and an act of indemnity passed, we are determined not to lift an anchor; and the grievances of particular ships must be redressed." [54]

The Board had waited a long time, and they were gentlemen not used to be kept waiting: they had dined, and the meal will not have been barren of fortifying wine. The new petition stiffened their spirits; no more weak conciliation: they decided to resist. The rascally fellows should accept what had been offered, and all would be pardoned: otherwise the dreadful terrors promised by the Articles of War would be visited upon them. Punctuality at the office, administrative habits, a knowledge of the natives of Sumatra, and service experience, all came to the after-dinner conclusion, always a comfortable one, that the Fleet was really sound, but just for the moment suffering from the presence of a few agitators; the rest were poor simple men misguided by rogues scheming for some ulterior purpose. They had not, we have not yet, learnt that, as Burke said, agitators are symptoms, not causes. The Board conceived a bold, dashing plan of slipping the cables and taking the ships to St. Helens, leaving only a few of the worst behind. They summoned the chief officers of the Fleet, Bridport, three Admirals, and sixteen Captains, to meet them the next morning, the 20th. They were full of fight; they would show strength.

But, alas, their spirits were damped by what the officers told them in the cold light of day. Any attempt to move a single ship without the permission of the Delegates would be futile. It was not a question of a few agitators, but of every man jack of the Fleet. Far from resisting the demands, they had better all be granted. The Board's stiff knees bent before this advice. Reluctantly—for Spencer still trembled at the idea of supplementary estimates, though Pitt was to write to him that midnight, "The amount of the expense is comparatively of no consequence" [55]—the First Lord and his colleagues decided to raise the pay of A.B.'s and ordinary seamen to what was demanded,* to grant marines the same pay on sea as on land, and to restore the pound to sixteen ounces—or, if short, to give an allowance. But face must be saved; a chance could still be clung to: there *should* be landsmen, and they *should* get a shilling a month less advance than ordinary seamen. They were determined to make a point of that; but they said nothing about food, or leave, or Greenwich pensions, or the redress of particular grievances: those subjects were wrapped in discreet silence. Finally, all were to return to duty at once, and be forgiven, or else everybody concerned would lose smart-money, be disqualified for pensions, and be excluded from Greenwich for ever. There! they decided comfortably; all would be well now. They had conceded the most that could be expected of officials in their position, who must never give all they are asked for in case they should be thought weak. They would send a letter to each captain to read to his men, and then go home to London with the feeling of work well done as saviours of their country.

Early on the 21st the men were assembled on their various ships to hear the letter from the Board, and listen to their Captains' persuasive comments. They seemed

* The A.B. got 29s. 6d., which, after deductions were made, left him 28s.

satisfied. On the *Duke*, Captain Holloway even got so far with his men as almost to persuade them to return to duty; but, unfortunately for him, a cautious sailor at the back shouted, "Wait and see what the *Queen Charlotte* does!"—a call to order which cancelled Holloway's efforts. The same feeling was expressed on every ship: the men seemed pleased, but they would wait until their council had pronounced upon the message; the Delegates were even then collecting at their headquarters, those from the *Royal Sovereign* promising Gardner to send him immediate word of the result. With that the commanders had to be content. Gardner waited; it seemed to him that he waited a very long time, and he grew fretful, then anxious. He thought he would go across to harangue the Delegates and bring them to reason. He liked haranguing, and had done his best in this way when he had got the critical order to sail on the 16th: he had not been successful then: in fact, his "admonition and friendly advice"—stated in the strongest terms, in which the words "disgrace" and "mischief" occurred rather often —had been "rejected in a manner which hurt his feelings exceedingly": [56] but he might be luckier this time. It was all infernal nonsense, of course, the result of the Sunday schools giving people an education above their place in life, and the trouble was largely due to men like that fellow Spray on his own ship, who had been a chorister at Cambridge—and, one need hardly say, the newspapers.[57] But he knew how to talk to them. So, taking Pole and Colpoys with him, he rowed over to the *Queen Charlotte* and started talking, his argument soon being reinforced by a note Holloway brought from Spencer to say that refusal would be met by "condign punishment," and "utmost vengeance of the law," acceptance with "the forgiveness for which the Board of the Admiralty have solemnly and publickly pledged their faith to them." [58] All went swimmingly, Gardner talked the gathering over in fine hortatory style, and settled down to write a submissive letter to the Admiralty, which all the men would sign.

Then, suddenly, four Delegates who had been absent on shore burst into the proceedings. They were Joyce and Morrice from the *Royal George*, Glynn and Huddlestone of the *Queen Charlotte*. They had not had the benefit of Gardner's honeyed and manly words, but Spencer's message filled them with profound mistrust. Why this insistence on forgiveness? Who could trust the Admiralty's faith? Who could say that they would not be treated like the recent mutineers on the *Culloden*, who had been promised pardon and then strung up at the yard-arm? The only pardon they would accept as safe was that of the King himself; they would do nothing until this was in their hands. They held forth in this strain to the crew below and to the Delegates, who agreed with their view. No return to duty until they had the King's pardon! Gardner, once more exceedingly hurt, was furious; all his eloquence was wasted. He changed his tune; the sucking dove became a lion, and he started slanging the Delegates. They were "a damned mutinous blackguard set," he shouted; they were "skulking fellows," he roared, working himself into ever-increasing rage, "who knew the French were ready for sea, but were afraid of meeting them." Then, beside himself with fury, he seized one of the Delegates by the shoulder, shook him violently, and declared that he would hang him and every fifth man in the Fleet. Howe's cabin immediately became a scene of riot and tumult; the men hissed and shouted; Delegates and crew surged threateningly round the gallant Admiral and his companions: spotted shirts and striped jerseys, canary yellow and scarlet kersevmere waistcoats, overwhelmed the blue-and-gold of the Admirals, who were hustled off the ship in a highly undignified manner.[59]

The Delegates, eager to take the news to their expectant men, dropped hastily into their waiting boats, which radiated out to the other ships, soon, however, to cluster together again about the black and yellow sides of the *Royal George*. Things had been happening there. Joyce and Morrice had decided to call another meeting in their ship, and had hoisted the signal, a red flag. The officers were appalled. Not knowing this was the concerted sign, they let their imaginations run riot: the bloody flag was normally flown when going into action, now it could only mean revolution. They did their utmost to prevent the abhorrent signal from going up, clutching at the ropes, arguing and wrestling with the men; but finding they were powerless, Captain Domett, in a last disgusted effort to salve his pride, hauled down the flag which represented Bridport, who in turn swore that he would never hoist his flag on the ship again, to expose it to such insult and disgrace. Gathered together once more, the Assembly, rattled by Gardner's outburst, showed its teeth; it ordered the guns to be mounted, and the Fleet prepared for action. The officers were kept in closer, but still respectful confinement (a few of the more hated ones were sent on shore), and a watch set as though the ships were at sea in presence of the enemy.[60]

Then, to make sure that nothing would go amiss among themselves, they circulated

A CAUTION FROM THE DELEGATES TO THE FLEET.

The settlement of a business of such vast importance as the present is the most critical and ought to be attended to with the greatest wisdom, as ourselves and characters depends on our present conduct, therefore the following considerations are absolutely necessary as a security and bulwark against the fair speeches of designing men, who will use all their eloquence to defeat our laudable intentions.

First.—Indispensibly requisite that the prayers of our petition be fully answered.

Second.—That no verbal answer be attended to on our part.

Third.—That an Act of Parliament be passed for the augmentation of our pay and other articles in our petition.

Fourth.—That after the petition is fully satisfied, a petition be presented to His Majesty, and the pardon for the liberty we have now taken be received in due form, through the whole Fleet.[61]

Such a manifesto would prevent the men from slipping guilelessly back to duty.

Meanwhile Gardner and Pole had gone off to tell their news to Spencer, whom they disturbed after his dinner, at the house of Sir Charles Saxton. Gardner then, apparently,[62] made out the draft of a letter to the Fleet insisting on the validity of the Board's promises of forgiveness: but Spencer was dubious as to whether this was enough; the King's pardon seemed to be the only thing that would do, and surely, when so near success, it would be absurd to allow an idle suspicion—a suspicion of his own honour—to spoil all. He must get the King's pardon. So, without a moment's waste of time, he got into his carriage at midnight, and set off for London as fast as his horses would take him.

CHAPTER V

INTERVAL AT SPITHEAD

TO people endowed with lively imaginations, the mutiny seemed monstrous and sinister, not at all the simple protest of men who felt aggrieved. Captain Willet Payne of the *Impétueux*, for example, being ill at the George Inn, allowed full play to his rollicking fancy, which, as a fire-eating sailor and an accomplished rake, he found irksome in the tedious atmosphere of a sick-room. Scribbling down his mental adventures for Spencer's benefit, he decided that there were "secret *Jacobin* springs" behind the whole affair; the only thing to do was to try to create disunion among the mutineers, and it was he, it seems, who hit on the illusory idea of splitting opinion by inventing "landsmen." He also suggested making the shore batteries bristle with every gun and mortar available—Spencer fell in with this too—and inserting articles in the *Star*, which he said was the seamen's favourite newspaper, to express the nation's horror at the heinous event.[63] Young Lord Camelford, even less governed in character and imagination, rose to greater heights of the lurid. Just promoted lieutenant after a career of insubordination and super-romantic fantasy such as you might expect from the most harum-scarum of the eccentric Pitts, he warned Spencer that there was a horrid plot to kidnap the Board if it should venture on any ship.[64] *The Times*, as a Government organ incapable of believing that anything could really be amiss with the sailors' lot, was to put it all blandly down to our old friends the agitators, especially Joyce and the slippery Evans.[65] Lady Spencer, reflecting her Lord's anxiety, was alarmed at the amazing order that prevailed among the subversive spirits:

Alas! my dear Sir [she wrote to Windham on the 20th], we none of us know the end of this most awful affair. Lord S. writes in very low spirits. . . . Dundas, whom I have just seen, seems full as serious on the business as I am, and truly there is food for thought in the present prospect of things. The quietness of the men, tho' comfortable in some respects, yet in others is most alarming—it proves a steadiness in them to accomplish their object which overpowers *me*, whatever it may do other people. . . . That a mutiny of this extent should have been brewing for 3 months, and not one word of it to have transpired, is most wonderful. Surely, surely, it implies a great want of knowledge amongst the officers,[66]

an observation which was both shrewd and fair, coming from someone who had not seen Pakenham's letter.

To Lieutenant Philip Beaver, on board the *Monarch* in Portsmouth Harbour, who watched these things with an intelligent eye, and pondered them with the experienced mind of a man of thirty-two, the affair did not seem fantastic. Though well within the trouble (his ship being in harbour was not involved, however, till the 19th), he was not toppled off his balance. While being sorry that the mutiny should take place in war-time, he could not help admiring the "moderation [of the men] in so daring an exercise of illegal power," and their patriotism in declaring that if the French came out they would haul up the anchors and go for them. As the negotiations went on, he became more and more astonished at their "prudence and decency": they had been driven to do what they were doing by the folly of Lord Howe and the Ministry. He thought that the Board, instead of haggling, would have done much better to grant handsomely what would be forced from them in the end; and he wisely feared that "Lord Spencer and the other Lords of the Admiralty trifle too much and may make matters worse." The next day, the 20th, his opinion grew firmer; he believed that the Delegates had

been obliged to make use of some strong expressions towards Lord Spencer to convince him of the danger, which he did not seem to comprehend, and of the absurdity of that board since it has sat here, which had only made things worse.... The seamen still continue to conduct themselves incredibly well, performing the usual duties with alacrity, and behaving towards their officers with the greatest respect. I had always great respect for an English seaman; I like the character now better than ever.[67]

So much from a level-headed man to his sister, a man who really knew what it was all about. He at any rate saw no reason to assume Jacobins at work.

The country on the whole, after the first shock, was inclined to take the matter calmly; it regarded it gravely enough, but refused to be rattled into hysteria by anyone. After all, the sailors were extremely well behaved; they were ready to fight the French; they saw to the carrying on of trade; and when you looked at the demands they made, these were really very reasonable. In fact, in the main, public opinion was with them. The people of Portsmouth were so far curious rather than alarmed: it was great fun to walk about in your spare time and see what could be seen of the goings on, and gossip about it all. The affair, indeed, added to the gaiety of life by the presence of the Board, which treated them to a little extra pageantry. For when, on Wednesday, 19th, the Prince of Württemberg—who was about to marry the Princess Royal—came to Portsmouth to receive its freedom, Lords Spencer and Bridport, with Sir William Pitt, Governor, took him round the Fleet in all the gay panoply of the commissioner's barge. Who but Englishmen would have made a tour of state to show a foreign visitor their Fleet in full mutiny? or who but English sailors in mutiny would have turned out to salute the cruising dignitaries?[68] One hopes that his Serene Highness found his host's character a little more comprehensible after the display.

The newspapers varied, but were, on the whole, fair, when not gibing at the authorities for treating with a "convention of delegates," or a "representative government" established on board a British fleet. For example, the *London Chronicle* printed on the 19th:

> It is but common justice to say that the seamen have conducted themselves throughout the whole business with a sobriety, steadiness, unanimity and determination, that would do honour to a better cause,

the last phrase, perhaps, demanding too much selflessness in human beings. Another paper remarked that:

> ... a decent seasonable attention to the remonstrances of the sailors might have saved England from a calamity which no man could contemplate without dismay.[69]

It is true that in the *Sun*, which was the paper the sailors took in (and not the *Star*), there did appear on the 18th an odd squib, dated from "The Buoy of the *Royal George*, Spithead, Sunday, April 16th, 1797," and signed, "The Spirit of Kempenfeldt," which clanged all the tocsins of alarm; but it failed to make the burghers of England tremble. The authorship was never disclosed, but—well, was it not the very thing that the exuberant and ingenious Captain Payne had suggested to Spencer should be done? Is it beyond the bounds of likelihood that he should have anticipated his suggestion, given the example before laying down the precept? and that it should really have been dated from the George Inn, rather than from the *Royal George*? Whether by the gallant captain or not, the writer had much to learn in care of words and dignity of phrase from the men he upbraided. The alarmist appeal began, with a faint reminiscence of Mark Antony:

"Friends, Countrymen, and Fellow Subjects," to sum up after a deal of high-sounding trumpery:

> My brave Fellows! Be not deceived—calm reflection will soon await you—*Then* will you start aside from the unhappy path of disobedience designing men have surprised you into. ... [Does not that sound very like Payne?] Make known your wishes and wants in an official and re-

spectful manner and be assured the love your King and Country bear you will dispose them to give you every comfort and reward a grateful country can bestow, consistent with its existence as a Nation.[70]

The Delegates had no difficulty whatever in effectually demolishing the spirit; brave Kempenfeldt was gone, they could take liberties, and they headed their reply of the 20th, which also appeared in the *Sun*,* with a quotation which, if not quite accurate, at any rate showed that they, too, knew their Shakespeare.

FROM THE LIVING TO THE DEAD.

Art thou a spirit of earth or goblin damn'd?

SIR,—In the *Sun*, of the 18th instant, we have seen your address, and which greatly surprised us, wherein we are accused of those crimes, which disgrace the name of a British seaman, and which may prejudice the minds of our countrymen against us; as we are called upon to make known our wants and wishes in an official and respectful manner.

Therefore, we, His Majesty's most loyal and dutiful subjects, wish to make known to the world that we have done so.

We, as subjects of a loyal country, presented our petitions to that honourable Earl, who wore the laurels of the glorious 1st of June, and who was in the hearts of British seamen represented as their friend; but sorry are we to say that we found to the contrary, in his not representing our petitions to the Lords Commissioners of the Admiralty.

But to convince our country at large, that there is not in anywise the least spark of republican spirit, we have caused to be inserted the most private of our concerns: sorry also we are to remark the words, "French agents," as our country may think, by that assertion, we now take into our arms the people that a British seaman detests the name of. But to the contrary, we have our country's good as much at heart as any other description of men whatever, and that our request is nowise injurious to our country.

We ask for that comfortable subsistence which our country can easily bestow, and that those barbarities which are practised by some (sorry, indeed, we should be to say the whole, as there are among us men of every description, both good and evil) be erased out of this well-instituted service.

* The editor was threatened that those responsible would be made to dance to a tune other than " God Save the King " if any burlesque whatever appeared.

We, the subjects of your address, coolly as the representatives of that body which has so long lain under the well-known Buoy, wish you to come forward in a fair and manly way, in your real and corporeal state, and try for one week if the scanty allowance on which we are obliged to subsist, will keep you in the spirited state which men of our description require, but are at this moment without the assistance of at least two-thirds of their pay; and our wives and families languishing in want, whilst this country, that abounds with plenty, ought to be ashamed at the word Want!

To the brave Admiral Kempenfeldt's GHOST,
Buoy of the Royal George, Spithead.

P.S.—If the clamours of justice daily echoing from the mouths of the loyal tars should again awake the SPIRIT OF KEMPENFELDT, let not his ethereal, but his corporeal part, make itself known, and we will convince him, that those who have made *Britannia rule the main,* know also their duty to their Sovereign.

Spithead, April 20, 1797.[71]

Could anything be neater, more completely crushing? It would be a tame, poor-hearted reader of the *Sun,* who would not be turned by this to sympathise with the sailors. You cannot talk in that controlled strain without being pretty sure that justice is with you; and besides, the Spirit of Kempenfeldt had been made to look ridiculous; so laughter was on the seamen's side.

This interchange, of course, was before the tumult that had ended Gardner's untimely exhortation, which had made the sailors, already suspecting they were being tricked, think that the Admiral, with all his threats of hanging, had something up his sleeve. For the moment their nerves had got the better of them, and hustled them to arms; but they soon regained the steadiness which so disturbed Lady Spencer. The events of the 21st may have given encouragement to some wild spirits among the men, United Irishmen perhaps, who panted for a general flare-up, but if so they were effectively damped down. So on the 22nd the Delegates wrote three letters, all of them of great restraint and dignity. The first of two to Bridport was a personal one, regretting the flag-striking incident of the day before, asking him to take up his command again, and referring to him as "the father of the Fleet": there was no officer in the whole Navy whom they would more willingly serve under, they said, disclaiming any idea of meaning to offer him personal insult. In the second letter, which was official, they explained that Gardner's speech of appeal to "loyal" individuals had looked to them very like an attempt "to sow division and mistrust in the Fleet" (there was nothing they resented more than insinuations against their patriotism). "But for the unfortunate cause above mentioned," they went on,

> there is every reason to believe that before this time every tittle of the business would have been settled; but at present it is the resolution of all not to lift anchor till every article is rendered into an Act of Parliament and the King's pardon to all concerned.[72]

The behaviour of the Board, in fact, following upon the early Admiralty message, pompous and inane, which Bridport had been forced to broadcast, had made them suspect the integrity of their lords and masters in the service. These august people, they felt, would fool them if they could. It was obviously necessary to make it perfectly clear to their Lordships that they would not on any account be fooled. So the third document of that day, while it thanked the Board for their generosity, for the satisfaction they had given to "every loyal and well-disposed seaman and marine," ended significantly:

> But we beg leave to remind your lordships, that it is a firm resolution that, until the flour in port be removed, the vegetables and pensions augmented, the grievances of private ships redressed, an act passed, and his Majesty's gracious pardon for the fleet now lying at Spithead be granted, that the fleet will not lift an anchor; and this is the total and final answer.[73]

That was unmistakable in its plainness.

"The grievances of private ships!" The seamen were probably as determined about those as they had been about the pay, and it was the point least likely to be listened to by the Admiralty, for it meant that the latter would have to admit tacitly that many of the officers were the most appalling bullies, who often resorted to outrageous tyranny to cover up their slackness and incompetence. They knew only too well that the charges made by the men were true. Admiral Collingwood, best of disciplinarians, who himself hated the lash, more than once told the Admiralty "that some of the younger captains (although admitting there were several honourable exceptions) endeavoured to conceal, by great severity, their own unskilfulness and want of attention, [and] beat the men into a state of insubordination." [74] Yet luckily for their peace of mind none of the petitions sent in by the men even faintly represented the horror of life on board, for, as the seamen of the *Nassau* had said, it was impossible for them to put it down on paper. They did say, however, that their captain was a tyrant, and that

> the next executor of this cruelty is our second Lieutenant, Mr. Pyewell, who in the night on his watch will make any one strip under his shirt and let him get two or three dozen either with a ropes end or else with the boatswain's mate's ratan. We might rather wish ourselves into prison or to be killed at once.[75]

A rattan being no mean weapon; but even such an emotional statement could not possibly convey much to civilians without experience of the physical reality behind it. On 19th April the whole crew of the *Nymphe*, two hundred of them, did rather better, declaring above their signatures:

> We are kept more like convicts than free-born Britons. . . . Flogging is carried on to extremes, one man received three dozen for what was termed silent contempt, which was nothing more than this. After being beat by a Boatswain's mate, the man smiled, this was the unpardonable crime. Another was flogged for not going up the rigging quick enough, and another for not sending him down as was supposed smart enough. In short the number that has been flogged for trifling offences would be too tedious to mention at present. . . . When engaged with the enemy off

Brest, March 9th 1797, they even beat us at our quarters tho' on the
verge of eternity and said I'll beat you until I make you jump overboard,
damn you, you rascal, etc. Jump overboard or be God Dam^d. I will not
send a boat after you. . . . Is this the way to encourage the service?

And they reported that another sailor on the same ship
"received two dozen for not having the number sewn on
his hammock." [76] Whatever the Board may have thought
about the best way of encouraging the service, or however
much they may have discounted these complaints, many
of the officers were certainly monsters of the worst kind.
"Captains there are," James recorded,[77] "who seemingly
delight in such work [flogging]; and who, were the cruise
long enough, would not leave a sailor belonging to the ship
with an unscarred back." Of one at least it is told that
he would stand gloatingly by while the delinquent writhed
in agony, and say, "By God, I'll show them who's captain.
I'll see the man's backbone, by God!" [78] The punishment
was so drastic that men had been known to throw themselves
off the yards into the sea rather than face the skinning they
were promised as a reward for being down last—which they
probably were if they were up first. For there was no
limit to what the captain could do to make men's lives
unbearable, nothing sometimes he did not do ; and Marryat
was not far out when he told of the captain who ordered
five or six dozen for spitting on the quarter-deck—a filthy
habit, no doubt, but one which might have been subdued by
gentler methods. The most ghastly of all the cases of
tyranny, which really argues that an obsessed man was in
command, is that of Captain Pigot of the *Hermione*, who, in
the West Indies in September 1797, threatened to flog the
last man down from the yards. Two topmen, in their terrified anxiety to avoid the ordeal, fell from the mast and broke
their limbs; whereupon Pigot ordered, "Throw those lubbers
overboard!" That night the maddened sailors rose, and
murdered their captain with nearly all the other officers.

To be flogged was to be tortured. The first stroke laid on by a brawny boatswain's mate, as hard as he could at the full length of his arm, would always jerk an involuntary "Ugh!" out of even the most hardened unfortunate "seized up to" the grating at the gangway; six blows tore the flesh horribly, while after a dozen the back looked like "so much putrefied liver." After a time the bones showed through, blood burst from the bitten tongue and lips of the victim, and, expelled from his lungs, dribbled through his nostrils and ears. To make sure that the standard of hitting was maintained, the wielder of the cat would be changed after every two or three dozen, and the blood was wiped off the thongs between each stroke to prevent them sticking together. To be flogged through the Fleet to the tune of the "Rogue's March" meant almost certain death, if not on the spot, a few days later; and on being sentenced to this fiendish punishment, an offender was usually offered the choice of being hanged. A severe flogging smashed a man; he was ill for weeks after it, and rarely recovered his self-respect if he originally had any good in him.[79] The Regulations did certainly lay down that a dozen strokes on the bare back was to be the maximum, but nobody took any notice of the rule; two or three dozen were usual, a hundred common, while the infliction of three hundred was by no means rare.

Yet throughout the mutinies the men never raised their voices against flogging as an institution, though it was infamous, and futile as an instrument of discipline: they even carried it out themselves, though not outrageously. What they did object to was its abuse; and, as the men of the *Pompée* wrote to Howe:[80]

My Lord, we do not wish you to understand that we have the least intention of encroaching on the punishments necessary for the preservation of good order and discipline necessary to be preserved in H.M. Navy, but to crush the spirit of tyranny and oppression so much practised and delighted in, contrary to the spirit or intent of any laws of our country.

They went in constant fear of a horrible ordeal for some trifling offence, for ceremonial flogging, carried out in all the forms with the reading of the Article of War against which the man was supposed to have offended, and the raising of everybody's hat out of respect for the King's ordinance, was not the only doom that could overtake a man without warning. Any officer, even a midshipman, could unmercifully beat, or have beaten, about the head, arms, and back, any wretch with whom he momentarily lost his temper, a pastime known as "starting," which was carried out with a knotted rope until its wielder was weary. Had this state of things been rare, so much need not have been said here, and would not have been said by the men; but, in fact, the humane officer was the exception, to whom the men were touchingly grateful; usually he was little better than a sadistic devil.

If the piteous testimony of the men may not be convincing, there is that of an officer, James Anthony Gardner, said to be a calm, good-natured man, not given to either over-excitement or squeamishness, and always ready to say what good he might about his brother officers. Commissioned to the *Salisbury* in December 1782, he described her as "an old devil of a ship, properly called the Hell Afloat," recording of her that

> this was the most hateful and disagreeable ship I ever had my foot on board of. Mast-heading upon every trifling occasion. The senior mid-shipmen (with the exception of a few) were tyrants.

Transferred after two years to the *Orestes*, he found that her lieutenant, Thomas Jeynes,

> was without exception the most cold-blooded bad fellow I have ever met with. I have seen him thrash the men with the end of a rope until he was tired, making use of the most abusive language.

Nor was his next ship, the flagship *Edgar*, any pleasanter, for there the Admiral "used to play hell, and turn up Jack, and would spare nobody." Similarly in the *Queen*, the first lieutenant, Constable, was "a devil of a tyrant." Once, when Gardner was "starting" the crew of the jolly-boat for slackness in getting it out, Constable shouted at him, "Damn my eyes, sir! That's not the way; you should take a hand-spike and knock their brains out." And even if the advice was not meant to be carried out literally, it shows the sort of atmosphere in which the men lived.[81] Nearly everywhere, then, there was the same system of terrorism, and apart from the flogging and starting there were minor forms of tyranny and bullying, such as mast-heading, gagging with an iron block, making a man ride a gun with his feet tied underneath, and giving him harassing or disgusting duties to perform endlessly. A man's life could be made a perfect misery, and was, we are told, on seven ships out of nine.

It was far better to serve under a martinet, a "smart" captain, than under a slack one, for in the former case there was less unrestrained brutality; punishment might be severe, but it was regulated and had some show of justice. It was no good the captain being kind-hearted unless he kept his subordinate officers in order, for otherwise the seaman's life might still be a continued agony of apprehension, as in the *Glory*, which sent in a petition on 17th April 1797:

> It is our unanimous desire that Lieut. Fitzpatrick and Lieut. Hicks be dismissed out of H.M.S. *Glory*, as the former has in every means behaved tyranically to the people with ordering them to be beat in a most cruel manner . . . beating, blacking, tarring, and putting the people's heads in bags to the mortification of the whole ship's company, also striving to affect and discontinue the genteel kind behaviour of our well wished for Captain. These are faults which in all probability through their proceedings for the time to come is the ready way to the ruin of the British nation.

Grammar may have been weak in the *Glory*, but the sense was sound, and indignation gave the words strength. The

Ramillies, again,[82] objected against petty tyranny, their lieutenant, Trench, keeping them for long hours on unnecessary work (after cutting their grog, too), such as raising and lowering the boats twelve and fourteen times, having kept them at work from four in the morning till ten at night: and after all that, perhaps, making the men carry their hammocks on their backs for hours together. Trench was helped in his amiable pursuit by Lieutenant Simmonds. In the same way, it was not to denounce their captain, but their lieutenant, William Compton, that the crew of the *Minotaur* petitioned: he beat them, they said, most unmercifully. "It is impossible to insert in this sheet the many acts of cruelty and the many men that has run [deserted] from this ship through his ill-usage." One need not continue the list: complaints were all but universal; but we may add the pertinent one of the *Duke*, whose company stated that they had been cruelly maltreated, and begged that certain of their superiors might be "replaced by officers possessed of more humanity."

Mercifully it was not all so unrelievedly grim and hopeless; some of the officers were decent men, who understood that discipline must be based on affection and trust, and not on fear. These officers were duly loved by their crews, who wished to follow them from one command to another. One round-robin, for example—a round-robin was signed in a circle, each man writing towards the centre to avoid priority—runs as follows:—

> We the company of His Majesty's ship *Vestal* having heard that Captain MacDougall late of His Majesty's said ship being appointed to the command of the *Asia*, would be very happy to sail along with him which is the petition of your honours most obedient very humble servants.[83]

Sometimes when a good captain left his ship, the sailors would scrape together what small mites they could from their pay, and subscribe to buy a small piece of presentation plate;

and, as we shall see, Admiral Duncan was so loved by his men that they declared themselves ready to do anything for him, down to the shedding of the last drops of their blood. Many of the officers knew about their men, regarded them as fellow-creatures — Pakenham, for instance, and Beaver—but there can be no possible doubt that the general conditions at sea were abominable, tending to the utter degradation of both body and spirit.

It is small wonder, then, that the men insisted upon the redress of grievances on particular ships. The question of punishments had not been put forward in the decorous negotiations between the Delegates and the Board, for obviously discipline in itself could not be argued about; and besides, the men did not object to discipline as such, only to its shocking abuse; the complaints were against individuals. Besides, the Admiralty had been so long and so fruitlessly bombarded with petitions on the subject of brutality, that it was clearly no use to appeal in this way. Bridport, as a supremely sensible man, asked for complaints; at least the *Minotaur*, in sending some in on 24th April, said they were "informed by the Delegates of the Fleet that your Lordship will receive any grievances from any of the ships under your command." Their objections sound well justified, and in one part reveal a further piece of mal-administration. In this they arraigned their surgeon, Bell,

> for inattention and ill-treatment of the sick and wounded and not being qualified, as we can judge by several accidents happening in the ship. . . . And for not visiting the sick for two or three months together, and when visiting has often been observed in liquor, and not serving to the sick such nourishments as is allowed by Government, and for the want of which many men has died in this ship. There as been men went down to him for relief when sick, and he as told them that a flogging would do them most good.[84]

Some of the doctors, of course, did their work well, and were regarded by the men as their best friends; but many of them were of the kind typified by Bell—sodden, rough and incompetent.

So with a growing consciousness of power, power made plain by the whole trend of events, the men, while waiting for the effect of their "total and final" answer, which had followed the Board to London, harboured their resentment, and nursed their determination to get the "special grievances" redressed. While happier folk on land carolled that Britons never, never should be slaves, the very men who ruled the seas were being treated, as they said, like Turks, cowed with curses and blows, fretted by ignominy and contempt, the bitterness of their lives only occasionally tempered with a shred of kindness. They would obey orders with alacrity, they would treat their officers with respect, but they would not forget. Outwardly restrained, they were simmering underneath. Yet in this period of uneasy waiting the leaders kept absolute control, for they possessed faculties which very seldom go together—the capacity to work the feelings of men up to a state of revolt, combined with the power to direct the course of events after the first explosion. They seem to have judged with almost perfect precision how far they could go; but the old life, they swore, would never come back: they had had enough.

CHAPTER VI

UNTIMELY EFFECTS OF PROCRASTINATION

WHILE the Fleet, in controlled excitement, was waiting out its time at Spithead, Lord Spencer was tirelessly busy. Arriving in London at nine o'clock on the morning of the 22nd, he saw Pitt, insisted upon a Cabinet council being called at once, with the whole Admiralty Board in attendance, and at five o'clock, with Pitt and Lord Chancellor Loughborough, drove off to see the King at Windsor, where a council was called at nine. There and then they made out the proclamation of pardon, which George III signed and sealed. The Admiralty messenger rushed up to London with it, had a hundred copies printed before midnight, and carried them off damp from the press to deliver to Sir Peter Parker at a quarter to seven on the morning of St. George's Day, 23rd April.

Parker promptly sent for the Admirals, who consulted with him till eleven, when they returned to their ships, and copies of the proclamation were fetched from the flagship by the various captains, to be made known to the men. Bridport himself read the one on the *Royal George*, and made a speech in which he promised a general redress of grievances; whereupon the crew cheered lustily, and pulled down the sinister ropes from the yards; then, before very long, the Admiral's insulted flag appeared once more on the topgallant masthead.

But the red bunting still flew jauntily on the *Queen Charlotte* and on the other ships, for in these the men were not quite so sure. Suspicion had entered so deeply into many of their minds that they cynically imagined that the supposed pardon might be a fake. What had happened to the *Culloden's* men was vivid in their memories. They decided to wait until they knew what the Assembly would have to say about it, and the Delegates were soon summoned to the *Queen Charlotte*, where the applause had been somewhat muted after Admiral Pole's reading of the proclamation. Decision was again delayed by the absence of Patrick Glynn, and of Valentine Joyce, whose family lived in Portsmouth, and who had not, presumably, been present at the happy scene of reconciliation on his own ship, the *Royal George*; but after a little time they were conducted on board with all the pomp and pride of ceremony. While the tension grew among the officers and men alert for news throughout the Fleet, the debating Delegates came slowly to the conclusion that it would be safer to see the original draft of the pardon; it was not until this had been fetched from the flagship, and they had seen the King's own seal upon it, that they agreed to be satisfied. As a sign that every one was appeased, the crew of the *Charlotte* manned the yards in their best blue and white, and roared communicative huzzas to the other ships; and at last, at about six, the only yard-ropes which yet remained were removed from the *Mars*, which, with the *Marlborough*, had shown some reluctance to come in.[85]

The crowds gathered on the beach and quays could see to some extent what was going on; but it was not till the ever-busy Captain Holloway of the *Duke* came on shore at about seven, "to announce the happy tidings to the anxious spectators waiting the result on the platform," that they were altogether released from dread. "All the boats from the other ships followed, and the seamen in each on landing declared the business most happily settled. . . . The intelligence was received with the most excessive joy by the people on shore," [86] who no doubt celebrated far into a noisy night this convivial conclusion to St. George's Day. The next morning a portion of the Fleet dropped the few miles down to St. Helens, and four days later most of the rest joined them to wait for a fair wind to put to sea. The *Ramillies*,

Marlborough, *Minotaur*, and *Nymphe*, still refractory on account of the detestation in which they held some of their officers, stayed behind at Spithead, under Colpoys in the *London*, and were detailed to take station near the Lizard when the battle-fleet went to harry the French. The mutiny was virtually over.

In the opinion of the country it should have been over long before, and would have been if the authorities had acted with common sense. Scornfully referring to the council at Windsor, the opposition papers remarked that:

> It would have been wise and dignified that this council had been held on the first explosion, instead of attempting to chaffer and bargain with the fleet. The moment of negotiation was when they had first made their representation to Lord Howe. ... It was hoped that the whole affair would be an awful warning to ministers, how they presumed to trifle with the petitions of an aggrieved people.

They went on to say that "there is an insult in indifference, which is more painful to a spirited man than injury," but did not fail to point out that injury was there too in the undischarged warrants for pay "lying in vast masses" in various dusty pigeon-holes in London.* But mercifully all was now settled, and the country could once more rest its head comfortably on its pillow.

At least so every one supposed; and all would have been so but for the dilatoriness of the Government, and the contrary winds which prevented Bridport from getting out his ships. The Admiralty itself lost no time: it sent a memorial to the Privy Council on the 22nd, telling them of the promised increases of pay and provisions; but the Council, apparently not realising that they were sitting on a tub of

---

* Neale, 47. From the *Commons Journals*, 52, p. 503, we learn that on 25th April 1797 (the date is significant) the Navy Office estimated the debt of H.M.'s Navy, as it stood on 31st December 1796, to be as follows:—

Due to pay the men unpaid on books of ships paid off .	£435,395	15 2
To ships in sea pay on aforesaid 31st Dec. . . .	973,324	12 9

gunpowder in the middle of a crisis, and that swiftness was of crying importance, spoilt it all by setting in motion the slow-grinding wheels of the normal Circumlocution Office methods of legislature. They appointed a committee to consider the proposals, as though they could not have got straight to business by sending a proclamation to be ratified by Parliament at once. "Was this a period for petty form-alities and official procrastination?" Fox was later to ask the House indignantly: "Was it necessary to suspend a business of such importance that the ministers' clerks might have leisure to form their estimates according to rule?" As though every one had not known what the result would be; as though the active part of the Council had not themselves framed, and been agreed upon, the proposals![87] But even so, the committee considered, no doubt very wisely and importantly, and then they considered again, with the result that they did not report until 3rd May, already a fort-night after the pardon and the promises. The next day the estimates were ready, and Pitt said that he would bring them before the House on Friday, 5th: an unlucky date to choose seeing that the House was not to meet until the 8th! So there was another week gone, and nothing done. Mean-while elsewhere things were happening, and the place was St. Helens.

The sailors, wind-bound in harbour, had plenty of time to think, and as they thought, suspicion ate further and further, ever more convincingly, into their minds. Why was there all this delay? It must be that some hanky-panky was going on. They had no notion that constitutional law-making was a cumbersome business, likely at the end to be long-winded also, and not a simple, easy matter, such as writing out a trade bill. Moreover, it seemed plainer to them every day that the reply to their "total and final answer," issued on the 24th, had not been very encouraging. Its tone, for one thing, suggested that the sailors were a lot of ungrateful dogs for whom quite enough had been done in raising their pay. In satisfaction of their request for fresh meat instead of flour when in port, they were told shortly that it "cannot at this time be complied with": as for vegetables, "instead of asking for more, they ought to be most thankful for that with which, at a great expense to the country, they are now supplied." There was to be no addition to pensions on account of the new great burdens to the public in the way of increases in wages; in the matter of complaints they were graciously informed that these might be made to the commander-in-chief, who would duly appoint courts martial; and to this the Commissioners added sublimely that "their Lordships are inclined to hope that all animosities have ceased, and that the complaints which were brought forward in a moment of ill-humour may now be suffered to drop." [88] It is doubtful if the phrase "a moment of ill-humour" appealed to the sailors' comic sense as it may at this distance to ours; at all events the answer was damnable in tone and silly in substance. The seamen therefore muttered as they pondered; but if they became sullen, they did nothing to disturb the equanimity of the high and mighty deciding their fates in London.

All the same, a decided note of warning sounded from Plymouth. On the 26th, the crews there in the squadron under Sir Roger Curtis mutinied in sympathy with, and apparently in accordance with instructions from, their comrades at Spithead; at any rate they did it neatly, picturesquely, and without a hitch. The next day Captain Squire, of the *Atlas*, wrote to Sir John Orde, the officer commanding at Plymouth, to say that his crew were ready enough in returning to their routine duty, but would not be patient for more than three or four days, in which time, they had no doubt, the expected Act of Parliament would be passed. Orde forwarded the letter to the Admiralty, and while telling them that Squire guaranteed the loyalty of his men for this short time, expressed a strong hope, which should have spurred the authorities on, that the Bill would have gone through by then.[89] But even this hint, if they ever saw it, did not hasten the majestic pace of the "ministers' clerks." Meanwhile, on the 28th, the men at Plymouth, growing restive at hearing nothing, decided that they must get into close personal touch with their friends at Portsmouth, and that the best way to do this was to send them a deputation. But how? There was the problem, for they would have to ask for an Admiralty boat, and it might be refused them. What then? The leaders at Plymouth addressed a letter to the crews of the ships in the Sound:

28th April 1797.

BROTHERS OF THE SQUADRON,

We are one and all unanimously agreed if our request is not complied with immediately for a cutter to go round with the Delegates to Spithead to know the issue of this affair, we are determined to get the ships under weigh immediately to proceed there.[90]

It was a bold threat, and the Delegates apparently knew it, since they did not give the captains a chance of calling their bluff.

For they were not granted a cutter, and they did not sail the squadron up-Channel to Spithead. What they did do was rather tamely to hire one of the Portsmouth cutters, and man her with two Delegates from each of the rebellious ships, the *Atlas, Saturn, Majestic,* and *Edgar.* Yet their send-off was inspiriting enough. About five o'clock on the evening of Friday, 28th, the deputation left Hamoaze. When abreast of the *Saturn* and the *Atlas* (their "Parliament Ship") the crews tumbled up from below, crowded the gangways and forecastles, and saluted the adventurers with terrific cheers, which were returned; after which the cutter went spanking up the Channel under a crowd of canvas. The men they left behind behaved extremely well, with great sobriety and scrupulous respect for their officers, "in short, [with] that kind of regularity that is altogether unusual, at and after the payment of wages"; for their Delegates promised to be back on the Monday evening. When these representatives got to Portsmouth, six of them went to interview Sir Peter Parker, from whom they demanded and got assurance that the Fleet had satisfactorily settled its differences with the Admiralty. They all went back happily on the Sunday, six by one of the passage vessels, two by land express. Yet not altogether happily; for the two Delegates who had gone to St. Helens and visited the *Queen Charlotte* and other ships came away with a flea in their ear: the crew of the *Royal George* had damned them up and down for leaving their ships, told them to go back at once, and added that if they found them loitering at Portsmouth they would infallibly hang them.[91]

Far from regarding the Plymouth affair as symptomatic, and doing all they could to soothe the men while the "Seamen's Bill" was being prepared, on 1st May the Admiralty sent down to the captains of ships an order which was "a masterpiece of folly." [92] It annoyed the officers considerably, since it accused them by implication of pilfering the best of the men's supplies (which was not altogether untrue), and insisted on the better regulation of medical stores; but its main purport was that discipline should be tightened up. The captains were to see that "the arms and ammunition belonging to the marines be constantly in good order, as well in harbour as at sea"—a thing which had never been done before, and which could have only one meaning; moreover, the order concluded by saying that the officers were to be ready "on the first appearance of mutiny to use the most vigorous means to suppress it, and bring the ringleaders to punishment." [93] The men in command, on the spot, knew there would be the devil to pay if that got out, and were as reticent as they could be about the order: they were like men in a powder store, into whose horrified hands the authorities had thrust a lighted fusee.

Yet the Admiralty may have thought that their exhibition of sheer imbecility was a brilliantly effective creation of the intellect when they heard how an attempt at mutiny in the North Sea Fleet had been overcome by a spirited application of discipline. On the afternoon of 30th April, Admiral Duncan heard the men, who were swarming on the fore-castle and fore-shrouds of his ship, the *Venerable*, give three unauthorised cheers. He immediately mustered the officers and ordered the marines under arms, for every one knew what this sort of hurrahing meant. He was profoundly grieved that the men for whom he had always done so much should behave in this way, and he was also very angry indeed. He was bursting with rage as he heaved his gigantic frame forward "to know the cause of such improper conduct," and it was only with the greatest difficulty that his chaplain was able to prevent him running his sword through one of the men. It was not long before this tower of fury got his men under control, and rated them so soundly, and so humanly, that when he asked them what they had meant, they could only answer meekly that they thought there was no harm in doing as their friends at Spithead had done.[94] Duncan forgave them; they were his children, and that they meant no harm he knew by the letter they had written on the 27th:

Venerable,
27th April 1797.

The seamen of the North-sea fleet beg leave to return their grateful thanks to the Lords Commissioners of the Admiralty, for their ready compliance with the humble request of their worthy companions in the Channel Fleet. At the same time to convince their lordships of our united and steady support of his Majesty and our country, we will at all times risk everything that is dear to man. Have only to regret, from the situation of the enemy we are opposed to, it has not been in our power to show the nation we wish to do our duty and honour to our country and worthy commander-in-chief.

Seamen,
Yarmouth Roads.[95]

The affair seemed to promise well, and everybody was pleased, especially Lady Spencer, who wrote to Duncan, on 3rd May, from the Admiralty:

My dear Admiral,

You must allow me to thank you for your kind letter and obliging attention to my request, and I am the more eager to do this because, in the same page on which I return you my acknowledgments for these favours, I have an opportunity of expressing to you my delight at your dexterity and spirit upon certain cheerings on board the *Venerable*. The success attending such well-judged and vigorous conduct makes me lament that we have not more Adam Duncans. However, since we can't cut him up into several pieces (tho' there is certainly enough of him to make many reasonable-sized men), we must be contented with having one of that name who will keep the North Sea fleet in good order. God bless you, my dear Admiral.

Believe me sincerely yours,

Lavinia Spencer.[96]

But on the very day that Lady Spencer wrote these charming things to her Gargantuan friend, a debate took place in the House of Lords, with a wholly unexpected result. The Duke of Bedford, cantankerously in opposition, asked if the ministers had any communication to make on recent occurrences in the Navy. Spencer answered that he was not charged by the King to make any communication to the House, nor did he foresee that any communication would be made upon that subject. Apart from the obvious consideration that the Government did not want to prejudice the question while a pertinent Bill was being concocted, no minister wanted the limelight turned on to this business: least of all would Spencer want to produce his somewhat too revealing correspondence with Bridport. He hoped that

75

everything would be hushed up and no more said. Howe then rose and gave a summary of the affair so far as it had touched him, regretting that the subject had ever been brought under discussion. Lord Grenville, Foreign Minister, told the Duke of Norfolk that he would oppose any motion for papers as being impolitic; whereupon the Duke of Bedford growled that he would try to find some means of calling for them. Really it was quite an innocuous debate, merely an opposition sticking pins into a Government; but its effect in the Channel Fleet was disastrous.

For the somewhat garbled versions which appeared in the newspapers gave the sailors, quivering with suspicion, the firm idea that either the ministry or Parliament meant to go meanly back on the promises the Board had made the Delegates. What did Spencer mean by saying he did not expect to have to make any communication? It was all very mysterious;* they had waited and waited, and nothing had happened, till now—this! As early as 30th April a watch-maker on the *Mars* had gossiped with the surgeon's mate while he worked in his cabin, and told him that the men thought the Admiralty were trifling with them; and, finding he had a gullible listener, went on to make the good man's flesh creep by saying that the sailors meant to take the Fleet into Brest! [97] Thus by the time the reports of the debate had had time to sink in like acid on an appropriate base, the men were fizzing with the certainty that they had been cheated. It seemed so obvious that one of the Delegates was heard to say "that those who had power took them for fools, or vagabond knaves; but they would convince them that they were neither, and that they would not be so treated." [98] On 5th May the men of the *Queen Charlotte* were hailed by

* Perhaps they were still further excited by incendiary handbills diffused among them by revolutionaries; but as no single one of these has ever been found, this is a gratuitous assumption to make. There is no need to postulate anything of the sort to account for the men's state of mind.

a boat from the *Mars* from which the men shouted that Parliament was going to throw out the Seamen's Bill, and for proof chucked a bundle of newspapers through a lower-deck port-hole.[99] It is not as though the *Mars* was led into any excess by unduly excitable or seditious Delegates, for of the two, both at that time A.B.'s, one was promoted midshipman that very month, the other quarter master's mate the next September.[100] The simple truth is that the men profoundly mistrusted either the Admiralty or their power to get the Bill through.

As soon as Bridport got wind of this inauspicious feeling among his men, he did his best to soothe it by reading them out a copy he had just received of the Bill the Privy Council had drafted. But at this stage such a "proof" did no good. The sailors, in a state of "preternatural suspicion," were firmly convinced that Parliament had every intention of rejecting it; and their suspicion became a certainty when it leaked out that on 1st May the Admiralty had sent down a very ominous order. In fact the men on the *Duke* were made so desperate by dire rumours of what the order conveyed, that they made up their minds that, by hook or by crook, they must see what it was all about. They did, in the event, adopt direct methods. They burst into Holloway's cabin and insisted on seeing the order; but Holloway, realising what a dangerous document it was, had destroyed it. The men, however, were not to be baffled. They seized their captain, and sent a message to the Admiral demanding a copy, and swearing that if they did not get it they would either hang Holloway, or subject him to "a degrading punishment," by which they at first meant flogging, afterwards to soften their intentions to ducking. This was flagrant, raw mutiny, but Bridport was helpless: he gave up the order, which was without loss of time hastily sent from ship to ship all round the Fleet to add fuel to the already mounting flame.[101]

The leaders on the *Queen Charlotte*—if they were the

leaders—acted promptly, and at once began to weave anew the close net of a disciplined mutiny. From that ship a note was sent round:

> This is the sole agreement of the fleet, that our matters is not fulfilled. We are still to a man on our lawful cause as formal. We have come to an understanding of Parliament, finding there is no likelihood of redress to our former grievance. Therefore we think it prudent to obtain the same liberty as before. So untill our matters are comply'd with we are determined not to go to sea.
>
> P.S.—There is *Marlborough* and *Nymphe* in a wretched condition. If Admiral Bridport does not comply with these measures and forward them, we will take the speediest methods.[102]

The last words have a grim sound. The two ships named, we remember, had been left behind at Spithead as being more refractory than the others; and small wonder, since the captains of both ships were in the habit of belabouring their men about the head with a speaking-trumpet.

All the next day the Fleet was in a state of fevered activity; the men of the *Incendiary* transport even cheered, and were restless with insubordination; boats with messages or Delegates went ceaselessly between the ships, in which opinion was hardening, and determination rising to a height at which it could look possible violence in the face without faltering. Thus the *Ramillies* wrote to the *Glory* on the 7th, perhaps as a circular:

> BROTHERS,
>
> Our ideas relative to the dilatory proceedings of Administration in not passing or even of bringing in any kind of forwardness an Act of Parliament to ratify the promise made by the Lords Commissioners of the Admiralty for the increases of our wages, etc., are as follows:
>
> They mean to lull us into a supposed state of security relative to their good intentions towards us by granting us a temporary increase of provisions, etc., which 'tis true they have already done, with no other view than to keep us in the dark as to their intentions respecting the main points in view. If they once divide us and get us upon different stations, be assured they think they can then make their own terms. They know we

are no politicians, but at the same time our late proceedings have convinced them that we are not entirely bereft of rationality. We all know that without an Act ratified by Lords and Commons, the promises of the Lords Commissioners of the Admiralty are of no avail. Why, then, delay the passing of such an Act, and endeavour to amuse us with needless procrastinations and evasive subterfuges?

P.S.—We are well assured that the Seamen's Bill is hove out, particularly meeting the disapprobation of Lord Spencer, etc. We have this from good authority. If you receive this letter and approve of it, let a pair of white trousers be hung from the sprit-sail yard arm as a signal of approbation.[103]

The Lords Commissioners might have been flattered to feel that they were capable of such masterly depths of cunning; and probably after this note had been read a pair of white trousers did flutter gaily in the breeze, but something more alarming than the exposure of a garment happened when the *Royal George* got a message from the *Pompée*:

Our opinion is that there [is] not the least reliance to be placed in their promises, which, sorry as I am to say like, our oath of fidelity is broke if we do not remain unshaken until the whole is sanctioned by an act of Parliament. Now, brothers, your steady friends the *Pompées* beg of you to give them a final answer, and whatever may be your proposals, we one and all will never deviate from being determined to sink or swim.[104]

This caused such murmuring and seething, that Admiral Pole, who had transferred his flag and joined Bridport on the *Royal George*, saw fit to address the crew, and urge them to wait patiently. The ferment subsided; but if Pole thought that the matter was over, he was very much mistaken. The men had waited a whole fortnight now, which in their ignorance of the majesty of legislation they supposed was time enough for their Bill to have been passed a dozen times over—an opinion fully shared by the opposition in Parliament—and were angrily determined not to be bamboozled any longer.

CHAPTER VII

BLOODSHED

EVER since the 3rd of May, when he had been told (wrongly, as it turned out) that the French Fleet had sallied out of Brest, Bridport had been waiting for a favourable wind. At last, in the early hours of Sunday, 7th, the breeze veered easterly, and he could have sailed out. But now, just when the chance had come, he knew that it would be useless to hoist the signal to weigh, since it was plain as the flag at his mast that the men would not stir until they had their Bill. The day was to prove him right, and no later than nine o'clock in the morning.

At that moment, an outbreak of preconcerted hurrahing was carried across the waters of St. Helens from almost every ship, the seamen gathering at the forecastles, and on the tops, shrouds and booms, to propel this new signal of cheerful defiance. The men of the *Pompée* told their captain they wanted their rights confirmed by Parliament, and taking a boat against orders—the marines refusing to interfere—made a tour of the Fleet. The *Mars* sent a boat to the *Queen Charlotte*, and when the captain of the latter ordered it away and called out the marines, the marines refused to obey, the crew broke out in active mutiny, and told their captain that he was deprived of his command until the Act should have gone through Parliament. The men of the *Glory*, after cheering for "an act of Parliament and an honest three pounds of pork," refused duty. It was the same all over the Fleet. The men on the *Royal Sovereign* took possession of Sir Alan Gardner's cabin, and, saying the Admirals had deceived them, seized all the arms and ammunition on the ship. On the *Defence*, indeed, there was some reluctance to join the fresh movement; but the crew, threatened by the guns of the *Pompée* and *Glory*, once more reeved the yard-ropes and roared their submissive cheers. By about eleven o'clock the Fleet was as it had been on 16th April—the men in control, the yard-ropes in evidence, and the Assembly gathered in the state cabin on the *Queen Charlotte*.[105] The blow was almost more crushing than Bridport could bear; this was the reward of his patience!

> I have endeavoured [he wrote to the Admiralty] to prevent this mischief by every argument in my power, but without effect; and I cannot command the fleet, as all authority is taken from me. . . . My mind is too deeply wounded by all these proceedings, and I am so unwell that I can scarcely hold my pen to write these sentiments of distress.[106]

Unluckily he could not relieve his feelings by telling the Admiralty what he thought about the delay, and their "unfortunate order," as Gardner had been bold enough to call it, of 1st May.

The Delegates were brisk enough about their conference on the *Queen Charlotte*, and at about midday set out in a procession of boats to row the three miles or so across to Spithead, where four line-of-battle ships and several frigates and small vessels were placidly lying. At about one o'clock Captain Griffith of the *London* came sorrowfully to disturb Admiral Sir John Colpoys, who was his uncle, with the news that things at St. Helens were as bad as they had ever been. Colpoys made up his mind that he had had enough of these breaches of discipline. That very morning he had had another Admiralty order from Sir Peter Parker instructing officers to act promptly and severely upon any hint of such a thing, and had strengthened the effect of this upon his mind by choosing this day for the monthly reading of the Articles of War after divine service. His spirit was tuned up to an exhilarating firmness, and since Bridport was not at hand to tell him not to be a fool, he determined to try what he had been prevented from trying on 16th April. He at once had all hands turned up on deck, asked them if they knew what was happening at St. Helens, and on their telling him they did not, went on: "Well then, let me know if you have any grievances remaining." They answered, "No"; but the question was ambiguous. Colpoys thought he was asking them whether their grievances had been satisfied, which they had not been, and the men seem to have thought he was asking them whether they had any new ones. Colpoys then asked if the Admiralty had not granted all they had expected, even more than all, and the men replied, "Yes"; but this did not mean that they were satisfied with the way Parliament was treating their affairs. Deluded by this double misunderstanding, the Admiral thought he had his men with him, and, coming to the point, said: "I now pledge myself, if you follow my advice, that you shall not get into any disgrace with your brethren in the Fleet, as I shall become responsible for your conduct." He then had all the boats hoisted in, and sent the bluejackets below (some of them, however, remained on deck forward), with orders to run in the lower-deck guns and shut the port-lids, so that there should be no communication with the boats as they came alongside. The hatchways were closed, and the entries guarded: officers and marines were armed, and stationed in various places, especially at the sally-ports, a proportion, however, staying with Colpoys on the quarter-deck, facing the sailors who had remained above on the forecastle. The gallant Admiral, in all the stubbornness of fifty-five and with a great experience of naval discipline, was thus prepared to defy the oncoming forces of insubordination, and watched the ominous approach of the boats from St. Helens with a confident eye.

The Delegates first went on board the *Marlborough*, the captain making no resistance, where they told the crew to get rid of the officers against whom they had a grievance, and to take the ship down to St. Helens. As the sound of

their oars came to the ears of the seamen cooped up in the stuffy 'tween-decks of the *London*, these began to show great excitement; they tried to push up the hatchways, and were resisted by the officers, who called out to their commander to ask if they were to fire if necessary. Colpoys shouted back, "Yes, certainly; they must not be allowed to come up till I order them." When the Delegates came alongside, they were warned off by the sentries, but then cried out an appeal to the crew, now intoxicated with the ardour of tussle.*
The men on the forecastle began to move; some of them started to unlash a gun to point it at the quarter-deck, but the first lieutenant, Peter Bover, threatened to fire if they went on. They desisted, all but one, who, made of bolder stuff, dared Bover to fire, and went on freeing the gun. Bover promptly took him at his word, and the man fell mortally wounded. The men seething below rushed up the hatchways crying "Blood for blood," were fired on by the officers, and fired back; there was general confusion, shouting, trampling, and explosion of firearms. Several on both sides were wounded, among them a Delegate, three sailors fatally, and on the other side two or three marines including an officer and a Midshipman.† The marines themselves, all except two foreigners, deserted to the other side, or flung away their arms, upon which Colpoys ordered the officers to retire, and called to the men to come aft across the decks, which, according to one of the Delegates—they had scrambled on board as soon as the firing ceased—were as red as during a battle. That there was not more bloodshed was due to Colpoys' instant acceptance of defeat, and to the steadier men, who, with forbearance and common sense, stopped the firing.

* Mr. Gill suggests they may have been intoxicated with rum; but seeing how sternly discipline was kept, and that the *London* was a good ship, this is most unlikely.

† These numbers are uncertain; the returns differ. The man Bover killed was not a Delegate, as is always stated.

But the affray was not yet over, for Peter Bover had been seized and hauled forward by a yelling crowd of sailors frantic to make him pay with his life for killing their comrade at the gun. A yard-rope was rove, the noose thrust round his neck, and they were about to string him up when Valentine Joyce, hurling himself through the dense pack, flung his arms around his neck, and screamed out above the wild tumult, "If you hang this young man you shall hang me, for I shall never quit him"[107]; and one of the topmen shouted out that Bover was "a brave boy." This caused a moment's hesitation, during which Colpoys, seeing what was happening, and being a gallant gentleman, dashed forward into the middle of the excited, smoke-begrimed mob, to take responsibility for Bover's action, clearing his way through seamen furious from the heat of the struggle, and "overboiling with rage and fury at seeing several of their wounded and dying shipmates weltering in their blood." He stood up square on the forecastle facing the seven or eight hundred enraged countenances, facing too the scores of weapons perilously pointed at him within a finger-twitch of going off. In that white-hot tension anything might have happened: hell itself might have been let loose in a wild massacre of officers, or setting the ship on fire. Suddenly from the body of the surging, gesticulating mass a hoarse voice roared out threateningly above the din, "You're a damned bloody scoundrel!" Colpoys steeled himself for the crash; but, most paradoxical thing in this paradoxical mutiny, the sailors instantly lowered their firearms, and hustling their intemperate comrade, shouted out, "How dare you speak to the Admiral in that manner!"[108] and made as though to duck him. It was not authority that had been smutched, but the whole great naval tradition dear to the men: never before had a British admiral been so insulted! The highly charged tension relaxed; there was a slight pause, and then the quiet voice of the ship's doctor, whom the men liked, was heard persuading them to listen to Colpoys. The latter, on the opportunity like a flash, called up all his powers of rhetoric to explain that Bover had been acting under his direct command, and that he himself had been obeying orders, "very recent instructions," from the Admiralty. "Orders? What orders?" the men clamoured, and defied him to produce any; and only on his insisting that he was telling the truth, was he allowed, under escort, to go to his cabin to find them.[109]

To give hot blood time to cool, Colpoys spent as many minutes as he could in hunting for his keys, and returned with the document through a forest of such vehement dark looks that, though he was relieved to see that the rope had been removed from Bover's neck, he had little hope for himself. In the interval Valentine Joyce had boldly adjured the angry multitude to be calm, and Mark Turner, a Delegate from the *Terrible*, who had served with Bover before, had put in sturdily for him; and as he was a solid midshipman of thirty-seven, his partisanship would weigh. One of the *London* men, too, had argued in his favour with "manly eloquence"; but what really saved him was the fact that he was a favourite with the crew.[110] The men, then, having previously tucked away their pistols and made all safe, Colpoys read the obnoxious order, upon which he, Griffith, and Bover were marched off to their cabins, to be kept in close confinement pending court martial; and the bloody flag once more displaced at the masthead the Admiral's serener banner of St. George.[111]

The plan of the Delegates was at this point perfectly cut and dried. They had two objects in view, both of an offensive-defensive nature, bold and far-seeing, but at the same time cautious. The first, obviously made more important than ever by the affairs of that day, was to force unpopular officers to quit their ships: this would show that the men meant business, and at the same time prevent feelings becoming exacerbated so far as to produce more incidents of the kind that had reddened the decks of the *London*. The men acted without hesitation, as James Anthony Gardner, for instance, now second lieutenant on the *Hind* frigate, was to discover, somewhat to his surprise. He had the first watch that evening, and all seemed quiet up to midnight, when he was relieved by the master. But at about three bells in the morning watch he was urgently sent for by the captain, and, rushing up on deck, he found the whole ship's company in process of being harangued by his superior, who, "in the most impressive manner" he could attain, was urging upon his men the fitness, the dutifulness, the merit, and the beauty of returning to obedience. But the men failed to be impressed, or at least would not budge. Gardner, indeed, thought them vacillating, and considered that if this had been an isolated mutiny, the stout fellows "would soon have driven the scoundrels to the devil"; but what could one do when surrounded by line-of-battle ships all "acting in the same disgraceful manner"? How disgraceful Gardner had further driven home to him when, not long before eight, a paper was handed in naming the captain, purser, and certain other officers, including himself:

> GENTLEMEN [it read], it is the request of the ship's company that you leave the ship precisely at eight o'clock. As it is unanimously agreed that you should leave the ship we would wish you to leave it peaceable or desperate methods will be taken.

It was no earthly use to fume or fuss; there was nothing to do but go below and hastily pack. Near the time stated the expelled officers were told that everything was ready; their trunks were taken for them, and they went down to the barge among ranks of silent men, each armed with a cutlass. They battled towards the shore in the teeth of a north-eastern gale, and it was not until nearly four hours later that they were landed on Point Beach. A harsh, long-drawn experience, bitter to the spirit, and bitter to the flesh in that howling wind; full expiation, surely, for the venial sin of "starting"; and as a final ignominy, the boat's crew refused to carry their officers' baggage farther than the edge of the beach. Had they not been warned by the ringleaders that if they did they would be handsomely ducked when they got back? Gardner, however, who had heard this threat, was prepared. He told the bowman, and one or two others whom he believed to be "great scoundrels," to hump their traps to a hut only a few steps from the boat, and, showing them his pistols, said: "You understand me." They did, the traps were duly carried; but it must have been poor satisfaction for the shivering officers—and the men were actually ducked.[112]

The Delegates' second object was to concentrate their forces. They already had the idea that the Admiralty would try to divide them, "get them upon different stations," as the crew of the *Ramillies* had said; and they had come to Spithead partly to get the ships there to join them at St. Helens. How general this idea was can be gathered from a letter written by the crew of the *Prince*, in Curtis's squadron at Torbay:

Torbay,
8th May 1797.

Ship Mates,

In consequence of the affair which has taken place at Spithead highly concerns the Navy in general, and we think it a duty incumbent on us all since it is brought forward we ought to carry the same into effect the opportunity now offers to do ourselves some service in freeing ourselves from the tiranny and arbitrary power that is Comd over us. It appears thay have ordered us here to separate our connection as much as possible from Bridport's fleet, and in case any step should be taken by us that you will act in conjunction with us and not be said you shrink back from maintaining your rights and privileges.

PRINCE ALL HANDS.[113]

a letter which apparently crossed a message from St. Helens telling them to come there. Concentration, then, was the main object of the move, but it would also prevent any possible fracas between the sailors and the troops. The latter were now all prepared for action at Portsmouth; there were ten thousand of them, the garrison ready for a siege, with the drawbridges up and the guns laid; even "the old, crazy castle of Southsea" had its quota of troops.[114] It would be as well to be out of contact.

On the 8th, therefore, most of the ships, large and small, went down to St. Helens, having got rid of their unpopular officers. Yet not all of those who stayed behind were disliked: Captain Talbot of the *Eurydice* frigate, for example, was very much loved by his men. The crew were told that if they did not go down to the Isle of Wight the *Marlborough* would fire on them; Talbot's orders, on the other hand, were to stay at Spithead: neither crew nor captain would disobey orders, so, to the regret of his men, Talbot had to leave them. They were not, however, separated for long. It had been the policy of the Delegates during the first mutiny to let the big ships bear the weight of the contest, leaving the smaller vessels to go about their duty; and to this policy they reverted. Thus after a day or two the frigates returned to their old anchorage: whereupon the men of the *Eurydice* wrote, with a charming wholeheartedness and an almost lyrical impulse:

> Captain Talbot, with the same cheerfulness that we joined in promoting the general good, so we now join in our earnest wishes and desires that you will once more join the flock of which you are the tender shepherd. We wish by this to show you, Sir, that we are men that loves the present cause as men ought to, yet we are not eleveated that degree to neglect our duty to our country or our obedience to you, and as the line of battle ships means to settle the business, the command of the ship belongs to you, sir, which command we, the ship's company, resign with all due honour, respect and submission hopeing you will always continue to do as you have heretofore done, to hear a man's cause as well as an officer's.[115]

On the 8th, however, the roads were left empty except
for the *Royal William*, Sir Peter Parker's ship, which apparently never joined the mutiny as a unit (though certain of
the men did); the remainder, with or without officers, made
for St. Helens, some of them failing to display that nice
accuracy in navigation, particularly at the tricky entrance
to the harbour, expected of the British Navy. Excellent men
as the captains of forecastles might be, it was not in the
difficult art of manœuvring a sailing ship that their virtue
lay, especially in the hurricane that it had come on to blow;
and more than once the ships riding at single anchor were
within an ace of fouling one another.[116]

The wholesale expurgation of officers began on the 7th,
and went on for two or three days. The *Marlborough* and
the *Nymphe* joyfully ejected their trumpet-wielding captains
and other officers: Captain Holloway and the officers of the
Duke were compelled to obey a peremptory missive:

GENTLEMEN,

You are desired upon the receipt of this that the undermentioned persons
quit the ship upon the receipt of this, never to return again, except the
persons with a mark against their names who is to return when everything
is settled to the satisfaction of the fleet. You are to depart out of the ship
directly,[117]

only six out of the twenty-one names having a cross against
them. Over a hundred officers were put ashore, including
Admiral Gardner, hardly a ship failing to yield its sacrifice.
Sometimes they were treated with delicacy, given due warning, honourably borne away in the captain's barge, and
perhaps told they might come back when all was over: from
other ships, such as the *Glory*, they were suddenly bundled
out without notice or respect. That ship, in fact, lost all her
officers. Throughout this turmoil Bridport, impotently
calm—at least as calm as he could manage to be—was receiving reports of calamity, as from the captain of the
Terrible:

8th May.

I beg leave to inform your Lordship that I am just come on shore from H.M.S. *Terrible*, the command of that ship having been perfectly taken from me, and finding that I had no longer any authority over any part of her crew, they have hoisted the Red Flag to call the Delegates on board, and on the arrival of four of them, seized all the arms in the wardroom, and in the officers' cabins, immediately after which they declared it to be their determination that myself and all my officers, except the Master, Surgeon, Purser, three warrant officers, and one Midshipman should quit the ship.[118]

The people of the *Mars*, finding that one of their officers kept a brace of pistols loaded in his cabin, came to the conclusion that all of them were bellicose, with the result conveyed to Bridport by their commander:

9th May.

This is the first opportunity I have had of communicating to your Lordship the mutinous conduct of the crew of H.M.S. *Mars* by turning me and the officers named on the other side out of the ship yesterday morning after having taken possession of all the arms and placed additional sentinels over us all Sunday night, and prevented my having any communication with any person except the First Lieutenant and Master, and with those a very short time, and upon going out of my cabin in the morning I was stopped by a sentry, and told it was the ship's company's orders that I was not to go upon the Quarter Deck. I am sorry to say the Marines have taken a very active part in this mutiny.[119]

The marines, indeed, forgot their function and acted with the seamen; and not on the *Mars* alone, for, while he was dressing in the morning, the Captain of Marines on the *Queen Charlotte* had a note thrown on to the gallery directing him to leave the ship at once.

It was not that the men wanted to be officerless so as to pursue fell designs unhindered; it was only that some of the officers had made themselves hateful. Indeed it was a little invidious to be uncommanded, and on the 11th Bridport was handed a request which may have cheered him:

MAY IT PLEASE YOUR LORDSHIP

That we *La Nymphe's* ship's company are perfectly satisfyd with what was agreed on by the fleet. But as we wish to shew the world that we Love Discipline and Good Order to be established on boar[d] us we humbly hope your Lordship will send us immediately a Captain and two Lieutenants, that we may not be hinder'd from proceeding with the fleet when ordered to sea.

We remain your Lordship's humble servants,

La Nymphe's SHIPS' COMPANY.[120]

A similar plea was addressed to Nepean by the crew of the *Stag*. The men, it is clear, never regarded this affair as a mutiny, but as a combination[121]—one of the very earliest in the history of the Labour movement—to get a just reward for their toil, and a betterment of the sub-human conditions of their lives.

Portsmouth, Southsea, Gosport, were filled with officers bewailing their misfortune, or besieging Sir Peter Parker with prayers for help. The sight of them did not reassure the people of those towns, who surged on to the platform to see wherries, boats, cutters, rowing or sailing in to deposit batch after batch of homeless officers of all ranks, and be thrilled by the sight of boat-loads of sailors each sporting a brace of large pistols, a cutlass, and a cartouche box. "The horror and confusion of this town are beyond description," the *London Chronicle* reporter wrote from Portsmouth, giving every atom of news-value to what he could pick up: "The mind of everyone is almost in an indescribable state," he went on: the Fleet was going to St. Helens for the trial of Admiral Colpoys! It was comfortingly true that the seamen kept the masters on board "to fight under them if an enemy's fleet should insult our coasts," and threatened to go to sea to meet the French without officers,[122] but this did not make up for the piratical figures at the wharf-side, nor for the bloody flags waving from the mastheads. There was a sense of violence in this outbreak: it was all most unlike that friendly first mutiny which the Prince of Württemberg had been conducted round, as though it were a mild diversion. Tempers, they knew, were up, for the sick at Haslar had been so incensed by the events in the *London*, that their behaviour towards the wounded marines and officers who had been brought in there warned the authorities to move them somewhere else.

What the country was most agitated about was the fate impending over Colpoys, Griffith, and Bover; the tensest interest centred on the *London*. Would the sailors' court martial condemn these officers to death? In the dismayed capital there was something like a panic, and the most absurd suggestions were made for saving the situation, among them that the King himself should at once go to Portsmouth and, playing the wounded sovereign, plead the men back to their duty![123] There was some cause for alarm, for fierce deliberations were going on among the Delegates gathered on the *Mars* while the anxious officers awaited the outcome in the cabins of the *London*. The Assembly did not go so far as to appoint a secretary to keep the minutes, but one can guess from the current rumours that a tussle racketed backwards and forwards for hours. It was natural that some of the men should be hot for revenge— you do not see your friends shot down without wanting to have somebody's blood for it—and on the 9th the *Morning Chronicle* reported:

> Admiral Colpoys was tried yesterday by the delegates on board the *Mars* for Murder and found guilty.

But one may be sure that the more level-headed among the Delegates did not want to shed more blood; humanity apart, it would entail reprisals, and make hopeless any prospect of pardon for this new mutiny. Yet the scales do not seem to have tipped on the happier side until John Fleming, the A.B. of twenty-five who had been elected extra Delegate of the *London* to replace the one who had been wounded, made a decisive statement, which he either read to the Assembly, or sent before going across to the *Mars* to take his seat as a representative. In this remarkable letter he thanked his electors for the most flattering proofs of their opinion of his abilities to act as a man and a Christian ought to do—the phrasing is his own—and went on:

Permit me now to speak for that ship's company whose confidence I enjoy. In the first place, had they followed the momentary impulse of passion, and wreaked their vengeance on that unfortunate gentleman, a few minutes would have brought to their recollection the amiable character he always bore amongst them, and I am confident would have embittered the latest moments of their lives. Now, my brethren, your general cry is "Blood for blood." Do you mean that as a compliment to us to assist us in following error after error? If so, it is a poor compliment indeed; or do you, let me ask you, think it justice? I hope not; if you do, pray, from whence do you derive the authority to sit as a court over the life of even the meanest subject? The only answer you can give me is, that you are authorised by your respective ship's companies. But is that authority sufficient to quiet your conscience for taking the life even of a criminal, much more that of a deserving worthy gentleman, who is an ornament to his profession in every respect; I can almost safely say you will say "No." But if you are to be influenced by your ships' companies, contrary to your own opinion, I am but a single individual among you, and before this hand of mine shall subscribe the name of Fleming to anything that may in the least tend to that gentleman's prejudice, much more his life, I will undergo your utmost violence, and meet death with him hand in hand. I am, nevertheless, as unanimous as any member of the fleet for a redress of your grievances, and maintain that point with you all, so long as you are contented with your original demands, but the moment I hear of your deviating from these principles, that instant I become your most inveterate enemy.*

Such a letter, worthy of a Privy Councillor, must have shaken the wilder spirits among the Delegates, especially as Fleming accompanied his signature with the words "Per desire of the *London's* ship's company." At all events, on the evening of the 9th, a message was sent to the *London*

* See Appendix III.

that Bover should be released. He remained on his ship, the men of which bore him no grudge.

> I have been [he wrote to his family on the 11th] in a most critical situation, but all is well again; I was fortunately much beloved by several of the ship's company, and that alone has saved me; their respect for me has increased much since the business.[124]

But what was to happen to Colpoys and Griffith was still undecided, though on the 10th the *London Chronicle* told a relieved world that

> Admiral Colpoys has been tried by a Tribunal instituted by the seamen, the verdict of which is to the following effect:—"That in every part of his late conduct on board the *London* man of war he conducted himself as became a British officer; he is therefore free to reassume the command of his ship, or decline it, as he thinks proper."

The unlucky reporter was wrong again.

CHAPTER VIII

BALM—AND SOME FRUITLESS RESEARCH

IN the midst of all the flurry and excitement the "Seamen's Bill" at last came before Parliament, not in all the array of a statute, but as a financial resolution. The shock of the new mutiny, which had come as a complete surprise, had made it clear to the most departmental mind that the greatest speed was essential. Of all the men taken unaware, Spencer had been the most shocked. On the 6th he had written to Bridport:

> I am truly happy to find that at length tranquillity and order seem to be perfectly established in your squadron. . . . We have had a very severe lesson in this business, and I trust all the officers in the Fleet will feel the effect of it.[125]

The lesson was to be severer still, and by the time Bridport had received the prematurely complacent message, the mutiny had broken out far more violently than before. No one, of course, not even the most virulent enemy of the Government, dreamed of opposing the resolution which came up on the 8th, embodying a supplementary estimate of £372,000 for the current year; it was not, after all, such an enormous addition to a war budget of twelve and a half millions. But what stimulated the ire and the loquacity of the opposition was that the Government asked for a silent vote, as though in this way they could slink out of any discussion of their early mismanagement and subsequent bad handling! Fox and Sheridan were not going to let slip such a golden chance as this, and the debate was lively enough to arouse the drowsiest habitué of the gloomy benches at St. Stephen's. Fox swelled with an accumulation of decorous invective as his wide mouth poured scorn on the Government. How could ministers expect blind con-

fidence when they had so blatantly shown themselves worthy
of none at all?—who had displayed, in fact, "a degree of
guilt or incapacity, or both, that has led us to the brink
of destruction." He made terrible lunges over the fatal
dilatoriness of the Council, and was brilliantly seconded by
Sheridan. The resolution, naturally, was passed, but the
wordy battle was fought next day in the Lords, and again in
the Commons, generalled this time by Whitbread, who later
brought a vote of censure against Pitt on this issue. After
more fulmination by Sheridan, who pointed out that the
sailors were very properly suspicious of promises, and that
a resolution was only a promise and would probably not
satisfy the seamen, Pitt moved to bring in a Bill to make
the resolution law. It was brought in on the spot, rattled
through all its stages, and sent up to the Lords, who had been
asked to wait; and indeed, after passing the Bill, they post-
poned their adjournment until a message came to say that
the Royal Assent had clinched the affair.[126]

A copy of the resolution had been galloped down to
Portsmouth for showing the Fleet, in the hope of allaying
the agitation. Unluckily, the sea was running so high that
boats could not get near most of the ships; but fortunately
among those in more sheltered waters was the *London*, and
the document was taken on board. It was read in triumph
by the men, who immediately promised to release Colpoys
and Griffith. On the Thursday they, with Bover, were
summoned on shore for a civil trial by the court sitting as
coroner's jury upon the body of a wounded man who had
died in Haslar Hospital. The crew were unwilling to give
Bover up, fearing the result, but he promised he would
come back, and on a verdict of justifiable homicide being
returned, the matter was closed. Yet not altogether; for
the men throughout the Navy felt such resentment against
Colpoys that on the 14th, after many flattering remarks
from Spencer, he was ordered to strike his flag and go

ashore.[127]   Even the next year, when he was appointed to another ship, the feeling against him on the lower-deck ran so high that the appointment had to be cancelled. He was never employed at sea again.*

Bover, on the other hand, though implored by his friends not to risk his life by going back to his ship, persisted in rejoining it, was received with three cheers, and requested by the crew not to leave. He assented, and continued to serve on the *London* till promoted to commander in February of the next year.[128]

The mutiny, however, was not yet over; the men would not, and indeed could not, return to duty until a fresh Royal Pardon had been obtained for the dire offence of the second outbreak. And it would have to be a very embracing one, for the Admiralty order of the 1st, combined with the way Colpoys had acted upon it, suggested clearly to the seamen that as matters now stood the instigators would be hunted out and vindictively hanged. Red flags still flapped viciously at the mastheads, the officers were nowhere in command, and the authorities were on tenterhooks owing to disturbing news of unrest at the Nore. Some very definite, even flamboyant step would have to be taken to set everything right again, and prevent the disease from spreading. A picturesque vision of the fitting end came in a dazzling gleam to either the King or Pitt: Howe, the venerable Lord Howe as plenipotentiary, armed with lavish powers to treat with the men, occupied the centre of the canvas; his prerogative would extend to the redress of grievances, and even as far as the royal one of bestowing universal pardon. It was an Academy picture of the best kind, but to some it was worse than shocking. Burke, in his final phase of last-ditch Toryism, was furious, and wrote to that now somewhat tarnished oracle, Windham:

---

* Griffith, however, became an Admiral and a Knight, after himself taking the name of Colpoys.

But among all the parts of this fatal measure the Mission of my Lord Howe has been by far the most mischievous. Had a great naval commander been sent down—*Gravem pietate et meritis virum quem*—to awe the seditious into obedience, it would have been the best thing that could have been thought of; but to send the first name in the Navy, and who had been but lately a Cabinet Minister and First Lord of the Admiralty, at upwards of 70 years of age, to hunt among mutineers for grievances, to take the law from Joice, a seditious clubist of Belfast, and to remove by his orders some of the principal Officers of the Navy, puts an end to all hopes for ever. Such mischief need not to have been attended with so much degradation.[129]

Burke was so deeply self-ingrained with his own terror that he was ready to sniff sedition anywhere; and Windham, no doubt, gave strident tongue at this false scent. But still one wonders if it occurred to him to ask Burke who he thought might have been capable of aweing the seamen into obedience? To most people, however, the idea of sending Howe seemed to smack of genius: they were not troubled by the thought of degradation, they wanted the business cleared up. Surely the sailors would listen to their once-worshipped Black Dick; and, after all, some may have thought that, since his lack of attention, to put it mildly, had been partly the cause of the outbreak, it was poetically right that he should figure as the balm to heal the running wound. So on the 10th Howe made what was for him, cramped by age and infirmities, the heroic journey to Portsmouth, taking his wife along with him.

It is doubtful if the project of sending Howe as *Deus ex machina* seemed quite so beautifully apt to Bridport; it must, in fact, have been wickedly galling. Here was he, who had borne the ardours of the day, who had indeed been swamped by a storm which need never have burst if Howe had only had the sense to let him know it was gathering, superseded at the last moment, when honour and glory were about to descend, by the intolerable old fool himself. Addington and Spencer sent him emollient letters, sweetly explaining that they could not help this development, that the sailors had been promised Howe, and that therefore they must have Howe—not, perhaps, the most tactful form of excuse. But Pitt wrote from Downing Street on the 10th:

> ... It was thought best to make this a civil commission in order not to interfere with the military command of the Fleet, and at the same time to give the commission to a distinguished naval character, though not with any naval authority or functions. ... I am sure you will continue to contribute your exertions with the same zeal and public spirit which you have shown under such trying difficulties to bring this arduous work, if possible, to a happy termination.[130]

Bridport may not have been a brilliant sailor, but he was, as he showed all through the mutiny, a man of unruffled sense and great moral courage; that he was a man of unusual generosity as well is revealed in his reply. He swallowed the affront, put his pride in his pocket in the good cause, and wrote to Pitt the next day:

> *Royal George,*
> St. Helens,
> 11*th May* 1797.
>
> My dear Sir,
> I feel myself much honoured by your most obliging and affectionate letter of yesterday's date.
> I hope the appearance of Earl Howe, at Portsmouth, will fully answer the expectations of the public by restoring regular order in the fleet at Spithead and at this anchorage. His Lordship will find me ready to give every assistance in my power to obtain this most important and necessary object, which I hope the measure will produce without delay. In many respects we are better than when I sent to the Admiralty yesterday, but still the authority is in the hands of the people.
> I have had my dear Sir a most anxious time, and much to encounter with, and if I had not kept quite calm and composed, the consequences would have been more alarming.

He had, after all, a right to say that; and then he let Pitt hear his private mind on the behaviour of the Board, and of the Admiralty with their fatuous orders:

I have always considered peevish words and hasty orders detrimental, and it has been my study not to utter the one or issue the other. I wish that rule had guided the conduct (of) those in higher situations, as I think it wiser to soothe than irritate disturbed and agitated minds.

While I have the honour to command his Majesty's Fleet, I shall steadily pursue this line of conduct, and to the last moments of my life it will be my pride as well as my duty to manifest my loyalty to the King, and my rooted attachment to our excellent constitution.

    With perfect respect and regard
        I have the honour to be, my dear Sir,
            Your faithful and affectionate humble servant,

                                    BRIDPORT.[131]

The stage, then, was cleared and set for the last act, appropriately, and perhaps a touch sentimentally, with the old hero coming to appease his naughty children, and, helped perhaps with a sugar-plum or two, to make them all good again.

But in every theatre work goes on behind the scenes, which the public drinking in events from the front knows nothing of; and in this theatre it was undertaken by an amiably indefatigable young magistrate called Aaron Graham, who travelled down to Portsmouth at very much the same time as Lord Howe. Known to be painstaking and fired with patriotism, he had been relieved from his duties at Hatton Garden, and sent to ferret out what really lay behind the mutiny: for just as at the present day there is a type of mind which cannot believe that everybody in England is not perfectly happy unless he has been deluded, poor fellow, by some subversive, probably Bolshevik agent, so in 1797 there were people who could not understand how sailors could fail to be contented with their lives unless seditious—Jacobin or Irish revolutionary—elements had been at their horrid work. Of such was Thomas Grenville, brother to the Marquess of Buckingham; he had considered the egregious order of 1st May to be "very proper," and wrote as pondered thoughts of the second mutiny:

I cannot help fearing the evil is . . . deeply rooted in the influence of Jacobin emissaries and the Corresponding Society.

I am more and more convinced that Jacobin management and influence is at the bottom of this evil.[132]

One wonders if he would not have changed his mind if he had been rated for a month, say, as Ordinary Seaman on an average ship: he might have discovered other roots equally deep, and a not contemptible power of management.

Burke, we have seen, cast dark looks on Ireland as a main source of the trouble: Joyce was a seditious "Belfast clubist." He had, it was said, been a tobacconist in Belfast, conveniently shipped away to cut short his subversive activities; but there is no proof whatever of this, and since he was only twenty-six, and his family had evidently lived in Portsmouth a long time (he was himself born in Jersey), it is likely that he has been confused with someone else. There were, it is true, a good many Irishmen in the Navy, as has often been pointed out, though not in the proportion usually assumed; * and among them there must have been United Irishmen, men sworn to damage England, the tyrant country, at the cost of any crime, as some small measure of revenge for the ugly atrocities England was perpetrating in their country, at this time given over to brutal ravage. But that United Irishmen led the mutiny, or had any hand in it, is another matter altogether. No doubt they joyfully helped to stir up dissatisfaction, and eagerly adhered to the cause; but after the organisation was achieved, they were probably a nuisance rather than a help to the leaders. Beyond doubt there were revolutionaries in the Fleet; they may have provided a Delegate or two, but the questions were: Had they any

* The Naval and Marine forces in 1797 totalled 120,000. From 1793 to 1st Nov. 1796 the total of Irishmen enlisted for these forces was 16,515. It is usually calculated from this that the Irish made up about one-eighth of the Navy; but such a result makes no allowance for the considerable wastage of war, nor for the enormous number of desertions. One-twelfth would be nearer the mark.

influence on the sailors as a whole? Could you say they were the cause of the mutiny, or could you deduce that they would have any effect on the seamen's actions in the future? And if this was a revolutionary outbreak, who were the people on land directing the proceedings?

These were the baffling questions to which Graham, full of confidence, came to discover clear answers. What he learnt would be sent to John King, Under Secretary of State to the Home Department, by whom anything of value would be submitted to the discerning eye of the Home Secretary, the Duke of Portland. Graham apparently arrived on the 11th, and, bursting with zeal, did not give himself an instant's rest from the very first moment: he neither sat nor stood still from breakfast till seven o'clock; and since he added, "I have hastily devoured my mutton chop," he evidently gobbled only a stand-up dinner before dashing out again to see what he could see, or ferret out what he could smell. His best plan, he thought, would be to detach one or two of the Delegates from the rest, and "through them tracing the incendiaries (if there are any) who have been wicked enough to stimulate the seamen either to a beginning or a continuance of their disorderly behaviour." He was optimistic: "Hopes I have—and great ones too," he wrote, "of being able to secure the evidence of Joyce of the *Royal George* and Melvin of the *Pompée*"; and if he founded his hopes on rather flimsy material, that is an attitude proper to youth. The direct approach, he saw at once, would be useless, too crude; he must display ingenuity and guile, and the brilliant notion struck him of worming his way into Joyce's secrets through family influence:

> The mother of the former [Joyce] I have completely the possession of through the management of a lady of this town who can also if it should be found necessary, prevail upon the sister to join her influence to the mother's, and as the father likewise is said to belong to the Invalid Corps in the

garrison, there can be little doubt of his assistance being had if it should be wanted.

An opportunity occurred—or was it engineered?—when Joyce's mother was reported ill: it might be easy to get hold of him then, for who knew what unlockings of the heart the pleadings of an ailing mother might not procure? But Joyce came attended by a great bodyguard of sailors, and remained obstinately silent about any sedition-mongers; so the management of the lady of the town reaped a barren harvest.

Melvin might be easier to catch and to pump; someone who knew him intimately assured Graham that the Delegate would peach if he could be sure of his discharge from the Navy—"his present disagreeable situation." Graham took it that he was authorised to make Melvin—a Sunderland man, thirty-four years of age—a tempting offer; "and as to pecuniary considerations," he added nobly, "they will never stand in my way." But Melvin provided thrilling revelations no more than Joyce did: perhaps it was that, having been promoted Quarter-Master only two months before, he did not find his situation disagreeable after all; or else, perhaps, he knew of no sedition.

But Graham was not easily balked, and obviously enjoyed the fun of detective work. He betook himself incognito to every likely and unlikely place, talking to every one —to sailors, dockers, publicans—peering about everywhere, and hobnobbing in Haslar Hospital, on the beach—where he found all the sailors most attached to the King and panting to fight the French—and at pot-houses. If from vague hearsay he gathered that a suspicious character was prowling in the Isle of Wight, he instantly sailed over to investigate. He was never idle for a minute. Plying his busy avocation he crossed the harbour to Gosport, "searching backwards and forwards (as you would do for a bank-note) 8 or 10 times a day." It was all useless, he drew blank every time.

But he did get one exciting hint that a sinister incendiary

was at work somewhere. An acquaintance flew to tell him of an adventure he had met with. When walking about he had noticed a sailor idling outside a public-house with a girl. They had been approached by another sailor, on closer inspection a very queer sailor, with unsullied hands, neat footwear, and a clean white shirt peeping indiscreetly out from below his tarnished chequered one. This pseudo-sailor went up to the honest tar and asked how the mutineers were getting on; and when he was told that they were doing very well, thrust a guinea into the fellow's unexpectant hand, and slipped away. "Damn him!" the astounded sailor remarked, "I don't know him, by God!" The girl, however, who evidently had realistic views, and knew that lost opportunities do not recur, at once said, with sound feminine practicality, "Never mind; let's go and have a drink." And that was all, for though Graham's informant pursued the mysterious stranger, he never caught another glimpse even of his heels.

The worst of it, Graham found, was that every one was brimful of information; it was most distressing.

> So great is the abominable itch (among all descriptions of persons) for inventing something new, and so common is the practice of circulating as a matter of fact what is considered only as a story of the day, that treason itself might easily be planned, executed, and publicly talked of long before it would be seriously noticed by the magistrates.

For instance, the rumour that seditious pamphlets were being distributed among the seamen. Everybody took it for granted that they were, but nobody had ever seen one, and no magistrate, captain, or admiral could ever produce one; and seeing how difficult and dangerous it was to get such things printed, the result is not surprising. Whether this proved that the magistrates had grown careless from the too frequent cry of wolf, or that there were no pamphlets, Graham could not determine. But the point did not matter, for in the end he was forced to admit failure all along the line, since he never ran a single quarry of any kind to earth: and at any rate, incendiaries or no incendiaries, the men remained inconsiderately loyal.

> I am persuaded from the conversation I have had with so many of the sailors that if any man on earth had dared openly to avow his intention of using them as instruments to distress the country his life would have paid forfeit. Nothing like want of loyalty to the King or attachment to the government can be traced in the business.[133]

It was all very sad for persons like Grenville, and perhaps for those who felt that a startling, possibly lurid discovery would exonerate the high and mighty from a charge of maladministration. Lord Howe, on the contrary, may have been relieved: he knew where he was with sailors, while Jacobins and United Irishmen would be another kettle of fish altogether.

CHAPTER IX

GALA DAYS

AND in any case the business was not going to be so easy. The men had tasted power, they were still uncertain whether the authorities really meant to play the game with them, and Howe, the old idol, had shown in March that one of his feet at least might well be made of clay. But the aged Admiral, though bowed under his infirmities and his glories, put his whole heart into setting matters right: if the business had been a little his fault, he would at any rate make up for it a hundredfold now; he would spare neither his flesh nor his spirit, and the latter, blown into a blaze by a tremendous exercise of will, would emit one final illumination before it went out for ever.

He did not waste time, or even rest at Portsmouth, but at once had himself rowed across the Solent to St. Helens, where he boarded the *Royal George*. It was not altogether certain in what temper he would be met by the crew. The day before, Wednesday, 10th, Bridport had loyally distributed copies of the healing Act of Parliament, but even so it was not by any means sure that every one was appeased. The men of the *Mars* and the *Duke* were inclined to be stiff-necked, those of the latter ship especially, attempting to incite the Fleet to further demands, possibly on the point of the distribution of prize-money. They insisted on interviewing the Assembly, which poured cold water on their ardour, upon which they made pilgrimages to all the other ships to try to stir them up, but in every instance met with rebuffs; far from being allowed to board the ships, they were greeted with torrents of picturesque seafaring abuse, punctuated with shouting and hissing. The fever on both these ships appeared so dangerous to the temporary commanders of the Fleet, that they stationed guard-boats near by, and forbade all except official Admiralty communication with them. For the general feeling of the Fleet had crystallised into something peaceable, which was probably well expressed by the crew of the *Robust*, who sat down to compose a work of high, not to say high-falutin, literature, to air their minds —and their talents; and even if it is "singularly free from grammatical restraint," it was certainly found none the worse for that:

Robust,
11*th May* 1797.

The favours and goodness our officers confer upon us, are such as can be equalled by few officers in the fleet; and that is our just and grateful sense of the officers of his majesty's ship *Robust*. Is there a man so poor in spirit, that praises such as we have without imitating the actions worthy of them?

How pleasant would be the toils of war, did all employed in it meet with the same recompense! [Was this a side-glance at prize-money?] It is our deeds alone render us worthy their indulgence, and preserve their good opinion. To inform you with how much ardency we wish to serve them, if ever accidents fall in our way, we are thoroughly resolved to lead them into the paths of glory; and they might rest assured that all of us will rejoice in an opportunity of testifying our duty, affection, gratitude, and submission, which we flatter ourselves they will not hereafter disapprove.

We are, with the utmost respect and submission,
    Your Honours' eternally devoted servants,

Robust SHIP'S COMPANY.[134]

But it is unlikely that Howe should have seen this before stepping upon the flagship: if he had, it may have done something to sustain him at that first awkward moment of meeting Bridport, who, very correct, very aloof, was waiting to receive him.

Black Dick then talked to the men of the *Royal George*. He had first of all to re-establish himself in their confidence as the sailors' friend, and then to convince them that the Act really was water-tight, that the Admiralty meant to deal squarely by them, and that the Royal Pardon was all-embracing. From the first he dealt with them as man to man; there was no getting upon the high horse for him, or refusing to recognise the authority of the Delegates, as there had been on the part of Spencer's Board when it had come down in April. His own intuition guided him there, though it may have been strengthened by the advice of Lady Howe, a woman of "discretion and excellent understanding," according to Benjamin Franklin. But apart from all other difficulties, there was one that lay deep in the old hero's nature, and a grave one in the circumstances—sheer incapacity to state his meaning directly. He meant what he said honestly enough, but it was not always easy to discover what, precisely, he had tried to convey.* As an Admiral who knew him well remarked: "Lord Howe possessed a very peculiar manner of explaining himself, both in correspondence and conversation;" so it is not surprising that his conference on the *Royal George* took three whole hours. He then went on to the *Queen Charlotte*, to preside in his old state cabin under conditions his queerest nightmares could not have foreshadowed, and finally tackled the recalcitrant *Duke*. That was enough for the day: he had arrived at Portsmouth only at eleven o'clock, and had done work which would have been creditable in a man far less than seventy-one years old.

The next day he spent doggedly going from ship to ship, till he had been to every one, arguing, explaining, cajoling. His patience was infinite, his manner at once sympathetic and sorrowful. He explained in long, tortuous phrases, of which the men understood the spirit if not always the meaning, how blameless the Admiralty had really been; that

* For instance, in approval of an officer's actions: " Your conduct with regard to the despatches, testified so correct a judgment in every part, that, if my concurrence in opinion with you on the propriety of it will convey all the satisfaction you do me the favour to intimate, you are free to indulge yourself in the enjoyment of that consciousness to the fullest extent."—Barrow, 118, where other examples may be found.

nobody had ever dreamt of not keeping faith with the sea-men; and then—so he reported—he made the men aware of the enormity of their behaviour. He declared that he must have an expression of the whole Fleet's sense of this before he would proceed in the matter, and wrote that he only left the Fleet "under agreement with the Delegates that the sea-men, at large, should request, in suitable terms of decency and contrition, my interposition to obtain the King's pardon for those transgressions." The sailors were for the most part far too realistic to boggle at forms or formalities, and willingly made such a very mild gesture of humiliation; but on what mattered they were stubborn. The wording of the pardon Howe found to be the most tricky point of all: it contained the word "promise," and the sailors, having made up their minds never again to be "amused or diverted by fair promises," would have none of this specious word. The phrase, "we do hereby promise our most gracious pardon," had to be altered to, "meaning further to extend our most gracious pardon"; and if this involved sending the draft back to be altered, this could not be helped. The men were so difficult about points such as this, which seemed to Howe mere pettifogging, that he suspected there must be some agency at work to put a spoke in the wheel of reconciliation: he knew "the too easy facility of working upon the unsus-pecting minds of the well-disposed seamen." [135]

Thursday and Friday, then, the indomitable old man spent in being rowed from one ship to another, climbing up and down ladders, making long and tiring speeches, listening no doubt to still longer and more tiring arguments, till he was so fatigued that he had to be lifted in and out of his boat. He decided that on the 13th he would himself be visited, and appointed the Delegates to meet him on the *Royal William* at Spithead. It was there, he decided, that he would receive petitions from the crews about their officers, for on this point of "particular grievances" the Delegates had been firm as a rock; they would no longer be commanded by bullies. Since they expressed an "unalterable adherence" to these changes, Howe again saved face by demanding that each petition should be a prayer to His Majesty to indulge them with the appointment of other officers. The sailors did not mind, in fact they rather welcomed the procedure; they could state their reasons, and prove that "their complaints were merely tendered to show that they have not acted from a spirit of disobedience, but that they meant to represent what they deemed just ground of complaint."[136] What happened on the *Royal William* might be the test of Government good faith.

At a quarter-past ten the procession of boats containing the Delegates was seen swinging across from St. Helens; an hour later the petitioners climbed on board, and within a quarter of an hour Howe was received on deck with full honours. It was not, however, until noon that the Earl invited the anxiously waiting Delegates into the Admiral's cabin, where after two hours' talk the "treaty," as some contemptuously called it, was agreed upon.[137] Howe had been unable to make a stand: in fact, he had not tried very hard. What, after all, could he do, in the circumstances, when the petitions he received from the ships were of so clear a nature, so determined and yet so decorous?

> Our first Lieutenant, he is a most Cruel and Barberous man, Beating some at times untill they are not able to stand, and not allowing them the satisfaction to cry out. If your honr. be pleased to look Round you may find many ships that Want men and as wee want another ship by grantg one Wee will Remain In duty Bound to Remain
> Your Ever lasting Servants and petitioners,
> SHIP's COMPANY OF THE *Amphitrite*.[138]

It was clearly the officers and not the men who were in the wrong; and, as Howe said, "However ineligible the concession, it was become indispensably necessary."

The diehards were furious against him for giving way on this point. Are men to dictate who shall command them? they asked indignantly. Then farewell discipline! But it had not been discipline the men had objected to, only its hideous perversion. Howe, for form's sake, offered them courts martial on officers complained against, which was the regulation procedure suggested with such a lack of humour by the Board in reply to the early petitions. But the men naturally rejected this: the insufferable delay apart, they knew what the outcome would probably be, what it had so often been in the past. Not that there was anything deliberately malign or unfair in such courts martial, but that the dice were inevitably loaded against inarticulate sailors bringing a complaint against an officer who probably had a tongue nimble enough to argue his case, with judges, moreover, who were of his own kind, and who would, even if unconsciously, sympathise with him rather than with the men. Besides, courts martial at this date would only inflame passions, by raking up old scores, and add to the excitement. Howe undoubtedly did the sensible, the humane, and the statesmanlike thing: all through he had shown that at last he realised the implications of the mutiny, and in dealing direct with the Delegates he gave the first example of the proper way to settle industrial disputes. Such an innovation, in the Navy, too, of all places, revealed surprising imaginative powers. And besides, the unflinching dismissal of fifty-nine officers and warrant officers, including one admiral and four captains, was the very thing to impress the men with the sense that the Government was going to play fair, and also to show them that the country had confidence in its sailors. And as a final answer to those who have heaped obloquy upon Howe, it can be pointed out that he had been instructed to let the officers go, rather than fail in his mission:[139] and that the officers themselves did not want to return.

About half of those, then, who had been landed so humiliatingly at the beginning of the week were allowed to rejoin their ships, among them Sir Alan Gardner, whose crew, by deputation, begged him to come back. He was greeted home with three terrific cheers as he stepped on to his quarter-deck, and these—the temptation to harangue was irresistible—incited him to make "a very pathetic speech," telling the men how eagerly he longed to see justice spread an equal mantle over officers and men alike; but he grumbled privately at the "cursed yard-ropes" still being there. Peter Bover, as we know, came happily back to the unlucky *London* and reported to his family, a little incorrectly:

> ... The delegates have finally determined not to receive any of the officers that have been turned on shore from the ships, and insist that no two of them shall ever be appointed to the same ship. You see "it is an ill wind that blows nobody good," and I am peculiarly lucky in not only remaining in the ship, but likewise enjoying the most thorough confidence of the ship's company, who, I am happy to tell you, are, in common with the rest of the fleet, most excessively enraged at the idea of any republican agents stirring them up to sedition, and are unalterably resolved not to meddle with anything but what they have already asked, and which immediately concerns themselves only.[140]

The deposed officers did not suffer; they were placed on full pay until they could be employed again on other ships.

Aaron Graham might have saved himself a deal of bustling about, and idle gossip at street corners, if he had heard Bover's view on the loyalty of the men, their detestation of republican principles; and perhaps the letter of submission the too fervent *Mars* sent to the rest of the Fleet might have disappointed him:

> Our intentions were to act with the fleet: nor had we any other intentions, being convinced our grievances would be redressed. As to our captain and officers, we esteem and respect them for their humane behaviour, and consider ourselves as happy with them as with any other men in the service. We also beg leave to remark, that no set of men in

his Majesty's service are more attached to their sovereign and country, and are ready to defend their cause to the last drop of their vital blood, than are the

SEAMEN OF THE *Mars*.[141]

There was, in short, no effective sedition in the Fleet; and Howe himself put his finger on what might have given rise to the notion when he described his labours as having been to quiet "the most suspicious but most generous minds I think I ever met with in the same class of men."[142]

The conference on the *Royal William* had completely cleared the air; more than the air, indeed. It had broken to smithereens the poor barricades of pride set up by the Board, for the "total and final answer" had been totally and finally acceded to—pay, food, leave, redress of grievances: all that was needed was a solemn ratification in the form of the King's pardon. It was arranged that on the next day, Sunday, the Delegates were to meet the Earl on the *Royal William*, and then, at this final solemn conclave, the whole business would be concluded. Howe had done a good day's work. But still his labours for that day were not yet over, for in the afternoon eight ships of the line sailed into Spithead, alarmingly flying red flags to proclaim that they were in full defiant mutiny. This was Curtis's squadron from the west, which, on receiving the exciting message of the 7th from Spithead, had obeyed that summons rather than the Admiralty order to put to sea, which had arrived too late to prevent the insubordinate dash eastward. Howe immediately went on board the *Prince*, at some risk to himself, to seize this fresh bull by the horns, once more taking up his interminable task of persuasion; and soon the squadron, seeing that everything was settled, agreed to return to duty, but—they were going to get some fun for their trouble—they first insisted that sixty-five officers and warrant officers should be cast out of their ships. All then was over except for the rejoicings.

But there was to be plenty of those attending the great and glorious reconciliation which was to make that Sunday a gala day. A dense fog hung over the Solent that morning, and when Sir Peter Parker went on board the *Royal William* at twenty past nine, nothing could be seen of what was going on at St. Helens; but at ten o'clock the Delegates' boats could be discerned through the mist rowing "in two lines in great regularity." A few minutes later Lord Howe's figure broke through the veil, close at hand, upon which the Delegates turned out the guard to receive him. At twenty past they were admitted to the Admiral's cabin; but the meeting failed of its intended glamour, for the pardon had not arrived, and at eleven o'clock the Delegates re-emerged with nothing done.[143] However, it was sure to come that day, and to make up for the disillusion it was arranged to have a superbly jubilee procession the next. At midday Lord Howe went ashore again, to be received by an immense multitude shouting itself hoarse with acclamation. As he came near the Governor's house—where he was staying—Joyce came up to him to ask at what time he would like the procession to start. Howe, all courtesy, answered that the Delegates' time would be his, and did not flinch when Joyce named seven o'clock as the hour when the tide would serve.

Encouraged by Howe's tone, Joyce then turned to Lady Howe, who had come to meet her husband, and begged her to honour them with her company, assuring her that she need have no qualms: to which Lady Howe answered that she was not in the least afraid, and would be delighted to come. Matters being on this social footing—mutinies, yard-ropes, shootings, and other disagreeables swept out of mind—Howe then invited Joyce into the Governor's house to drink a glass of wine with him, an invitation which the "seditious clubist" accepted "with a manly freedom, unaccompanied by the least particle of familiarity or rudeness." [144] To round off these amenities news was received through the Admiralty telegraph—an ingenious means of communication by signal—that the revised pardon was on the way; and indeed it arrived that afternoon, the messenger having made the journey in the record time of four and a half hours. All was prepared for the grand finale. Everybody was rapturously pleased; the whole town of Portsmouth, with Gosport and Southsea, was in boisterous holiday mood: the only person at all irritated was Bridport, who had kept very mute and invisible throughout the proceedings, and girded at the extra delay which prevented him from carrying out the order to put to sea which the Admiralty, still without a grain of tact, repeatedly sent him.

The whole affair was a tremendous success, and went off without a hitch—more like an armistice rejoicing than the end of a grim and dangerous mutiny. Early in the morning —Monday, the 15th of May—the Delegates rowed over headed by the boat of the *Formidable* cheerfully flying the Union Jack. They landed at the Sally Port (adjoining what is now Victoria Pier), and marched up to Sir William Pitt's house, their bands alternately playing "God Save the King" and "Rule Britannia" with all the gusto of early morning, an exercise in which they were soon joined by the band of the marines. They were invited into the house, partook of refreshments, appeared on the balcony to the vociferous crowds below, and in fact hugely enjoyed their now honourable notoriety till it was time to make a start. At about eight the high and mighty were ready, and all made for the Sally Port once more, near which a curious incident occurred. It was noticed that Joyce was accosted by four men in plain clothes, with whom he talked a little, and then took along with him into his boat. They were sailors from the Nore, where another mutiny had broken out, and they had come, somewhat belatedly, to arrange collaboration with their fellows at Spithead; [145] the best argument for them, Joyce thought, would be to see what was happening that banyan day. So everybody embarked, to the accompaniment of lustily blaring bands. The first boat flew a Union Jack at the fore, and contained the sailors' enthusiastic instrumentalists ; the second, which was the Royal Barge, conveyed Lord Howe reclining in solitary, almost regal grandeur, and this was followed by one containing Sir William Pitt and the Lieutenant-Governor, seated amid the glitter of their aides-de-camp's uniforms ; then came Lady Howe with Lady Pitt and other ladies, while the marines' band of music brought up the rear. The Delegates' boats, with the crews arrayed in their smartest clothes, formed in line ahead on either side; and as each row of boats passed the platform an impressive shooting off of guns stunned the ears of the crowds which blackened the beaches, eagerly watching the whole gay procession dwindling away towards St. Helens.[146]

The peacemaker went first to the *Royal George*—upon which Joyce introduced his visitors from the Nore—and there, on the quarter-deck, read out the Royal Pardon. It was shown to such few seamen as could read, and when these had expressed their approval, it was passed round for the illiterate majority to see, and to gaze upon the Royal Seal attached to it, which to them was the surest of guarantees. Even ministers, full of duplicity, could not get round that. The enthusiasm was immense; the crew gave vent to three ear-splitting cheers, tore down the now outmoded yard-ropes, and replaced the bloody flag with the Royal Standard.[147] So far as they were concerned the mutiny was over, and the other ships, observing these portents, joyfully followed suit. But Howe, for all his years, was not going to leave the job half done, and visited nearly every ship ; and still not content, in the afternoon he had himself taken to Curtis's squadron, where things were yet uncertain. The *Prince*, however, instantly accorded him a guard of honour, and after a short time displayed the Union and Standard under a royal salute as a signal that that squadron too had returned to perfect obedience. Officers old and new boarded the ships everywhere, amid hearty cheers, and once more order reigned in the Channel Fleet.

But the fun was not quite over yet. Wearied almost to death, Howe landed at the Sally Port at six o'clock: he was so exhausted that he had to be lifted from the barge. The Delegates, who had rowed back in three lines abreast in the most perfect order, not only refused to allow mere beasts to draw his carriage, but hoisted·him, far too spent to walk, upon their shoulders, and bore him triumphantly to Sir William Pitt's house, the Union Jack symbolically held fluttering over his head all the way. Every yard of the road was crammed with crowds such as Portsmouth had never yet seen, cheering themselves husky in uproarious efforts to drown the din of the *feux de joie* rattled off by the West Kents, the South Devons, and the marines: the powder which had been provided for a possible (but very improbable) tussle with an invading horde of sailors being thus burned as incense at the noble ceremony of reconciliation. And then Richard, Earl Howe, once more the old beloved Black Dick, threw off the hero to become the host, and entertained the Delegates at dinner in all the forms;[148] and if there were toasts and speeches, as probably there were, they will have been shorter and less boring than usual. At last, as the ending of a long day, the men, filled with peace and good cheer, rowed their way back to St. Helens in the moonlight, singing perhaps the ballad of the occasion:

> The tars of old England have long toil'd in vain,
> From the time of King Charles down to the present reign:
> But their royal master their wages doth raise,
> So join, British sailors, in King George's praise.
> The fleet of Lord Bridport, the terror of France,
> Petition'd the throne that their pay might advance.
> Their petition was granted, each grievance redress'd
> In the heart of each seaman great George he is bless'd.[149]

And then the Delegates prosaically reported for duty.

At last, on the 17th, after a month's delay, Bridport put to sea. It had been a stimulating because successful mutiny; the Fleet was the better for it, with happier men and worthier officers, and no grudge felt. At least, none was shown on either side. Bover is witness that the men felt none. And at the very end, on the 14th, the myopic Admiralty itself had gone so far as to make a sensible, even a generous gesture. In an order of two paragraphs, issued to all flag officers, captains and commanders, they promulgated an act of total oblivion for all or any deeds of disobedience, mutiny, breach and neglect of duty, and ordained that no seaman or marine should be "disquieted by any reproof or reproach" in respect of such deeds.[150] This order was loyally adhered to; there was no victimisation of any kind—so far from it, indeed, that several of the Delegates were promoted within a year, one of them that very month to the rank of midshipman.[151] The only people who, perhaps, were disillusioned were the sailors who had come from the Nore to concert great actions. One of them, who had never been in favour of the mutiny, ran away; one stayed a while in Portsmouth; the other two, with the documents of peace which Howe had given them, returned sadly to a far less pleasant scene.[152]

PART TWO

THE FLOATING REPUBLIC

CHAPTER X

THE POT BOILS

TOWARDS the end of March, at the time when the urgent feelings of the men in the Channel Fleet were working up and crystallising out to produce "the breeze at Spithead," a village schoolmaster named Richard Parker was bundled out of a debtors' prison in Scotland, and deposited at the Leith rendezvous for naval recruits, a quota-man for the county of Perth.

The commander of the tender which was to take this obvious unfortunate to Sheerness was immediately struck by the polish of his manner, and more still by the look of the man. Thirty years of age, of medium height and well built, swarthy, with vaguely aquiline features marked by large dark eyes expressive below his black hair, which he wore long, there was something about the arch of the brow, the set of the nervous lips and chin, and the indrawn cheeks, which, added to a general delicacy, marked him out as very different from the usual seamy scum which oozed from a debtors' prison. He was desperately poor, he explained unnecessarily, a married man pursued by ill-luck, trying to make a living by forcing elementary knowledge into the skulls of snivelling infants; and being caught in usurious toils, had accepted a quota of twenty guineas to gain his freedom. Yes, he had been to sea before; he had even, indeed, been a midshipman in the *Mediator* in 1783, and had earned some prize-money. That was all he told Lieutenant Watson of the Leith tender: there was a good deal more to tell, but Parker was all on edge, his nerves were frayed, and he was so depressed by the prospect that lay before him, so tortured, perhaps, by the consciousness of his failure in the past, his vision of himself as a pawn of misfortune, that on the journey to Sheerness he sought an end to his troubles by throwing himself overboard.

Life might well have seemed to him a hopeless game, though it had begun invitingly enough. Son of a well-to-do baker of Exeter, he had, when only half-way through his education, insisted on going to sea, where he had at first done passably well. Then illness had struck across his plans, and perhaps a neurotic temperament. He had transferred from the Royal Navy to the merchant service, gone to Africa, to India, where he had engaged in trade; returned, married, and then, as though the sea must have him, had re-entered the Royal Navy, once more as a midshipman. Unluckily, in 1793, he had been goaded into a very trifling act of insubordination by a superior officer, and, though God knows the provocation had been bitter enough, his reaction of the mildest, he had been court martialled and disrated. Even so he might have done tolerably well, for he was applied for by the captain of another ship, who saw in him a likely petty officer; but illness had once more interfered with his hopeful views, and he had finally been discharged on the ground that he was incurably rheumatic, though there is a suggestion that the trouble was mental. His efforts to make good in Scotland had landed him only in jail, so that—clearly the sea must have him—he was forced to sell himself into a life of which he too well knew the hopelessness and the horror.[1]

But even his wildest forebodings, dark enough to make him momentarily prefer death, could not have rivalled the actuality which met him on board the *Sandwich*, where he was unloaded with his fellow quota- or pressed-men when the tender arrived at Sheerness, and upon which he was rated as supernumerary A.B. The *Sandwich* was an old corpse of a ship, built in 1759, and though once a splendid vessel, proud bearer of Rodney's flag in the West Indies, she now stank with decay. Her full complement in war was

about 750 men; but at this period, to her harbour flag-
and depot-ship complement of 400, she added some 1100
to 1200 supernumeraries, recruits of various kinds, and men
paid off from other ships, waiting for transfer, all crammed
into a vessel rather smaller than the *Victory*. One has a vision
of writhing humanity, like worms crawling over one another in the fœtid pot of a boy-fisherman; but no lurid
imagining of what this ship was can outdo the report the
ship's doctor made to her commander, Captain Mosse,
himself perturbed at the loathsomeness of it all:

Sir,   22 *March* 1797.

The infection which has existed for some time in His Majesty's Ship
Sandwich under your command having of late become more virulent, and
resisted the methods that have been taken to check it, which is solely
owing to the ship being so crowded, I beg leave to acquaint you that it is
absolutely necessary to reduce the numbers of men already on board.
Those men that are at first seized with the contagious fever, which has so
alarmingly shown itself, are in general very dirty, almost naked, and in
general without beds (having lost them either by their own indolence, or
the villany of their companions) . . .

I feel myself peculiarly called upon to point out the little avail of pre-
scribing medecines to unhappy sufferers, who are so bare of common
necessaries and compelled to mix with the throng by laying on the decks.
The number of sores, scalds, and other unavoidable accidents, which the
awkward landsmen are liable to, often degenerate into bad ulcers, which
cannot be readily cured on board, owing sometimes to their own bad
habits, but oftener to the foul air they breathe between decks; besides
being frequently trod upon in the night from their crowded state.

Sir, it is my professional opinion, that there is no effective remedy, but
by considerably reducing the number that have been usually kept for
months in the *Sandwich*, for sickness and contagion cannot be prevented
by any physical means where fifteen or sixteen hundred men are confined
in the small compass of a ship, many of whom are vitiated in their habits
(as) well as filthy in their dispositions. The circumambient air is so im-
pregnated with human effluvia that contagious fevers must inevitably be
the consequence.

Untoward fortune has often placed me in situations where I could not
practice my profession agreeable to its principles, or the feelings of my

conscience, but I never was in a situation more replete with anxiety, than the present as Surgeon of the *Sandwich*. I have only to add that the whole of the evil herein stated originated from the ship being crowded with supernumeraries, and those men permitted to remain such a length of time on board to the very great detriment (both physically and morally) of His Majesty's Service.

I am, Sir,

Your most obedient and humble servant,

JOHN SNIPE.[2]

This was no hysterical outburst from an overtired worried doctor, haunted by the horror of being unable to cope with the impossible, but a sober statement designed and fit for the eye of officialdom: or so at any rate Captain Mosse thought, for he forwarded it to the Admiral Commanding at the Nore, adding in his covering letter, "The surgeon's statement is, I am sorry to say, a true picture of our situation."

To the decent men in the service such a pestiferous ship must have appeared as physically abominable as any prison —we know what prison conditions were in those days—and morally many of the men were actually prison rabble, who had either come out of durance, or richly deserved to be put there. For "it was then a common practice with the London police when they got hold of a confirmed rogue, but lacked sufficient evidence to convict him, to send him on board any ship known to be in want of men, in order effectually to dispose of him."[3] It was degrading for self-respecting seamen with good records to be herded body to body with such filth, and they were, moreover, exasperated by knowing that many captains on other ships had applied for experienced men whom they knew, and on whom they had their eye to make petty officers of, only to be refused.[4] This alone was cause enough for a gruelling sense of wrong—to know that you might be enjoying better conditions and better pay, and yet be condemned to horrible companionship, to foulness and disease. And if the riff-raff might not find it altogether amiss to live in this way (apart from the ulcers and the fevers, and the being trampled on at night), some of them might well see in such conditions a heaven-sent opportunity for exercising their talents as blood-warming demagogues. But probably the most powerful influence in causing disaffection was the presence of a large number of quota-men, who, better educated, resented being treated worse than animals, being styed and fed like swine, and often treated like swine by superiors, who, sometimes irresponsible, acted under the protection of a ferocious code known as the Articles of War, which, incidentally, had been read out on board the *Sandwich* on 2nd May. They also, discontented for themselves, would help to foment discontent among the seamen. The wonder is not that there was a mutiny, but that the patriotism of any man should have survived conditions one might think made on purpose to damp it down to extinction.

If the *Sandwich* was the worst instance of squalor that could be found, the men in the other ships at the Nore, and in the North Sea Fleet generally, shared the discontent made plain to the nation by their brethren at Spithead; all were victims of the same system. Since they were ripe for revolt, whether conscious of it or not, the events stirring in the Channel Fleet naturally caused the intensest excitement, and roused hopes which glowed so bright that they became extravagant. That the seamen as a whole sympathised with the first mutiny had been made plain enough at the time by the behaviour of the sailors on Duncan's flagship; but the men in the North Sea area remained quiet, waiting restrained on the event, until the renewed and fiercer outbreak at St. Helens.

It was, in any case, difficult to organise a mutiny at the Nore. The ships stationed there did not form a unified fleet, designed to go into action as a unit. When the mutiny began, there were only three line-of-battle ships at the Great and Little Nore, the depot-ship, the *Sandwich*, and two others under orders to join the North Sea Fleet: the remaining eight ships, one of which was merely a floating battery, were of the frigate class, scattered at the Great and Little Nore, and in and about Sheerness. These ships were continually changing, being detailed for convoy or escort duty; there was no possibility of careful preparation, or ensuring cohesion, as there had been at Spithead. Yet the men at the Nore felt they must do something, if only to show that the whole service was at one in feeling with the Channel Fleet. And by hidden means, before the affair at St. Helens was over, they had got together some kind of organisation, arrived at some sort of agreement on how they would act, in spite of the temporary and shifting nature of the squadron, in spite of the sailors of the different ships not knowing one another, and at having to venture largely in the dark. Perhaps they received a message from Spithead, as the men at Plymouth had done, which would argue that someone at Spithead could be certain of at least one correspondent at the Nore; but it is more likely that the outbreak was due to a spontaneous impulse. Their grievances were the same, and they were burning enough; they knew the matter was in suspense; they, too, had it in their minds that the Admiralty was not above playing fast and loose: a demonstration from them might clinch the business. The fact that they were not led, were not acting on any carefully conceived plan, and had, as will be seen, no clear objective or clear views of what to do, in itself attests the strength of their emotions, their bitter sense of being wronged.

That these emotions existed was, on 12th May, made plain enough to their officers, who had expected nothing, some muttering on the *Inflexible* a few days earlier having been suppressed. On that day, a court martial, which had begun on the 3rd, was continuing to sit on the *Inflexible* to judge the case of Captain Savage, who had lost his ship;

and it was not until it had duly assembled, many officers being thus out of the way, that the men made any movement. At half-past nine, however, when the crew of the *Sandwich* were given orders to clear hawse preparatory to unmooring, they climbed into the rigging and gave three cheers, a demonstration which could mean only one thing: the pot had boiled over. Their admiral, Buckner, and Captain Mosse, were at the court martial; no steps could be taken with respect to them, but the mutineers ordered their first lieutenant, named Justice, to quit the ship. This done, they sent a boat to the man-of-war lying next them, and asked them to discharge their most obnoxious officers, an invitation which was promptly carried out. The success of this move being seen, the mutiny soon became general.[5] Boats rowed hurriedly from ship to ship to summon Delegates on board the *Sandwich*,[6] where before very long a committee was set up which declared itself to be in charge of the Fleet, and soon took steps to make this claim actual.

The moment he was expelled his ship, Justice took the news to the court martial, which at once broke up. Admiral Buckner gave the *Sandwich* a wide berth and went straight to Sheerness, but Mosse returned and boldly faced the music. The men, he found, were quiet: they could afford to be, for they were in complete command. They had assumed possession of the keys of the magazine, storerooms and so on, and had posted sentries with cutlasses on the decks and gangways. On reaching the quarter-deck, Mosse told the boatswain to call the men aft to retail their grievances, but cries of "No, no!" answered the call. Mosse then went forward to the fore-hatchway, where he found those whom he supposed to be the leaders; and going down among them he asked them why they were behaving in this "irregular" way, and told them that if they had any grievances he would redress them as far as he could. They answered that if he went back to the quarter-deck, ten or a dozen of them would form a deputation to him; but they thought better of this, and shortly sent him a message to say that he must wait for the return of the Delegates, who had gone to visit other ships. He could do nothing. The acting captain appeared to be the Master, who played the go-between betwixt him and the crew, and when the men demanded the arms, he could not prevent them from seizing them and storing them below well out of reach of the marines. He noticed that all the time they seemed to be strict in their discipline, copying, apparently, the behaviour of their comrades at Portsmouth; but here the Delegates did not yet presume so far as to instal themselves in glory in the state cabin.[7]

By the end of that day the seamen were solidly in possession of the whole fleet, with the uncertain exception of the *San Fiorenzo*, a frigate which had arrived that afternoon from Spithead. Since she came from the storm-centre where such heartening things were happening, she was cheered by each ship as she passed on her way to Sheerness; but the cheers were a trifle premature, for her crew, pacified by what had occurred on the Portsmouth station, obeyed their captain's order not to return the cheers. This was chilling, but all was put right the next day. In the morning, seeing that she was the only ship not in a state of mutiny, the powers thought that it would be convenient to continue within her decks the adjourned court martial on Captain Savage; but soon after the court had assembled, a posse of armed boats arrived from the other ships, vehemently demanding two men from her as delegates, and making it plain that the *Inflexible* would expect to be cheered as she passed out later in the day on her way to the Nore. The captain of the frigate hastened to the place where the court was assembled, so as to report this alarming news to the President; he was closely followed by the Delegates, who then declared that one of the objects of their visit was to take charge of Savage, by whom they placed themselves;

but when they were firmly told that they had no business there, they meekly withdrew. This futile gesture proved a certain indecision in the men from the very beginning, both as to their ends and as to their means; it betrayed a lack of confidence, especially as the Delegates rowed away without doing anything further. But meanwhile the *Inflexible*, with all her sixty-four guns, was coming magnificently out, under the command of her captain of the foretop, the officers having been politely deposed or disrated, the captain himself, half humorously, perhaps, having been granted the rank of midshipman by way of keeping the ship duly officered. As she drew near, it was seen that the tompions were out of her larboard guns, and that the men were at their quarters; but still the *San Fiorenzo* gave no sign of complying with the mutineers' injunctions. When, however, the great ship was abreast of the frigate, she fired a shot which cut away the foot-rope of the latter's jib-boom, upon which the crew of the *San Fiorenzo*, seeing that their fellows meant business, gave the cheers of adherence, and the *Inflexible*, content with her somewhat forcible conversion, passed on without firing another round.[8]

That day, the 13th, the mutineers spent in organising their affairs, which by the 16th were in thoroughgoing order. They drew up a code not unlike the one which had ruled at Spithead, a code which began by stating "Unanimity the only means of gaining the end in view," and went on to say that strict discipline was to be maintained, no "private liquor" was to be allowed, that respect was to be shown to officers, and that duty was to be carried on as before. Again, although all "unsuitable" officers were to be despatched ashore, no master or pilot was to be allowed to leave his ship. The circular declared with undue optimism that an early communication with all the Delegates would tend to bring about a speedy remedy, and concluded rather oddly, but, after all, democratically, by suggesting that each ship might add any clause which should seem to it proper to procure the preservation of good order.[9] Besides supporting the central committee, each ship in due course appointed its own junta of twelve to govern it, one of whom was elected to act as captain; and over and above these bodies there was brought into being, by election, a "General Committee of Internal Regulations," with a secretary and a clerk, which met on board the *Director* each morning, and apparently saw to the victualling of the ships. This was a matter of some urgency—indeed it was later to become a vital question —since most of the pursers, an unpopular race, had been sent to consider their sins on land. Discipline was rigorously maintained, for not only were red flags hoisted, but yard-ropes were rove as a signal that there was to be no laxity; and, indeed, all the while the Fleet was as well ordered in respect of routine work as at normal times. The junta on each ship acted as a court martial to deal with offenders, and carried out this duty without hesitation. One man, for instance, had his skin broken by twelve strokes of the cat for drinking too much, a negro, known as "Black Jack Campbell," and another man on the *Sandwich* were flogged "for getting beastly drunk with small beer"; [10] the *Repulse* recorded (but this was later) that "James Day stands charged with violating two of the most sacred laws enacted for the preservation and unanimity of the ship's company, viz.: drunkenness in the greatest extream, and neglect of duty." A petty officer was accused of the crime of inciting men to petition for leave to go ashore; a Midshipman Smith was charged with abusing a "brother" by kicking him, this malevolence being arraigned by a sailor who styled himself, "Counsel for the Crown." Luckily Smith's good character, and the evidence of the chief witness, procured a light punishment for him; he was confined to his cabin for twenty-four hours, and compelled to "ast Mr. William Johnson's pardon."[11] Only in one instance did the sailors show any vindictiveness, this against the boatswain of the *Prosperine*, whom for some crime or other they sentenced to death simply to frighten him, reserving him for a different punishment:

> He was disfigured with a large swab tied upon each shoulder, a rope round his neck, and his hands tied behind him: in this state he was placed in a boat, and rowed round the Fleet, with a drummer by his side, occasionally beating the "Rogue's March," the usual accompaniment of flogging through the fleet; he was then landed at Sheerness and marched through the Dock Yard and Garrison, guarded by a party of Mutineers; and when they considered him sufficiently punished and degraded, they let him loose, and left him without further molestation.[12]

But with all this, no attempt was made to compel authority to move; no demands were voiced, no manifesto issued or petition presented. It seemed to be a mutiny in the air, with no objective. There was, indeed, a good deal of pomp and circumstance about it, both under and on the level of public view. Within the ships the Delegates were busy, for knowing that a majority of stalwarts was not enough, but that an apparent unanimity at least was necessary, they offered the sailors what they knew would be the firmest shackle—an oath. They would visit a ship, and have the men brought one by one to the cabin, and there they would swiftly and in solemn secrecy read over to them a terrific avowal of faith, which was carefully prepared, and had been ready since the 6th:[13]

> I, A.B. do voluntarily make oath and swear that I will be true in the cause we are embarked in, and I will to the laying down of my life be true to the Delegates at present assembled, whilst they continue to support the present cause . . .

the man going on to swear that he would discover and report any activity subversive "of our present plan," or likely to fray the texture of "our present system."[14] When a sufficient number had sworn, so that their weight would be pre-ponderant, and secrecy hopeless, the rest were dealt with in batches. But what "our present plan," or cause, or system, might be, was left judiciously vague. It was all very stirring, but it seemed to lack direction: there is no doubt that the men felt deeply, some of them violently, and wanted something done, but nobody seemed prepared to tell them what that something was. The Delegates rowed about, sometimes processionally, in boats weighed down with blaring bands which wearied hearers with the repetition of loyal tunes such as "Rule Britannia," "God Save the King," and the now forgotten, though better musically and poetically, "Britons Strike Home": they marched up and down the streets of Sheerness tremendously armed with cutlasses and pistols, waving red flags, and they held meet-ings in the public-houses, The Chequers (now no more) being their favourite. Sometimes the meetings developed into gatherings which were more festive, and there may have been carousals on the *Sandwich*; but that was, for the moment, all. Even the topical poets had some difficulty in arriving at the essence, and would sing:

> Old Neptune made haste, to the Nore he did come,
> To waken his sons who had slept far too long.
> His thundering loud voice made us start with surprise,
> To hear his sweet words, and he bid us arise. . . .[15]

or:

> Then at the Nore the lions boldly roused,
> Their brethren's cause at Spithead they espoused,
> Each swore alike to King he would be true,
> But one and all the tyrants would subdue,
> Their gallant hearts the chains of bondage broke,
> Not to revolt, but to evade the yoke. . . .[16]

or rhymes about impressment, leaving it to be implied what they meant to do. But whatever may be dark, it is perfectly clear that the men felt they were existing under an intolerable burden of unfairness, stupidity and cruelty.

The fact seems to be that the mutineers of the Nore regarded themselves at this stage merely as auxiliaries to their comrades at Spithead. There the decisions would be made, from there the plan of action would be declared, and there, if anywhere, the sailors' battle would be won. Therefore on the 14th they sent four representatives to the Channel Fleet, who, travelling through London, and narrowly escaping impressment, arrived at Portsmouth, as we have seen, just in time to partake in the festivities which so joyously concluded the Spithead trouble. They returned from the gay reconciliation on the 19th, or rather two of them did, to be chilled by a bleaker atmosphere. They brought with them the relevant papers pressed upon them by Lord Howe, and the news that all was over. What, then, were the mutineers at the Nore to do? Were they humbly to return to duty and crave the King's pardon? They had to make up their minds, from motives one can only conjecture, and with results which became too horribly apparent to the people of Great Britain. For this mutiny was far worse, more threatening, more violent, and longer maintained, than that at Spithead. If that had been a breeze, this was a full gale.

From the beginning the conferences of the Delegates had taken place on the *Sandwich*, and before many days Richard Parker took the stage as leading Delegate on that ship. It was the *Sandwich's* boat which led the processions which rowed so noisily musical through the Fleet, and in it, occupying the place of honour, sat the smouldering, swarthy person of Richard Parker; it was his lithe figure which led the bands about the streets of Sheerness, to the admiration of the then friendly inhabitants; and when at last the Delegates sent out their ultimatum to duly constituted authority, it was signed "Richard Parker, President."

CHAPTER XI

"BETWEEN THE ACTING OF A DREADFUL THING . . ."

THIS swift exaltation of a gaol-stained nobody to the pinnacle of command of a fleet in rebellion has led fertile minds to suppose that Parker must have rejoined with the stark purpose of fomenting mutiny, bent upon mischief, emissary of some revolutionary club. But there is no reason to doubt the truth of the statements he made immediately before what he called his "extremely boisterous" exit from life at the end of the yard-arm, in which he explained how he had had his lurid greatness thrust upon him. Till the 12th he knew nothing about the mutiny; the cheers took him by surprise as he was innocently working in the carpenter's mate's berth, and when he ran up on deck he was astonished to see the forecastle guns pointed aft. He soon after went below, and only heard about the expulsion of the officers. He considered that the whole affair, with all its rash talk about hanging, was far too violent, and the next day expressed his opinions to Simms, the carpenter's mate. Simms agreed, and thought it a pity that some cool, level-headed person was not in charge. On the third day the Delegates invited Parker to join them in one of the starboard bays, given an air by being hung round with hammocks ; and in one day more he was asked to take the chair at their meetings. Then before he knew where he was, and without his making even a gesture, he found himself, in style and function, president.

It is easy enough to see why the men elected Parker to this dizzy height, though he had not been with them long. Here was a man of vivacity and intelligence, of much more education than most of them, who knew the ways of the

Navy, and had been an officer. He would be able to write a good letter, and talk on more equal terms than they could with the high and mighty. And obviously he sympathised with them. It is also quite easy to see why Parker accepted. He believed that the sailors wanted no more than to have their grievances redressed, and he thought their condition so appalling that their behaviour was justified. "As a human being," he wrote,

> I stand subject to human passion, the noblest of which is a tender *sensibility at every species of human woe*. Thus influenced, how could I indifferently stand by, and behold some of the best of my fellow-creatures cruelly treated by some of the very worst. I candidly confess I could not, and because I could not, fate consigns me to be a victim to the tenderest emotions of the human heart.[17]

It is no doubt true that he was not among the first movers of the mutiny; if he had been, it could hardly have flared up so soon, and perhaps it is true that he accepted his elevation with reluctance. Yet to a man of his temperament, excitable, neurotic even, the position must have seemed full of glamour. What a chance to be a great man, to benefit his fellows, to earn a glorious name! "I die a martyr in the cause of humanity" he was to declare—and he thought it. He believed in his mission, and saw himself also as a moderator of the seamen's passions: he would subdue, or so he dreamed, the too tempestuous feelings of the more fiery rebels, guide them into more temperate channels. But he had not, as he was to find out, the dominating qualities of a great leader; he was the tool of the hot spirits, and sometimes in his excitement allowed his own volatile emotions to carry him too far.

It was a difficult position for him, flung headlong into the tumult and bidden to direct it, for by the time he was made president matters had already thrust to a certain distance. Officers had been expelled their ships—from the *Inflexible*, for instance, the first, second, and third lieutenants, the master and the surgeon; the *San Fiorenzo* had been fired on, an act which amounted to levying war against the King; and all the ships had refused duty except for the essential routine. A certain manner had been adopted—the parading about the streets in all the panoply of war, heightened by a blatant atmosphere of violence. This last was most fiercely exhibited at the hospital, or sick quarters, where the Delegates, outraged by the treatment, or lack of it, vouchsafed their ailing fellows, adopted such a threatening tone that the surgeon bolted to quieter regions, and his assistant took refuge in the next world by cutting his throat.[18]

The situation was all the 'more uneasy because at that time nobody, not even the prime instigators, could tell what the object of the mutiny was. To show their solidarity with the men at Spithead, yes; but when the Delegates came back from there, the news they brought rather took the wind out of the sails of the leaders at the Nore. "Though it is honest, it is never good to bring bad news," and the Delegates were so incensed with MacCarthy, one of their emissaries, for carrying back the documents, that they seem even to have threatened him with hanging for disloyalty.[19] Yet, on his own showing, he was the "founder" of the mutiny on the *Inflexible*.[20] The result was, of course, infuriating, since a considerable sum of money had been collected to defray the expenses of the travellers,[21] who, instead of bringing back further potent incitements, had done no more than to buy "two or three pennyworth of ballads for twenty pounds," as Parker is supposed to have grumbled. At any rate, whatever they brought, it was not the material to support a mutiny with, and we might think that the sensible thing to do, since so much had been granted, was to cancel future proceedings.

But however much Parker may have wanted to do this, and there is no evidence that he had the wish, he would not have found it possible. For one thing, a special Royal Pardon would be needed to cover the offences the mutineers had already committed. But more important than this was the feeling of the instigators, or of most of them. They would look foolish if they were to cry off now; and, moreover, the men had been worked up to do something. Acts have a momentum of their own. The sailors were exhilarated by the atmosphere they had created, they were enjoying their liberty, their comparative freedom from the tedious duties of sea life, and their release from the perpetual threat of harsh punishment from officers they hated, and whom they had got rid of. Besides, were they to be outdone by their comrades at Spithead? Must they not add something to what had been gained there—for there were still many things they had at heart—and could not they too look fine in the eyes of the world by compelling the Lords of the Admiralty to come and bargain with them? It would be unbearable simply to return to duty with a sheepish grin like schoolboys sneaking back from playing truant.

Yet this is what the Government, and the people of England in general, expected them to do. They looked upon the Nore mutiny merely as a piece of natural ebullience provoked by the Spithead affair, which would subside as soon as it was known that Howe had settled the trouble. The Admiralty allowed it a few hours at most.[22] Probably many of the seamen too thought that the best course was to let all become quiet again, but if so they were overruled by their more imaginative comrades. Yet from the beginning the ultimate movers seem to have had some trouble in getting any approach to unanimity, as is shown by the elaborate procedure they evolved for administering the oath of "fidelity": their ostentatious parading, their music, their forming of numberless committees to involve as many people as possible in authority, all seem designed rather with the object of arousing enthusiasm, of "bucking the men up," than with any clear end in view.

They would now have to deal, somehow, with the cooling news brought back from Portsmouth. Parker tried to make out that the Act for the increase of pay was only an Order in Council; and when forced to retreat from this position, declared that the Act would be valid for only one year. The single grain of comfort they had got was Howe's promise that unpopular officers should be removed from their ships, and they proceeded to a more drastic purge, from which, among others, Captain William Bligh of the *Director* was one of the first to suffer. Bligh's ship had not been a happy one for some time, a state of affairs that might be expected under the man who a few years before had goaded the men of the *Bounty* to successful mutiny. As early as 10th April six men had refused duty, and had had their backs lacerated; before long others had shown an insubordinate spirit. Though on the 25th Bligh had published the proclamation granting increased wages, on 2nd and 3rd May he had felt it advisable to read out the Articles of War, and punish a further batch of men. The ship had come to the Nore to refit on the 6th, and when the men joined in the mutiny on the 12th, three officers had been promptly sent off.[23] Thus the further action the Delegates took on the 19th is significant, as is made plain by the letter Bligh wrote to the Secretary of the Admiralty:

SHEERNESS,
19th May 1797.

You will please to inform my Lords Commissioners of the Admiralty that this morning about nine o'clock, soon after the return of the delegates from Spithead, they came on board and declared to me they had seen Earl Howe, who told them all officers were to be removed from their ships who they disapproved of; they were in consequence directed to inform me in the name of the ship's company that I was to quit the command of the ship and for it to devolve on the first Lieutenant, who they in the same breath ordered to supercede me.

Being without any resource I was obliged to quit the ship. I have stated the whole transaction to Admiral Buckner, and now wait their Lordships' directions, being ready to meet any charge that can be brought against me or such investigation as they may think proper to direct.[24]

Such an action, the Delegates no doubt felt, would help to keep matters going.

They had to act quickly, because Buckner sent a message to say that he would come on board his ship, the *Sandwich*, that day, and notify the King's pardon on the terms the Admiralty had sent him on the 17th. This had to be staved off, and they returned an answer that they would wait upon the Admiral on shore and attend him to his ship. This seemed satisfactory to Buckner, who, however, had to wait till two o'clock, when a deputation led by Parker called upon him with a paper of grievances in their hand. It shows a certain degree of efficiency in council that they should have produced their demands so soon, demands which had, of course, to be in excess of those granted at Spithead; and there can be no doubt that the men felt that there were still some outrageous grievances which should be remedied, some alteration in naval rules which justice cried out for. They may even have been angry with their Portsmouth brothers for not having attempted to do more while they were about it. Buckner tried to argue with them. He was an old man— he had been made lieutenant more than forty years before, had been with Rodney in the West Indies, and was comfortably ending his days as Vice-Admiral of the White at the Nore—and he believed that he could reason with the Delegates. He discussed the demands, and, as he wrote plaintively in his report, "endeavoured with every means in my power to shake their resolution of stipulating for them. I had considerable hopes that I had succeeded in doing this," he went on, because they asked him to go off to the ships the next morning, when all would be satisfactorily settled. Buckner did not quite understand.

At all events, at nine the next day, the 20th, he set out for the *Sandwich* with two captains and a procession of the

Delegates' boats; and he became all the more full of hope since the crew of the *Clyde* cheered him as he went by with his flag flying. No doubt all would be well. But from the first there was a hitch. Nobody had been warned at what time he would be coming: they were not ready, and Parker was visiting some other ship. The remaining Delegates disagreed as to how he should be received. They had taken down his flag—they meant to rehoist it when he left the ship—and could they, they debated (it was a nice point of etiquette), receive him in state as an Admiral when he had no flag? So, instead of being shown full honours, he was only received as a private person, politely, with a common civility which in his position he could only regard as damned insolence. When Parker hurriedly came back he did little to reduce the Admiral's ruffled feelings, for though he apologised for the reception, the new commander of the Fleet kept his hat on as a symbol of his position.[25] It is possible that he might have done more than apologise, for both he and many men on the *Sandwich* were ready to man the ship and cheer; indeed a half-hearted effort to do so was made: but by this time "evil-spirited people had diffused into the minds of the ship's company that the Admiral was not competent to settle the existing differences";[26] and, moreover, the *Inflexible*, fearing weakness, had sent to say that if the *Sandwich* cheered the Admiral she would come alongside and sink her. Whatever the details may have been, it was plain that nothing could be done, and it is not surprising that the interview was "short and unavailing." "On my requesting they would attend me on the quarter-deck," Buckner wrote,

one of them was deputed to acquaint me that they still had something to settle, which they would lay before me in half an hour. Having waited a considerable time, they in a body brought me the enclosed paper, and declared with one voice *that they would not resign the charge they now had in their own hands* till the conditions therein stipulated for were complied with, and satisfied *by the personal attendance of a Board of their Lordships here*, which they insist they have a right to expect, there having been a precedent for it at Spithead.[27]

The men had evidently made up their minds: Buckner's attitude had perhaps helped to harden them, and there was nothing for the Admiral to do but to go away promising to send the paper on. The men disclaimed every idea of disrespect, but they drew his attention to the fact that they were a firm, compact body, determined to persevere in this point.

The document Buckner took away with him on his disillusioned return to the shore was, indeed, in the nature of an ultimatum, consisting of eight articles.

> Article 1st.—That every indulgence granted to the fleet at Portsmouth be granted to his Majesty's subjects serving in the fleet at the Nore, and on places adjacent.

That this would be allowed went without saying; but the statement shows that the men here also were profoundly suspicious of the Admiralty, and of the Government, especially of "Billy Pitt and Dundas," both of whom they hated.

> Article 2nd.—That every man, upon a ship's coming into harbour shall have liberty (a certain number at a time, so as not to injure the ship's duty) to go and see their friends and families; a convenient time to be allowed to each man.

This demand had been put forward at Spithead, but little had come of it; yet this lack of leave was certainly one of the seamen's most bitter grievances, and on every ground of fairness or humanity ought to have been remedied. A man joined for three years, a term which might be extended to four or even six, but sometimes he was kept for more than twelve years, any request for discharge being treated as an act of the greatest contumacy. All this time he was a prisoner at sea, drafted from ship to ship, serving often in unhealthy climates, never allowed to taste "the sweets of home," and so virtually dead to his friends and family. It was so obviously silly that when a ship came into port, and everybody knew that she would not put to sea again for some weeks, that a proportion at a time should not have been allowed on shore, that it seemed more than silly, it seemed malignant.

Article 3rd.—That all ships before they go to sea, shall be paid all arrears of wages down to six months, according to the old rules.

This was simply to ask that the regulations should be carried out, and is a severe criticism of naval administration.

Article 4th.—That no officer that has been turned out of any of his Majesty's ships shall be employed in the same ship again, without the consent of the ship's company.

Article 5th.—That when any of his Majesty's ships shall be paid that may have been some time in commission, if there are any pressed men on board that may not be in the regular course of payment, they shall receive two months advance to furnish them with necessaries.

This was aimed at preventing extortionate terms for credit being exacted by profiteering pursers; the poor devils of men had to have slops, and were at the mercy of official usurers: this was the one article Buckner said he would forward with wholehearted approval.

Article 6th.—That an indemnification be made any men who run, and may now be in his Majesty's naval service, and that they shall not be liable to be taken up as deserters.

The sailors must have known it was not very easy to grant this; the likelihood is that there were a great many deserters who had come back, and wished to have the constant fear of discovery and capital punishment removed.

Article 7th.—That a more equal distribution be made of prize-money to the crews of his Majesty's ships and vessels of war,

This was thoroughly just, and should have been granted without hesitation. The distribution was scandalous, and was not rectified for some decades. Even after the battle of Navarino, thirty years later, the Admiral commanding got £7800, the Able Seaman, 19s.!

> Article 8th.—That the articles of war, as now enforced, require various alteration, several of which to be expunged therefrom, and if more moderate ones were held forth to seamen in general, it would be the means of taking off that terror and prejudice against his Majesty's service, on that account too frequently imbibed by seamen, from entering voluntarily into the service.

There was a good deal to be said for this too, as anyone will agree who reads the antiquated Articles; and there is sound common sense at the end. The declaration concluded with due emphasis:

> The committee of delegates of the whole fleet, assembled in council on board his Majesty's ship *Sandwich*, have unanimously agreed that they will not deliver up their charge until the appearance of some of the lords commissioners of the Admiralty to ratify the same.
>
> Given on board his Majesty's ship *Sandwich*, by the delegates of the fleet, May 20th, 1797.
>
> RICHARD PARKER,
President.[28]

The game, real enough for one side at least, had started. What would be the answer to this move?

It was not for Buckner to say, though he could guess. He forwarded the demands, and also wrote suggesting that in the present distracted state of the seamen at the Nore, "it would be advisable to send no more recruits to the *Sandwich*, and to stop any ships in the Thames which should have gone to the Nore, since an accumulation of numbers would unavoidably add to the confusion that now prevails," [29] and he for one did not want his troubles added to.

When Nepean and the Lords of the Admiralty, complacently awaiting a soft answer, received and read the list of articles, they professed themselves "extremely surprised." They were shocked at the ingratitude of the sailors, who now, surely, were in sight of an almost Utopian way of life. They wrote to Buckner,[30] instructing him to refuse all the articles point-blank, except the first, which was already granted; as for the rest, the administration of the Navy was already perfect, or so they implied in bland diplomatic language: the fourth article they would not hear of discussing, for did they not leave such appointments to the discretion of commanders? They did not seem to realise that commanders were not always discreet, and that an officer rejoining a ship from which he had been ousted for brutality might be likely to wreak vengeance on his critics when he got back.

On receiving this letter, Buckner rewrote it in language almost as pompous and certainly more inflated than the original, explaining still more fully that their Lordships had not the least intention of journeying to Sheerness, and that deserters could only be pardoned by the King's clemency. His last paragraph, which is an unhappy re-phrasing of Nepean's words, is so lacking in humour that one hopes the seamen laughed, though one fears that it merely enraged them:

> When the seamen and marines at the Nore and at Sheerness reflect that the rest of the fleets have returned to their duty, and have proceeded to sea in search of the enemies of their country, their lordships have no doubt that they will no longer show themselves ungrateful for all that has been so liberally granted them, but shall strive who shall be the first to shew his loyalty to his king, and his love to his country, by returning to that state of obedience and discipline, without which they cannot expect any longer to enjoy the confidence and good opinion of their country.[31]

The sailors no doubt asked which had the most cause to be grateful, those on land or those at sea; and whether the confidence so amiably talked about by Papa Buckner was placed as he seemed to imply? It was essential for the country to be sure of its defences; the sailors could live without being patted on the back by those who allowed them the meanest pittance for reward, and condemned them to existences which most of them, we hope, had not the faintest conception of. But in case the letter should have had some effect on the weaker members of the Fleet, Parker thought it advisable to send round a circular informing them that the Delegates were determined not to relax their demands in any way.[32]

These pourparlers do not represent the whole of the activity going on. Since the mutiny had not immediately faded out as soon as the news of the Portsmouth reconciliation had reached the Nore, the Government began to treat the new outbreak seriously, and were filled with the determination not to be coerced this time, or inveigled into any weak conciliatory measures. Troops, two regiments of militia, were ordered to Sheerness, and marched in there on Monday, 22nd. Though it was difficult to disguise the meaning of that step, Buckner, in his usual somewhat flabby manner, did try to disguise it, and sent a letter to the Delegates declaring that this appearance of martial force was a mere accident, an innocent frolic, or perhaps an afternoon's perambulation: or so we conceive from Parker's answer to the Admiral:

> I have received your letter informing the seamen of the Fleet that it was not with hostile intentions that the troops appeared in garrison this afternoon. As I have not the present opportunity of consulting the opinion of the whole fleet, I must in justice say as to my own feeling it is an insult to the peaceable behaviour of the seamen thro' the Fleet at the Nore. And likewise the Lords of the Admiralty have been remiss in their duty in not attending when their appearance would have given satisfaction, until when no accommodation can take place.
>
> I am, Sir,
>
> Your humble servant,
>
> RICHARD PARKER,
>
> *President of the Committee of the Delegates of the Fleet.*[33]

This was a good answer, and the irrelevant conclusion contained a hint which might have been extremely useful if only the Admiralty could have had the sense to take it up. It was as though Parker were pleading with them for a little sensibility. The men, he was telling the Admiralty, wanted to feel they were being treated like human beings, and that a man-to-man confabulation might work wonders: the seamen were not prepared to fight—not yet: they wanted to be conciliated.

But if they were not prepared to fight, the Lords Commissioners were getting ready to put events to that issue, getting ready very silently and discreetly. Nepean wrote to Duncan:

(*Private and Confidential.*)

> ADMIRALTY,
> *May 22.*

MY DEAR SIR,

The ships at the Nore are in the most complete state of mutiny, and it seems to be very difficult to bring them to any reason without submitting to conditions which would be highly disgraceful. You know the state of your fleet, I believe, as well as anyone can do, and what use could be made of it. Do you think that you could depend upon any of the ships if you were to bring them up to the Nore, if it should be necessary to employ them in bringing two or three ships of the line over there to reason?

You may give me your private thoughts on this head, but the less they are communicated to other people the better.

> Yours ever most sincerely,
> EVAN NEPEAN.[34]

The men at the Nore knew nothing about this, but when they got the Admiralty answer from Buckner rejecting all their appeals, they began to think that action on their part might be necessary. And as a signal of determination, they hauled down Buckner's flag, which had been rehoisted, and replaced it with the red symbol of defiance.

CHAPTER XII

THEIR IMMOVABLE LORDSHIPS

THE red flag was a call to action, or was taken as such by the more turbulent spirits at the Nore; besides, whatever denial Buckner might make—and how unplausible the denial was—the sudden irruption into Sheerness of two militia regiments under General Fox smelt of challenge, even of direct provocation. Combined with the stultifying Admiralty reply, which seemed to bang the door on any possibility of negotiation, such a gesture invited the sailors to proceed to deeds. How far the Delegates led them, or to what extent the leaders were jockeyed into leading, it is impossible to say. "It is well known," Parker was to write, "what authority the seamen had over their Delegates, and in what a ferocious manner the Delegates were frequently treated for not according with every wild scheme which the sailors proposed to carry into practice."[35] Not from him, he was to say at his trial, had come the idea of hoisting the red flag; the extremists of the *Inflexible* had dictated the act. Petty officers as some of the Delegates were, they had many of them been kicked upstairs into their dizzier posts; they had lost in authority rather than gained, and had none of the hold over the men that distinguished Joyce and his assistants. They were, in fact, largely pawns, forced to be responsible figureheads behind which the real instigators sheltered. Parker, it is true, too volatile to be constant to himself, sometimes entered into the spirit of his "perilous situation," and showed a certain brittle bravado; but it was against his better judgment.

Thus, whether the Delegates prompted the rapid further developments, or whether they "acted pursuant to, and obeyed the injunctions of their constituents," remains doubtful; but the events, from which they could not dissociate themselves, do not. Boats with strong armed parties rowed out from each ship simultaneously, and, forming an organised flotilla, bore down on the harbour of Sheerness, with what purpose could only be guessed. It was soon seen that they had no designs upon the town; they swarmed over and seized the eight gunboats lying in the harbour, and with great speed brought them away. The display of force, the use of force, showed that the men were going to put their cause to the hazard of fighting it out, and they emphasised their intention; for as each boat came out to take up its moorings by the island of Sheppey, it fired a round at the fort as a symbol. The die was cast, if not for armed rebellion, at least for physical resistance.

To bring matters, and perhaps their ideas, to a focus as it were, the seamen at about this time consolidated their forces, and carried out a manœuvre similar to the one which had concentrated the Spithead Fleet at St. Helens. They gathered together the ships scattered about Sheerness and at the Little Nore, and joined them with the ships at the Great Nore, their formation being a double crescent with the captured gunboats at the flanks. Only one ship offered any resistance, the *Clyde* (thirty-eight guns), the crew of which was still obedient to their captain; but they were warned that if they did not unmoor, the *Inflexible* (sixty-four guns) would be brought alongside to compel them. The frigate submitted, but her captain and the pilot with great cunning had her moored on the outside of the formation, a place from which she might easily escape if opportunity arose: nevertheless, by the end of the day she was outwardly, at least, part of the mutineers' force; every man on her quarter-deck had a red ribbon in his hat, and every woman on board a similar decoration in her cap.[36] The only reply Buckner made to all this was to address another dulcet letter to the Fleet, pursuant to a fresh direction sent him that afternoon, which was merely a restatement of what had already been so barrenly said: the letter promised pardon, stated coldly that the Lords Commissioners saw neither "the propriety or expediency" of travelling to Sheerness, since they had not the slightest intention of "encouraging a repetition of demands by any further concession"; and it exhorted the men to be noble, to return to duty, and to chase the enemy.[37] Since this letter was as pompously worded as the former one, it proved equally futile. It was, however, politely acknowledged:

25 *May.*

To CAPTAIN MOSSE.

    I am commanded by the Committee to inform you that they have received through your communication the letter transmitted from Admiral Buckner to you, from the Lords of the Admiralty. I am further to inform you that no accomodation can take place until the appearance of the Lords of the Admiralty at the Nore.

    By Order of the Delegates of the Whole Fleet.

RICHARD PARKER.[38]

The visit of the Lords seemed at the moment to be the crucial point. It is evident that the sailors set enormous store by it.

Till this should be determined—for in spite of the haughty words the men still considered it was not determined—they were prepared to set stubbornness against stubbornness—and, since there was nothing to be done, to wait. So nothing was done, except that the mutineers made the most of their freedom, especially since the news from Plymouth, somewhat tactlessly insisted upon by a message the Admiralty sent by their semaphore telegraph, showed that there also the happiest of reconciliations with authority had taken place. Such news, far from weakening the men, merely stiffened them. Yet they did nothing very dreadful; they behaved, rather, like happy men let out on a holiday; but they began to alarm the inhabitants of Sheerness, and to make the rest of the country uneasy. They would crowd into boats in the morning, their headgear bedecked with large bunches of blue and white ribbons, the Delegates of each ship sitting in the stern-sheets without any mark of distinction, though the men who manned the barges wore round their hats, besides the gay ribbons, a broad band of blue paper with "Success to the Delegates of the Fleet" inscribed on it in gold. Red flags constantly flew from the tops of most of the barges. When all the Delegates were gathered on shore, they would hold conferences at some chosen inn, after which, with Parker at their head, they would march up and down the streets and along the ramparts, appearing to the inhabitants somewhat flown with insolence: for with music playing they flooded the streets in arms, red flags flying, "in all the pomp of parade."[39] Some men, it seems, went up to London to take legal advice, and flaunt their freedom in a wider sphere. On the 22nd John Blake of the *Inflexible* wrote to the *Champion* explaining how necessary it was to start a fund for the purpose of employing a "Law Agent" to help them in forwarding their scheme;[40] and on the 26th a man went into a London alehouse for a pot of beer, and there explained that he and another had come from the *Sandwich* to see Mr. Fitzgerald, an attorney who did business for the Fleet: a press-gang which had caught them had let them go on seeing their authority. He, certainly, did exhibit a mild sense of glory, if not insolence, saying that the Admiral and his officers "were thought nothing of [and that] he (putting himself into an attitude of self-consequence) was more thought of than the Admiral."[41] A pardonable piece of childishness. What most alarmed the officials, however, was the way the seamen fraternised with the soldiers, sweeping over the parade ground when they were at their exercises, "and in the very teeth of them along the ranks, shaking hands with their relations and friends amongst the militia."[42] Their reception seemed ominous.

FLOGGING AT THE GANGWAY

Cruikshank

LORD BRIDPORT
"Lodge's Portraits"

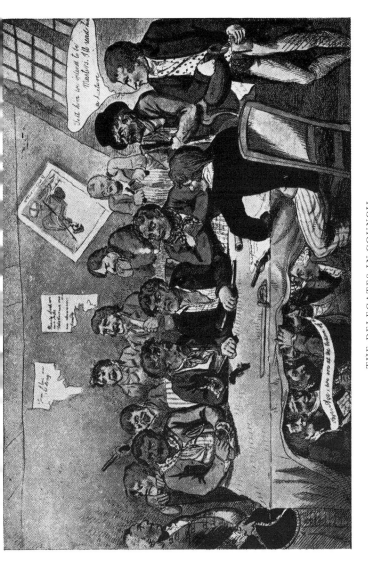

THE DELEGATES IN COUNCIL.

Cruikshank

THE EXECUTION OF RICHARD PARKER
From the print at the British Museum

It was most uncomfortable for the officers on shore; though cut adrift from their commands, they were still responsible, and felt they must do their best to put things right. But how could they? They had no power, even of persuasion. True, there had been little or no animosity expressed towards them, even if some of them had had to leave their ships with undignified speed: or so one would gather from the piteous appeal of a purser separated from his gear:

> Mr. Ellery, Purser of the *Proserpine*, will be much obliged to Mrs. Burbidge if she will desire Charles Nichols to let his boy put his pantaloons, two waistcoats and his coat into his dirty cloaths bag and give it to Mrs. Burbidge to bring on shore, he having no cloaths but what he has on: [43]

but then pursers were pursers, and other officers seem to have been treated with more respect, as, indeed, were all who remained on their ships. Those on shore continually met to confer, and again confer—there was little else they could do—and lost no opportunity of arguing with the men, offering them the King's pardon, and telling them how wicked they were.[44] As though that would have the least effect!

A curious incident which occurred on the 23rd should have made them see the futility of this kind of exhortation. Two marines, part of a Delegate's boat escort, had come on shore, got dead drunk, and had been arrested by the civil power and reported to the Port-Admiral as usual. When the committee heard of this, they hastily rowed ashore, demanded to see Buckner, and would take no refusal. An interview being granted at the house of the Commissioner, Captain Hartwell, where Buckner was colloguing with his senior officers, Parker, Davis (the "captain" of the *Sandwich*), and some others, were ushered into the presence. Parker demanded the custody of the prisoners (who would be punished by the seamen) on the ground that they be-

longed to the Fleet, to which Buckner replied that it was
precisely on that ground he was detaining them: whereupon
Parker, not too gently, told the Admiral that he had no
authority since his flag was not flying. "Parker," the Admiral
is reported to have said, making an odd, old-maidish appeal,
"my flag is struck; consider my feelings." To which Parker
answered, "I have feelings, Admiral Buckner, and I do
consider yours: I am sorry to see it, but it is not in my power
to prevent it."[45] But whatever may have been said, the interchange so incensed the worthy Captain Cunningham of the
Clyde, that he very nearly ran the usurping president
through. In the upshot, the deposed authorities, fearful of
precipitating an appeal to arms on such a small point,
especially as the outcome was doubtful, surrendered the
marines, with the pious hope that they might be confined.[46]

The mutineers, in fact, did not give a fig for Buckner,
who somewhat ruefully wrote to the Admiralty that nothing
he could say seemed to have any effect: the men did not
even take his messages seriously.

> All are clamorous to have the pardon notified them in a more solemn
> manner than they conceive the notification of it by me would impress it
> with (at least I am inclined to think that is their idea),[47]

he confessed to Nepean. They even treated him as a kind of
subordinate, and when the store ship *Serapis* came in from
Lisbon, they virtually seized it, ordered the commander to
moor his vessel under the guns of the *Sandwich*, and to
send Delegates on board, after which they were to despatch
a message to the Admiral *instructing* him to send out tenders
to remove the sick and the prisoners.[48]

Buckner had orders from the Admiralty to use force if
he found it necessary; but, luckily perhaps for himself, he
never saw the necessity. It is doubtful if the militia would
have been staunch at this date. As for help from the upper
reaches of the Thames, any illusion he may have had that it

would be forthcoming was soon dispelled. A cutter from the *Sandwich* sailed up to Long Reach, near Dartford, to be imitated on the 26th by armed boats from the *Iris* and *Brilliant*. Men from these boats landed at Gravesend, and though by this time popular feeling had so far turned against the seamen that they were captured by some of the townspeople, they were allowed to go again. Their object was to induce the ships lying in Long Reach to join them, and, in spite of firing from Tilbury Fort, they persuaded the *Lancaster* to make one of their number. The *Naiad*, however, refused. The next day they made another expedition, baffled by the guns from Tilbury, and again on the 28th, when two of their number were captured by the press-gang and sent to be imprisoned at Chatham.[49]

Such sorties, and the noise of the guns, began to arouse the fears of the populace: "the state of things on shore was one of preparation, terror and excitement." Comfortable folk on land began to behave as though invasion were imminent, and were encouraged to believe it was by seeing marines, infantry and artillery crowding into Gravesend and Tilbury, at which places the batteries were manned, and the furnaces kept stoked to supply large quantities of red-hot balls to discharge at invaders. It is true that Parker, or his insurgents, did toy with the idea of sending ships up the river to support those that wished to join the mutiny (such as the *Lancaster*, which had been unable to come down), and to free the river for all those who might wish to swell the throng at the Nore;* but nothing of this was ever apparent to the outside world, and any steps he might have contemplated were stopped by the action of the Admiralty.

For on the evening of the 27th there was a Cabinet meet-

---

* Cunningham says he detailed the *Clyde* for this work, but that the men refused, in spite of his harangues; but it is most unlikely that he would have selected a ship which he knew was uncertain, when plenty of others would be more willing.

ing to discuss what was to be done about the mutiny, for it was now clear that it would not crumble away of its own accord, and the Government was more than uneasy. Also an unforeseen difficulty had raised its head: the pardon they had offered the new mutineers was not valid! In the morning of the 26th, Lord Loughborough, the Lord Chancellor, had written to Spencer to say that the Spithead pardon did not apply, as it only covered acts committed prior to its promulgation. It turned out that the seamen had been right not to accept Buckner's blandishments. "I conceive," Loughborough wrote,

> that a new and more extensive pardon must be issued upon this case, and I should hope that some part at least of the difficulty arises from a distrust of Admiral Buckner's authority to give them a sufficient pardon;[50]

and it is within the bounds of possibility that the lawyer, Fitzgerald, had made the men quite aware of the flaw. The Cabinet therefore decided that a new pardon should be obtained and presented, and that, however deeply the Admiralty's honour was rooted in not going down to Sheerness, go down it should.

To Spencer the idea was intensely repugnant. His vaguely legal mind found it all wrong. Facts were facts, and rules were rules: why could not people respect the law? Once more the civil servant overlaid the humane man: he had learnt nothing from Howe, who on that very day wrote to the Duke of Portland:

> The extravagances of the seamen are not attended to, I think, in the manner they ought to be. We seem here to think that the *legal* authorities, with which we are vested, are sufficient to secure as well as to claim respect; and that the same impression we have formed on them cannot fail of operating with equal effect on our subordinates:

and was to write a few days later:

As to the neglect you describe of the seamen's complaints, I can only impute it to the incompetency of the persons who have the immediate superintendence in the department,

while in his opinion the sense of the officers in the ships with regard to the disorders was little less erroneous than that of the men.[51] But Spencer's mind was completely closed to that approach: his pride made him shudder at the humiliation of having to go down to Sheerness, as he declared in the almost tearful letter he wrote to the King asking him to sign the new pardon and declaration (which was immediately printed).[52] Nothing would have prevailed upon him to go, "but the extreme and urgent necessity of the case, and its being accompanied by an express determination not to add to the concessions already given";[53] sentiments with which the King unreservedly concurred.

So, late that night, Spencer, Lord Arden, Admiral Young, and the faithful secretary, Marsden, once more found themselves stepping into coaches, this time with the futile object, it would seem, of further irritating men whose tempers they had played no mean part in rousing. They slept at Rochester on the way, and arrived in the morning of the 28th at Sheerness, where they made Commissioner Hartwell's house their headquarters. Their presence was at once known on the ships, to the delight of the men, who felt they had scored an important point; but the Board made no motion towards the mutineers, settling down at once, in a good warm office manner, to discover from Buckner and the captains exactly what the state of affairs was. What they heard cheered them, for they gathered that the Fleet was by no means unanimous; that the *San Fiorenzo*, the *Clyde*, and five other small ships, all of which had hoisted the Admiralty flag on their arrival, were ready to dissociate themselves from their fellows. This determined the Board to persist in their wooden resolution, although the small ships had been soon overawed by their more hefty companions into striking the Admiralty flag.

That evening a crowd of Delegates surged round the door of the Commissioner's house; they were quiet, for they felt that the Board's visit was a sign of weakness, and if "every man's hat was decorated with red or pink ribbands . . . there was no huzzaing or music or any other sort of parade or noise." Expectant they certainly were, for they hoped at last to get contact, to be able to speak as men to men, to explain, to be treated as fellow-humans who, after all, were serving these high gods. But Spencer, "bent upon refusing every demand they had made with the haggling spirit of a slave merchant," [54] would not hear of seeing them, or of letting himself be seen. He would be majestic and aloof, the mysterious invisible power, as he had been at Spithead, with results that it had taken Howe a hard day's work to undo, though that aspect seems to have escaped him. He sent a message by Hartwell that he would see them only if they came to receive the King's pardon; otherwise he would communicate through Buckner, who, accordingly went to the door, and asked what they had to say. The familiar figure of their old, and perhaps too-little-honoured Admiral, was not what the men had come to see, and when he asked, "What did they want to see the Board for?" Parker, over-excited by the position he was in, knowing that the ranks behind him were not solid, and that it was now or never, said to the exalted messenger, "You are a man of sense, and know what is due to us: you know what we want." The men urgently demanded to see the Board, and it took some argument on Buckner's part to persuade them that this was quite impossible. Backwards and forwards the messenger went, till at last the men formulated their plea. They wanted the Spithead terms ratified for them, and a promise that the other points would be considered. Spencer, firmly astride upon his high horse, refused everything: nothing would make him budge: the only thing he could present to his mind as tolerable was the total submission of the men, and their humble approach to receive the Royal Pardon from his forgiving hands. The men trooped off, but that Parker really did say in retort to an admonition from Buckner, "You may all be ——!" is not very probable, especially as when Buckner told Parker that should the gunboat which threatened the loyal *Niger* open fire, every man on the gunboat would be excluded from the pardon, Parker had merely made a low bow. To round off the evening, the Board sent Mosse to sleep on the *Sandwich*, carrying with him a message to say that their Lordships expected to hear next morning that the Fleet had "accepted His Majesty's gracious pardon," and had returned to duty. They even named the hour of noon, though they did not propose to be pernickety about the actual time.[55]

Whether the Admiralty message got round all the ships the next morning is doubtful: it seems likely that it was from this time the Committee began to edit the news and messages sent them from shore. Some at least received it, and dissension was rife as to whether or not they should go on. On several of the smaller ships—the *Iris*, *Brilliant*, *Grampus*, *Espion*, and *Niger*, all of which Spencer had heard were well-affected—there was a struggle between the red flag and the white, now one, now the other, fluttering at the masthead, till at last the red prevailed; some more captains, too, were compelled to go on shore. On the *San Fiorenzo* and *Clyde*, indeed, the men cheered and ran up white colours when the captains read out the message, but here also the mutineers were triumphant, though not without help from outside; for the *Inflexible* got a spring upon her cable so as to veer round into position to fire a broadside into the *Clyde*, whereupon the captain, Cunningham, to avoid bloodshed gave up the unequal struggle, and the white flag rattled down. Mutinous as they were, however, the men wanted to make it quite plain that their quarrel was with the Admiralty only, not with the Crown, and since it was Restoration Day, they fired the usual salute; and though the red flag flew at the main, the Royal Standard stood out bravely at the fore. "Such," the disgusted Marsden exclaimed, "is their insolence."

Owing to the stormy weather the Fleet had not been able to communicate with the shore during the morning, but by two o'clock the wind had fallen, and a couple of Delegates showed themselves at Hartwell's house, merely to enquire, it seems, what terms had been granted their "brothers" at Portsmouth. They were given copies of the relevant documents, for which they are said to have expressed gratitude, though in what words, or whether what they said was more than common politeness, is not stated. Later, a whole band of Delegates arrived, briskly declaring that they would accept nothing short of their whole demands, to make plain that two could play at "I'm the King of the Castle." These were presented with a note, which they took away to one of their public-house rendezvous, and discussed about and about for an hour, at the end of which one of them brought a paper addressed to Spencer, telling him that the question had been put to the vote, and that a majority were in favour of going on with the mutiny. Upon which the meeting dissolved.

As the day was drawing to a close, the solitary figure of a dark medium-sized lithe man walked up the road to the Commissioner's house, and knocking at the door asked for an answer to the Delegates' last letter. It was Parker, inspired perhaps by some desperate hope that it was still not too late, that something might after all be done to batter through this horrible invisible wall which separated man from man, that some human touch might at the eleventh hour bridge the gap between the representatives of power and its humblest servants. Already he appears as a lonely figure: he could not be of the men; he was not among the rulers. On being told there was no answer he said nothing; he made a low bow and walked away, back to where the men who had elected him leader were gathering.[56] And when the Delegates returned to the shore in a body to get back into their boats, it was noticed that they carried a red flag before them, a thing they had not done from the time the Admiralty bunting had invited their allegiance, flying above the roof of the Commissioner's house.

CHAPTER XIII

DRAMA

SINCE no submission was forthcoming, the Board left Sheerness at half-past eight in the evening, to sleep at Rochester. But they did not feel that nothing had been accomplished. Spencer, indeed, felt more than a little pleased with the turn events were taking. Not only had dignity been preserved, but he had gathered that besides the ships already named, the *Serapis* and the *Pylades* were by no means staunch to the oath of fidelity, and that the *Director*, a ship of the line, was ready to desert. Marsden, writing after supper, as he said, as though to warn Nepean that he might be viewing the matter through wine-coloured glasses, was of the opinion that Parker's "assumed consequence began to give considerable umbrage" to the seamen, who might soon be expected to hang him by one of his own yard-ropes.[57]

But there was something more solid than hopeful opinions to buoy up the spirits of the Board. They had been accompanied on their outward journey by General Sir Charles Grey, "a fine spirited fellow and eager that the temporising system should be at an end," who had been left behind in command of the troops with full powers to take any step he might think useful. There was no doubt that he was full of fight, his mind bursting with heroic measures to resist an invasion. Under his vigorous eye every precaution was taken to protect the dockyard and garrison from attack; some of the gunboats, driven in from the Nore by stress of weather to seek shelter in Sheerness harbour, were to be seized; and though he was confident of the *morale* of his troops, one regiment was to be sent away to be replaced by two others. No armed vessels, it went without saying, were to be permitted to pass the batteries. Spencer was delighted, as he was by the fact that the two volunteer companies at Gravesend were regularly turning out on duty.[58] Further, he had taken steps to stop any ships up-river from dropping down to join those at the Nore; he was doing what he could to prevent the mutineers from getting into touch with sailors in other ports, and even thought of impounding all letters. In short, though the mutineers were behaving very well, offering no violence, and showing respect to all the officers that remained on board, he was inclined to treat them as full-blown rebels.

Besides, as we know, he had written to Admiral Duncan, with a view to using one part of the Navy against the other. But here was the fly in the ointment. Duncan had said in reply to the delicate suggestion that though it might be feasible, and that if ordered to do so he would try to bring his ships against the mutineers', the result was not at all certain. On the evening of the 26th, however, Spencer had sent Captain Bligh of the *Director* (who had plenty of time on his hands, having been expelled his ship) to consult with Duncan at Yarmouth, to tell him exactly what was happening, and to concert possible counter-moves. But in the meanwhile the news he had received from Duncan was, if not decisive, at any rate "very unpleasant"; still, though they were not what he had hoped for, he "rather feared" that the attempt to use one part of the Navy to subdue the other would have to be tried. "We must come," he decided, "to that issue at last."[59]

Well, he had done his best, and was even now doing all he could by cutting the mutineers off from their means of life. He had arranged that with Hartwell at Sheerness, and to make all sure, he caused Marsden to write to the Commissioner and Agent Victualler at Chatham:

ROCHESTER,
30 *May* 1797.

The mutinous conduct of the of some crews of H.M. ships at the Nore having rendered it necessary that no further supplies should for the present be furnished them, I am commanded by the Lords Commissioners of the Admiralty to signify their direction to you that no more stores of any kind should be sent off to the ships and vessels at that anchorage unless the demands for them should be approved by Admiral Buckner.[60]

This was the most far-reaching action that had so far been taken by either side.

Sir Charles Grey, however, was by no means so complacent as the Board: the service he was engaged in was naturally unpleasant, but then the mutiny was infamous—those are his own adjectives—and evil must cast out evil. But apart from this unavoidable aspect, "everything bore the most unpleasant and alarming appearance, proceeding from the indulgences (on what ground or idea I am at a loss to account) given to the mutineers," namely, their licence to make what noisy demonstrations they pleased, and to hob-nob with the soldiers on parade. He at once put a stop to all this, prevented the "miscreants" from coming into barracks, and in a day or two, indeed as soon as the Board had gone, forbade them not only the dockyard, but any part of the shore.

Worse still, the fort at Sheerness was hopelessly placed for the defence of the Arsenal. Why, "if you please," he protested (though being a good soldier he did not murmur a word till it was all over), ships of force could be brought within fifty yards of it, and the place was "in so wretched and ruinous a state" that it could not possibly hold out for many hours. The merlons were of brick, "and in such a tottering state that the firing on the King's birthday shivered them all to pieces," so that if the guns there had fired in defence, both men and guns would have been completely uncovered without the attackers firing a single shot.

Given a favourable wind and tide, ships could have passed the batteries of the fort in no time: and as to the outlying strong points which it would be essential to arm and hold, such as the Isle of Grain, there was no ordnance or artillery available.[61] Apart from the mutiny, such a state of affairs was a disgrace: it was true that it was a hundred and thirty years since the Dutch had captured Sheerness and sailed up the Medway, but England was again at war with the Dutch, and someone should have been hanged for criminal negligence.

But it is doubtful if Parker and his band were such desperadoes as all this suggests. Apart from the fact that the men were loyal, it is most unlikely that anyone seriously contemplated a *coup de main* on land: and if certain fiery spirits did clamour for it, Parker himself would have done his best to quash such a wild scheme. At all events on the night of the 29th he had enough to occupy him in domestic troubles, so to speak, to prevent any idea of organising an invasion from forming in his mind. Affairs were critical, since, for all the noise the mutiny had made, with its bands and its red flags, its flouting of authority, its ejection of officers, and its severe internal discipline, it had accomplished nothing at all. Even the visit of the Board, which had seemed such a crucial point, was only a Pyrrhic victory, worse indeed than another rebuff despatched from London would have been: it was no gesture of refusal made from afar, but a slap in the face. So much, too, had been promised from it. Far from its being material to make capital out of, the only thing to do was to minimise its effects as much as possible. But however much Parker might wish to do this, one glaring fact stood out: the mutineers would not be allowed to go ashore again, so even the pomp and glory, so heartening to people who have nothing else, would have to be abandoned.

Besides, the behaviour of the frigates on receipt of the Admiralty message had been disturbing in the extreme, especially that of the *San Fiorenzo* and the *Clyde*: it revealed a sinister lack of solidarity. He did not at all like the look of things; the men on those two vessels were too attached to their captains and there had been mysterious comings and goings between them. Here was he, a man of sense and judgment, sacrificing all, or at least risking all, to help men whose state had wrung his heart, who had appealed to him, and even made him their leader; and yet they were so unstable, so undecided as to what they wanted, that he did not know where he stood. Even the Delegates themselves had not rejected the Admiralty offer without contentions which had lasted an hour. But the gauntlet was flung; he had burnt his boats. He who had prayed the men to be moderate must now rouse and inflame them, bind them together by any and every means, cunning or demagogic, in his power. No, he could not trust those frigates; and he ordered a patrol of boats to row round them all night, and keep alert for anything untoward taking place.

He would have been still more apprehensive if he had known what had happened that day, and what action was brewing. On the 28th, the Board being advised of the feeling in those two frigates, decided to order them to Harwich to take on board the Duke of Württemberg and his bride; for the duke, having arrived in the middle of one mutiny, was about to take his departure in the middle of another. By some means the men of the *Director* had come to hear of this, and two of them had gone to Cunningham on the *Clyde* to tell him that their ship would join the frigates the next morning if she might take the lead. Cunningham had discussed this with Sir Harry Neale of the *San Fiorenzo*, and they had decided that the news was so important that they ought to delay their sailing, which they did, informing the Admiralty of their reasons. After seeing what a struggle there had been on board many ships, including the *Director*, as to whether the red flag or the white should prevail, the

Board, with hopes of a considerable defection, ordered the *Clyde* and *San Fiorenzo* to slip away as soon as they could, and make for Sheerness if they were not able to get right away. The captains therefore agreed to cut their cables at the same time, and arranged for a pilot to take them out.

Half an hour or so after midnight in the early morning of the 30th, Neale, snatching an opportunity between the rounds of Parker's watch-boats, rowed across to see Cunningham; but hardly had he reached his fellow-adventurer's ship than a message came from his own asking that the *Clyde* should cut her cable so as to give the *San Fiorenzo* room to swing, the former, we remember, having been able to take station at the extreme end of the crescent of ships. The cable was cut even before the messenger boat had got away, so promptly on the request, that another boat which had followed close on the heels of the first, and which contained the pilot rowing over to say that they were too late on the flood-tide to be able to make Sheerness, found the *Clyde* already a-weigh: more, her long-boat had been sent off to fetch Bardo, the mate of the Commissioner's yacht lying off Garrison Point, for him to take the frigate into harbour. The pilot, a tough Scot called M'Cullum, pluckily went back to the *San Fiorenzo*, braving what might happen to him should the Delegates find him there, as, now that the game was afoot, they probably would.

For a time, however, the *Clyde* was allowed to drift with the flood-tide. Nobody disturbed her; her Delegates were on board the *Sandwich* and so could raise no alarm; no attempt was made to set sail, which even on a dark night would have been noticed or heard, and the crew kept profoundly quiet. After a while a fore-sail was bent, and the wind coming round to the north-east, she was able to tack towards Garrison Point. Before very long, shouts of alarm, and a bustle on other ships, told them that the movement was discovered; the crash of guns overwhelmed the sound of wind and waves, but these were only signals, for the mutinous ships, riding the flood with their sterns towards the escaping frigate, had no time to tauten springs on their cables, and so could not bring their guns to bear on her. The gunboats along the shore were able only to echo the signal-shots, and hoist lights. The *Clyde* made westward little by little, and by the time the ebb-tide began was close to the Point, where Bardo came aboard in the jolly-boat, though his services were no longer needed. The noise of the empty cannonade had aroused the inhabitants of Sheerness, who, when the ship came off the Point at sunrise, greeted her with loud shouts of delight, the civilians being joined by hundreds of troops, shouting in such a manner as to leave no doubt either in Parker's or anybody else's mind as to where their sympathies now lay. But the men of the *Clyde* were so alarmed at what might happen to them if they were caught by the crew of the *Inflexible*, that it was all Cunningham could do to stop them in Salt Pan Reach instead of going on to Chatham. The ship was regularly cleared for action, and all hands were at their quarters throughout that night.

Cunningham had decided to send Bardo off to the *San Fiorenzo*, but this, of course, could not be done openly: the mutineers would have to be outwitted. He sent his lieutenant, Hughes, to the Dock Yard to beg for four riggers to go with him in a boat to the *Clyde's* old berth on pretence of seeking for the bearings of her anchors. Four men volunteered. Since the boat came from the Dock Yard on what was obviously routine business, the innocent mutineers were not half watchful enough, and, seizing a happy moment, Hughes smuggled Bardo on board the *San Fiorenzo*; upon which the riggers, panic-stricken at their temerity, pulled their boat lustily to the nearest point of the shore, two miles below their destination, where they deserted her, and ran to the Dock Yard as hard as they could in terror of a vengeful pursuit.

The *San Fiorenzo* made her escape about noon, choosing a time when the Delegates were away and most of the men throughout the Fleet piped down to their midday meal. Bardo, however, bungled the affair. A spring was duly run down the frigate's cable to veer her round in the right direction, but Bardo cut the cable too soon—or perhaps it was the fault of the men taking action the moment they heard the bos'n's whistle for dinner, which was to be the signal: at all events her head was in the wrong direction when the cable parted, and so, with the wind now blowing fresh west-north-west, the frigate could not hope to make Sheerness, and was forced to run for the open through the whole Fleet. She was raked by the fire of all the guns that could be brought to bear on her, and it was with rigging considerably damaged, and her main and fore chains a good deal knocked about, though with nobody hurt, that she got away with flags flying. Among the flags she flew, however, was the red, which was just as well, for, as it turned out, the crescent at the Nore was not the only danger spot for her. Bardo took her as far as he knew the channels, and then with a great deal of luck they fell in with a ship that had a pilot who could take her round the Goodwin Sands; whence she made her way to Portsmouth, capturing a French privateer as she went. On the way out of the Thames she met several ships coming into the mouth, many of which bore the red flag. The crew of the *San Fiorenzo*, taking no chances, cheered them as she passed.[62]

These desertions were a blow to dismay the leaders of the disaffected. Already the *Espion* and *Niger* at Sheerness had published their defection, and were being used in defence of the harbour; and to them were added those gun-boats driven in by the weather. Grey had got to work with energy. All the batteries in and about the fort which faced the sea were completely manned night and day, with soldiers always ready at the guns. To prevent any ships being taken out of the harbour, all the pier heads and projections from the Dock Yard were planted with guns, and sailors from the two docile frigates were detailed to man them and the gunboats. No one from the ships was allowed to land, and two Delegates who had actually gone ashore were held there in durance. It is true that these things did not matter much to the leaders, since they had not the faintest notion of attacking; and indeed the chief result of these warlike measures was to scare away the inhabitants of Sheerness: it was nothing to the sailors that the women and children had been evacuated from the town, and that the men had fled to safety unless business which could not be evaded kept them there.[63] Still, all this indicated that the Government was determined, and that the soldiers who showed fight, together with the civilians whose town was unpeopled, no longer sympathised with them.

Yes, the Government was determined, which was more than could be said for the sailors, who, as the struggles over the flags had shown, were disunited. Even on the *Sandwich*, when, the day before, the question had been put as to whether the mutiny should go on, there had been cries of "Give it up! Give it up!" [64] And no help was forthcoming. On the 24th a deputation of seventeen had been sent off to Yarmouth, in succession to four previous Delegates, to get the assistance of the Fleet there (both sides seemed to feel that the North Sea Fleet might be of decisive weight); but although they had seized the *Cygnet* cutter and sailed merrily away in her, nothing had been heard from them since. Thus there was internal weakening, and no support coming from outside. They were being deserted by their fellows. Not thus had they responded to appeals from Spithead! Would no help come? The Leith tender sailed in that afternoon: they would see what encouragement they might get from there. They

seized hold of Lieutenant Watson, dragged him like a cul-
prit, as he said, before their "infernal tribunal," and roughly
told him to keep his mouth shut when he tried to persuade
some of the seamen to return to their duty. Yet, and this
was the worst of it, a few of the Delegates seemed inclined
to take his advice, "declaring in the strongest terms their
regret at the situation to which they had reduced themselves."
It seemed many of the sailors, and even Delegates, would
have gone over to the Admiralty side had they not been
held back by terror.[65] In another way, too, the situation
seemed unstable. On some ships the electors ruled the
elected; on others the elected governed the men; and on some
of these, as was evident from what had happened with the
Clyde and *San Fiorenzo*, the Delegates simply did not know
what their men felt: they had been fooled by them, left
gaping astounded when their ships made good their escape.
It seemed that the mutiny would have to be abandoned,
however humiliating this would be.

But then, providentially, almost immediately after the
second frigate had got away, three line-of-battle ships were
seen bearing up-river towards the crescent of dubious ships.
As they came nearer it could be made out that they were all
flying the red flag: they must be, they were, ships from
Duncan's squadron come to help them. The situation was
saved, the mutiny could go on, it had every prospect of
joyful success. Who could stand out against the seamen
now?

CHAPTER XIV

YARMOUTH

IN sending Bligh to concert measures with Duncan, the Admiralty were pursuing the line they had proposed to themselves, with some misgiving piercing through the debonair phrasing, when Nepean had written to the Admiral at Yarmouth to suggest that his ships might subdue those at the Nore. Bligh's mission was, perhaps, all the more urgent, since Duncan's reply had not been inspiring. It appeared to be by no means certain how the men of the North Sea Fleet would behave. On the evening of 16th May, for instance, the crew of the *Albatross* sloop had been "very riotous and disorderly," and though the tumult had subsided, and the sloop sent upon its proper convoy business, it was not until the captain had threatened one man with a pistol, and the lieutenant had cut down another with his hanger, that calm had prevailed. Therefore it was not surprising that Duncan found Nepean's question required "some delicacy to answer." Having said this, he went on: [66]

> The fleet here continues to behave well, and I am sure will refuse no common service. At the same time, to call them who have kept in order to chastise those at the Nore, in my opinion would subject them to a disagreeable jealousy from all other parts of the fleet who engaged in this unhappy business; but for all this I don't shrink from the business if it cannot otherwise be got the better of; and this day, having occasion to speak to my ship's company, a thing I have lately practised much, from what happened last night I touched gently on what I might expect from them in support of my flag and self in the execution of my duty. They to a man said that they were ready and willing at all times to obey my commands.

What had "happened last night," 22nd May, was the refusal of the crew of the *Trent* to leave their moorings, on the ground that they had not got proper weights and measures. That affair had soon been settled, especially as Duncan had been determined to enforce his orders; and, he wrote:

I asked my people what they thought they [the *Trent's* people] deserved. Their general answer was that they should be made to go to sea; and if I would let them chastise them, they would. . . . Much harmony is in this fleet, which I think has kept us right.

Then, his outraged spirits getting the better of him, he continued:

I hear that people from the ships at Sheerness go ashore in great numbers and play the devil. Why are there not troops to lay hold of them and secure all the boats that come from them? As to the *Sandwich*, you should get her cast adrift in the night and let her go on the sands, that the scoundrels may drown; for until some example is made this will not stop.

God bless you and send us better times, not that I despair. This chastisement is sent us for a warning to mend our ways.

Such ferocious sentiments do not give a true picture of Duncan, who was actually most humane, much loved by his men, for the simple reason that he regarded them as human beings, and would talk to them as such. That he had their confidence he knew from the letters they occasionally addressed him, such as the one he received at about this time, entirely approving of his conduct, and declaring that "we will not, as long as life will permit, in any respect see either you or the flag insulted": while the postscript, which referred to the Nore mutiny, stated that though "it would appear unnatural for us to unsheath the sword against our brethren, notwithstanding we would wish to show ourselves like men in behalf of our commander, should necessity require."

This touching personal loyalty sheds a glory on men and Admiral alike. The truth is that Duncan, though stern for discipline, and never by any word approving of the men's subversive actions, in his heart of hearts sympathised with them; in his view the ways of the upper hierarchy were certainly in want of mending. Two years before he had addressed a paper to the Admiralty strongly recommending that the number of lashes should be limited, that grog should not be stopped, that unpleasant duties should be shared out, that more petty officers should be made, that leave should be regulated, tobacco, soap, and lemon-juice served, and that there should be a more equal distribution of prize-money: he had had, moreover, a few words to say on the subject of pursers. If the Admiralty had listened then, or remembered his advice when they went to Sheerness, the mutiny need never have been expiated in blood, which, if not innocent, was at any rate righteously indignant.

On the 24th the Admiralty, hearing that the Dutch Fleet was about to issue from the Texel, ordered Duncan to put to sea if the wind held easterly; apparently it did not, for he made no immediate move. On that day also the deputation of seventeen left the Nore in the *Cygnet* on their hortatory mission to Yarmouth, encouraged, it is reported, by Neptune, who sang to them:

> "Away, tell your Brothers, near Yarmouth they lie,
> To embark in the cause they will never deny.
> Their hearts are all good, their like lyons I say;
> I've furnished their minds and they all will obey." [67]

The Admiralty warned Duncan of their approach, and also that the four Delegates sent earlier had been tampering with his men;[68] no doubt it was through their instrumentality that Neptune had furnished their minds. On the 26th, therefore, the Admiral ordered the *Vestal* (twenty-eight guns), the *Hope* lugger, and the *Rose* cutter, to cruise between Lowestoft and Orfordness to intercept the visitors; and on the same day he decided to put to sea the next morning wherever the wind might lie.

By the time he gave the signal to repair on board he was

exceedingly anxious about the state of his Fleet; and, indeed, it was not long before ominous cheering was heard from the *Lion*. That morning she had sent a boat to the *Standard*, and though her men had not been allowed on board, the men on the *Standard* had refused to hoist their boats in. The *Lion's* men then attempted to seduce the *Glatton* and the *Belliqueux*, but without success, the *Glatton's* crew retorting to a threat that they would be fired on by shouting back the sooner the better, for they could fire as fast as their attackers. Duncan had called the captains on board to find how matters stood, and what would be likely to happen if orders were given to sail; he gathered that all the ships would obey, except the *Nassau*, which declared its refusal to move until paid. So far good, and even better when the men of the *Lion* and the *Standard* sent apologies for what had occurred that morning; but even so, Duncan felt he could not depend upon them, except, indeed, to fight the enemy. Of that there was never any doubt.[69]

It was not without qualms, then, that the Admiral put to sea at 5 a.m. on the morning of the 27th, with his whole Fleet except for the *Nassau*, which he felt it would be wiser not to tempt to disobedience. There were, however, other ships of which he was doubtful, especially the repentant *Standard*, loud in its demands for arrears of pay, and which he had thought of leaving behind also. For this was not the first time the *Standard* had given trouble. On the 5th the men had barricaded themselves in the bays, and pointed four guns aft. Duncan himself had rowed over with all speed; and the men had returned to their duty after he had shamed them with one of his stern, fatherly speeches. They had thrust a letter into his hand:

HONOURED SIR,

We are sorry to have recorce to this method of disclosing our minds to you, but nessesety demands it to clear ourselves from the infamous imputation of mutney being thrown upon us meaning no sutch thing but the comon caus of the British Navy we being allready the jest and redicule of this whole fleet likewise our boats cannot go on shore but the men are exposed to the scoffts and jests of others and accounted as men that cannot stand up for their own rights threatned that whenever the blessings of peace shall be restord to revenge themselves upon us wherever they meat us for our cowerdliness as they term it theirfore we hope Hond. Sir under theese curcumstances we have stated to you we hope you will not consider us as a rebellious or mutines set of people but as men who without failing in the least in their respect thay owe you and the other officers would wish to do their duty as such Honoured Sir if any cruelty be used against us and any of our lives be taken you cannot think will tamely suffer it no we wil have the life of the person if we suffer for it afterwards theirfore we intend not to die cowerdly but as men who will to the utmost verge of life not only defend their countreys cause but also defend themselves against any other internel enemies that may oppose.

That breathless and not very coherent sentence had seemed to express loyalty so long as the men could be preserved from ridicule; yet, as Duncan knew from the report of the captain the day before the outbreak, the crew considered that they were unduly in want of necessaries, and this deficiency had not yet been made up.

Moreover, one of his big line-of-battle ships, the *Adamant*, had been the scene of an outbreak, though he had so satisfactorily quelled it that he had told Vice-Admiral Onslow to transfer his flag there from the *Nassau*. On the 13th there had been the usual symptoms in the *Adamant*—the cheering, and the refusal to obey orders—upon which he had hurried on board, hoisting his own flag there. Facing the heated crew, opposing his solid bulk to the restless pack, he had said:

My lads, I am not in the smallest degree apprehensive of any violent measures you may have in contemplation; and though I assure you I would much rather acquire your love than incur your fear, I will with my own hand put to death the first man who shall display the slightest sign of rebellious conduct.

After a pause, which allowed the men to be quite clear in their minds that he meant what he said, he asked if any man ventured to dispute his authority, or that of any officer. One man actually had the almost unthinkable courage to take up the challenge offered by the colossal, determined figure, and came forward to say, "insolently" no doubt, as was reported, but still with enormous pluck, "I do." Without a moment's hesitation Duncan gripped him by the collar, and holding him over the side of the ship with one arm, said, "My lads, look at this fellow, he who dares to deprive me of the command of the Fleet!" There are times when it is well to use a giant's strength like a giant, especially if combined with a sense of humour; and this display was so irresistible that, though the laughter is not recorded, there was never again any trouble among the *Adamant's* delighted seamen.

But Duncan could not be sure of them as yet, and there was still another ship, the *Montague*, which had remained at anchor, and without permission, for reasons that her captain, John Knight, explained to the Admiral in agitated prose:

Montagu,
YARMOUTH ROADS,
27 *May* 1797.

SIR,
 It is with extreme reluctance and some pain that I am under the necessity to inform you that the company of His Majesty's ship under my command have to my surprise and mortification refused to a man to unmoor or carry the ship to sea untill they are paid up till six months. I have in vain remonstrated, assuring them that when the cruise was ended that application would be made for their being paid; they have thirteen months due, but they one and all quietly and deliberately said they had resolved by oath to abide by each other, and not to move unless to the Nore to be paid, except the enemy was in sight.

Knight wrote a similar letter to the Admiralty the same day, and with it enclosed a document "Signed by three of the most orderly men by the company's direction":

The ship *Montagu* is so leaky that she makes three feet water every 24 hours, and the decks leaking in many places, so that people's hammocks are wet very often, in so much that the ship's company are determined not to go to sea till she is docked or the leaks stopped and paid down* according to the rules of the Navy. And we do insist on another surgeon for the present one is very unskilful.

By order of the Ship's company,

ONE AND ALL.[70]

So the squadron was reduced by one more ship, and very nearly by another, for things had not gone smoothly on the *Repulse*. At the signal to unmoor the crew refused to man the capstan, and when

called on the quarter-deck to know the cause, they replied they had both pay and prize-money due, and would not go to sea. Captain Alms talked to the men for some time without effect; after some conversation in the waist with their officers they came aft and manned the capstan and we sailed.[71]

so Lieutenant Henry Carew of that ship recorded. In fact, the whole Fleet was uneasy; and even in the *Venerable* herself, at four o'clock that afternoon, there was an outburst of cheering from men crowded on the rigging, but this demonstration was promptly subdued by Major Trollope of the marines, who rushed on deck with his men, secured six of the ringleaders, and put them in irons.[72] The Admiral was profoundly hurt by this behaviour after all that the men had said to him, but took no further notice.

Duncan would not at this stage have found it "delicate" to answer the question as to whether his ships could or would subdue those at the Nore. The facts were too plain; and perhaps it was to save the generous-hearted and gallant Admiral a bitter sense of irony that fate caused Captain Bligh to arrive at Yarmouth when the ships had left, and in such circumstances that he dared not send after them the letters he brought: and what would have been the use?

* "Paid down": melted pitch poured along the seams, and with the oakum, to make the decks waterproof.

> We send you Captain Bligh [the Admiralty had written on the evening of the 26th] on a very delicate business, on which the government is extremely anxious to have your opinion. The welfare, and almost the existence, of the country may depend upon what is the event of this very important crisis, but till we know what we can look for from your squadron it will be very difficult for us to know how to act.

They were taking the matter seriously enough now: "the welfare, almost the existence, of the country . . ." that was not to put it too strongly; and they were soon to know what to expect from Duncan's Fleet without the intermediary efforts of Captain Bligh. On the 27th the Admiralty wrote to Duncan to prepare to attack the ships at the Nore; but before the letter reached him he was writing in heartbroken tones ("I am fatigued to death, and cannot hold it long"), "Sorry I am to repeat there is no dependence on any of us, I fear." "The Western fleet," he had just written, "has much to answer for; they have lighted up a flame that all their art will not suddenly quench, or I mistake it." The worst symptom was that in most of the ships the marines seemed to sympathise with the seamen. "I . . . have only further to say that I have lived to see the pride of Britain disgrace the very name of it." [73]

Yet at the time of his writing in this tone of despondency, on the 27th, things had not gone so badly: he had most of his ships with him, at anchor about four leagues from land, for since the wind was westerly, and thus of no use to the Dutch and French who wished to issue from the Texel, there was no need for him to make for the mouth of that river. But at about seven o'clock matters grew worse, for he received a message from the *Belliqueux*, to say that her crew was in great disorder, "and determined to send boats to the *Lion*, for what purpose I know not, but I am sure for no good." He therefore made the signal to weigh and stand out to sea, which his ships accordingly obeyed, except for the *Belliqueux*, which ominously made the signal of disability. Duncan meant to stand off till the next day, with the ships that would follow him, and anchored about two leagues farther out. The prospect was gloomy, but, on the other hand, he was probably encouraged by the visit he received at eleven in the evening from the lieutenant of the *Rose* cutter, who joyfully told him that he had captured the *Cygnet* the evening before, and caught all but three of the Delegates. The bulk were safely held in the *Hope* lugger, in which Duncan ordered they should remain, to be conveyed to the Downs in her. That at least was on the credit side.

In the course of the night, however, the *Lion* and the *Standard* "parted company," as the grieved Admiral put it, and early on the morning of the 29th he saw the *Montague* a long way to windward, standing towards the west, and rightly concluded that she was going to the Nore. As for the rest of the day, *The Times* reported, from Yarmouth:

> Admiral Duncan's fleet is now returning into these Roads, having been the whole time in sight of the town. The *Standard* and the *Lion* have come in and have hoisted the flag of defiance. The *Nassau* lying in our road has done the same. . . . The *Belliqueux* is come in and . . . hoisted the flag of defiance. It seems the men treat the officers in general well and perform their duty regularly.

That was the beginning of the general rot which gradually spread through the whole, though the mutiny here was more sporadic than in the other centres of the strike; no leader emerged, and there seems to have been little of that preliminary organisation which, perfect at Spithead, had been apparent, if weaker, at the Nore.

The order to weigh which Duncan signalled on the 29th was indeed obeyed, but reluctantly, and though the ships made eastward to begin with, they one by one deserted their Admiral, to his intense mortification. Never before had a British Fleet turned for home in the face of the enemy. Yet two big ships were loyal, his own—the *Venerable*—and the *Adamant*, over whose side he had held a squirming rebel; besides these there were two small ones, the *Trent*, which he had threatened to fire into, and whose loyalty is a striking tribute to his personality, and the *Circe* frigate. So Duncan held steadfastly on his course, and on 1st June anchored before the Texel. For three days the wind was in the east, and for three days Duncan blockaded the whole enemy armada ("14 sail of the line and 8 frigates with a number of other vessels amounting in the whole to 95," he wrote), with only two line-of-battle ships, and two tiny auxiliaries, making signals to an imaginary fleet in the offing. The ruse succeeded, the Dutch Fleet did not come out; but Duncan was determined that, should it do so, he would sink his ship with all her company, in such a position as to block the fairway, at a depth to leave the flag fluttering at the masthead above the waves.

Early in the afternoon of the 29th most of the ships were on their way back to Yarmouth: the *Glatton*, so fiercely loyal a day or two before, left at about one o'clock, going, not to Yarmouth, but to the Downs, where, however, she changed her mind, and in a few days returned to her Admiral at the Texel. On the *Agamemnon* the mutiny took the officers by surprise, the first they knew of it being the refusal of the men to answer the call of the boatswain's mate after their dinner. The officer of the watch, Fourth Lieutenant Brenton, at once reported what had happened to his commander, Captain Fancourt. Then

we went forward on the lower deck, and found the men had made a barricade of hammocks from one side of the ship to the other, just before the fore hatchway, and had left an embrasure on each side, through which they had pointed two 24-pounders; these they had loaded, and threatened to fire in case of resistance on the part of the officers. The captain spoke to them, but, being treated with much contempt, returned to the quarter-deck. A few minutes after a number of the people came up; some seized the wheel, while others rounded the weather braces and wore the ship, passing under the stern of the *Venerable*. The admiral made our signal to come to the wind on the larboard tack, the same as he was on himself. We answered with what was then called the signal of inability, being a flag half white and red over half blue and yellow, both horizontally divided. When the sails were trimmed on the starboard tack, and the course had been shaped by the delegates for Yarmouth roads, the captain went to his dinner with the officers, whom he had, according to the usual custom, previously invited, leaving me in charge of the deck, though without the smallest authority, if such an anomaly can be conceived. About half-past 3, Axle, the master-at-arms, came to me, and openly, in the presence of others, said, "Mr. Brenton, you have given the ship away; the best part of the men and all the marines are in your favour." I replied that I could not act by myself; that the captain had decided, and I feared there was no remedy. I, however, went into the cabin, and in a very clear and distinct manner told Captain Fancourt what the master-at-arms had said, and added my firm conviction that he was right, advising immediate measures to retake the ship, and join the admiral. His answer I shall never forget. "Mr. Brenton, if we call out the marines some of the men will be shot, and I could not bear to see them lying in convulsions on the deck; no, no, a little patience, and we shall all hail unanimity again." I quitted the cabin and walked the deck until my watch was out, too much irritated to say a word more.

On the following morning we reached Yarmouth roads, and joined three other ships, each having a red flag flying at her foretop-gallant-mast-head; the *Agamemnon* hoisted one also, which was called by the delegates the flag of defiance. During the whole of this time the officers kept charge of their watches, the seamen obeying them in any order for the safety of the ship, but no farther. A meeting of the delegates was immediately called, at which it was decided that the *Agamemnon* and *Ardent*, of 64 guns, and the *Leopard* and *Isis*, of 50 guns, should go to the Nore, to augment the number of ships at that anchorage in a state little short of open rebellion, but not with any view of assisting or being assisted by the enemies of their country; and it is certain that, had these put to sea, we should have immediately gone in pursuit of them with the same zeal and loyalty as at the beginning of the war.[74]

The last ship to turn back was the *Repulse*, which delayed till the 30th. There had been murmuring between her decks on the 28th, "but of no material consequence"; on the 29th the crew "began to be unruly but with a little persuasion it was got the better of"; however, on the 30th, at 8 a.m.,

> the ship's company told the captain they were determined to go into Port, and they took the ship from the officers and after various acts of violence carried her to the Nore.[75]

The mutiny of the North Sea Squadron was now at its most complete, but it was not, even at its height, universal.

Except for the *Montague* and the *Repulse*, the ships carried out what might be called a preliminary concentration at Yarmouth. The organisation, so far somewhat ramshackle, needed to be tightened up, and even developed. There had, as one might suppose, been some previous gathering together of the threads, the proof being that the "Outlines of the Articles of H.M. Ships *Belliqueux*, *Montague*, *Standard* and *Monmouth*" are addressed also to the *Adamant*, which had remained sturdily loyal. These "outlines" are not dated, but those for the *Agamemnon* were inscribed on the 30th. The rules were much the same as had governed at Spithead and the Nore: both sets of the Yarmouth rules insist that respect shall be paid to all officers, that duties are to be strictly carried out, that drunkenness shall be severely punished, and that although women might come on board, none might go off, unless, one set adds, "in a bad stat of health and no hopes of recovery." The *Agamemnon* decreed, "There shall be no quarrelling or fighting amongst ourselvs on any pretence whatever on pain of being severely punished": the rules of the *Belliqueux* and the others required that "No acclamations or noises or any expressions such as Grog be used and that good order and discipline be carried on untill this business is over." Apparently there were two meetings of committees on the 31st, one on the *Agamemnon*, the other on the *Isis*, but they resulted in almost identical documents, which expressed the resolution that it should be represented to the Captains and Officers that the Delegates so appointed are not to be understood as ringleaders of a Mutinous Assembly, but as men appointed by the majority of each ship's company, in order to prevent confusion and obtain as speedy a regularity of affairs as possible.

Thus once again the seamen insisted that their action was not a rebellion against authority, but a strike for better conditions of service, and that they were through and through loyal.

The intention of the Delegates appointed at Yarmouth was to ask their captains for the loan of a cutter to go round to the Nore; but there is no record that the bland request was ever made: perhaps it was refused outright, and thus the captains may themselves have forced the seamen to sail the squadron round to the Nore. Or perhaps the propitiatory visit of Admiral Sir Thomas Pasley, who had been sent by the authorities to persuade the sailors to return to duty, made it only too plain to them that nothing was to be got by staying at Yarmouth, and that they had better join forces with their friends. Neptune also appears to have been of that opinion:

> In Yarmouth next old Neptune raised his head,
> Awake my sons, the watery monarch paid (said?)—
> The torpid vapours from your souls remove—
> Inspire yourselves with true fraternal love.
> Unto the Nore repair without delay,
> There join your brothers with a loud Huzza.[76]

At all events, whether Sir Thomas or Neptune had anything to do with it, or whether it seemed the obvious policy, the sailors removed the torpid vapours from their souls, and ship by ship left the port to follow the *Montague*, led by the *Standard* and the *Lion*; these were the ships which, with four or five others, the *San Fiorenzo* had fled past with dissimulating cheers as she made her escape on the 30th. So by the 1st of June, all except four of the bigger ships, which were to follow later, were at anchor at the Nore, a considerable addition to that "floating republic," as it was called by the luridly imaginative *Courier*, a republic which owed temporary allegiance to President Richard Parker.

CHAPTER XV

MELODRAMA

ON 30th May, Captain Knight of the *Montague*, excellent commander of a leaky ship, trusted by his men, wrote to the Admiralty from the Nore:

> Since the date of my last letter the company of this ship have directed her movements, having put her in charge of the Master and Pilots . . . and have brought her to this anchorage.[77]

Such was the fact, but the laconic statement in no way indicates the ecstatic excitement with which the ships from Yarmouth were welcomed. There was no question of dragging the captains before "infernal tribunals," as with Watson of the Leith tender, nor of wildly tugging at the men to suborn them, since the ships already flaunted the bloody flag of defiance. But the moment a new recruit sailed towards them through the choppy tideway, she was joyously boarded by the Delegates, who "asked for grievances, ordered yard-ropes to be rove, demanded the keys of the magazine, and took the small arms to the forecastle." So at least it was on the *Repulse*, where, besides, though they behaved "very quiet to all the officers," they appointed two Delegates, Edward Thompson, captain of the maintop, who did not seem at all eager for the dangerous dignity, but was forced to assume it; and Richard Kent, who for his part was all alacrity, "active and eager like a Wapping attorney," [78] full of zest in argument, eager to buoy up or inflame, ready, in short, for any mischief.

To round off an action which was in itself violent, and might lead to a much more serious clash, a polite exchange of diplomatic compliments took place between high potentates:

To the Committee of the *Repulse*.   *Sandwich*,

31 *May.*

DEAR BROTHERS,

I have to inform you that in Council of the Delegates of the whole Fleet, they feel themselves greatly obliged to you for your speedily joining in the good cause we are embarked in. And by their orders I do hereby declare that from the bottom of their hearts they do thank you, and beg with brotherly love you will accept the same.

I remain, dear brothers,

Yours sincerely,

RICHARD PARKER,

President.[79]

The *Repulse*, not to be outdone in either formality or friendliness, acknowledged the communication:

(*Rough draft on the back of a punishment list.*)

DR. B.,

I have to inform you that the Commt. of this Ship is impress with the most sensible feeling of Gratitude on being 'formed by two of our Committee of your entire approbation of our conduct, in a cause which will never be erased from the minds of our Brother Tars. We, the Committee, are determined not to be influenc'd by the artful insinuations of our oppressors, nor be appeased untill our grieveance which has been too long standing is comply'd with.

I remain,

Dr. Brothers,

Your sincer.[80]

If this determination was real, Parker would feel that something might be done, even though his Brother Tars were somewhat vague in stating what precisely it was that they wanted.

Something might be done, yes; but what? There lay the Fleet, cut off from the shore, denied supplies, and apparently without hope of getting into touch with the authorities except by the dolorous way of complete submission. It was not within their view to attack Sheerness, or any other part of the land, since they were not waging war against the country: for the same reason they had no wish to sail away to some foreign port, since they were loyal servants of the Crown. They had asked for a discussion, and had been peremptorily refused; and the Admiralty, instead of facing them like men, had resorted to the mean trick of trying to starve them out. Perhaps, however, two could play at that game, for the Fleet in all its might lay at the mouth of the Thames, commanding the gateway of a capital which already at that date depended to a large extent on foreign trade for its subsistence. It seems that a blockade had been suggested a few days before, and the intention had become known, but the scheme had not been adopted. Still, now that the mutineers had been forced into defiance, such a challenge, not now to the Admiralty alone, but to the whole country, was surely justified, and might have a rapid and beneficent effect. But it was meant as a challenge only, to indicate what the seamen could do if they wished, "in order to show the country they had it in their power to stop the trade of the river; but had no intention of injuring their country."[81]

Accordingly, at nine o'clock in the evening of the 31st, Parker, accompanied by two other Delegates, proceeded on shore under a flag of truce, and, marching thus protected up to Commissioner Hartwell's house, delivered him what was proudly called "The Final Determination of the North Sea Fleet."[82] Though it was a declaration of immediate blockade, in point of fact for two days it remained only a threat—again, perhaps, the sailors were too optimistic—a delay which caused people in general to suppose that the threat would never materialise; they could not believe that the seamen would dare go to such lengths.[83] And at first it looked as though the optimists on this side were right, for nothing happened on the 1st except that Parker made a tour of his now large command, rowing round the Fleet to the accompaniment of music, which was drowned in the cheers vociferated from each ship as he passed.[84] On the

2nd, however, the *Swan* sloop was sent into the river with orders to direct to Parker at the Nore every ship that came in, except such as bore a pass signed, "R. Parker, President of the Delegates": but one ship not proving enough to cope with the traffic, she was supported first by the *Brilliant*, a rather larger vessel, and later by the *Standard*, a line-of-battle ship, with the *Inspector* sloop, the two latter representing the Yarmouth contingent.[85] Each of these watch-ships had its orders:

To the Committee,

    Hereby you are desired by the Delegates of the Whole Fleet to detain all vessels to and from the Port of London, those excepted whose cargoes are perishable, taking an account of the name of each ship.

    Given under our hand this 2nd day of June 1797 on board H.M.S. *Sandwich*.[86]

It had come to a trial of strength, or rather of doggedness, without violence.

The act, whether or not it was intended to continue it to extremes, was a desperate one, which no amount of glozing over could soften; and Parker at this time seems to have been in an excited, unstable frame of mind. It was not that the cheers, the intoxication of his position, had gone to his head, but that he had been over a fortnight, if not really in command, at least nominally at the head, of a mutiny which threatened the existence of the nation, and during this time nothing had happened to bring the mutineers a single inch nearer their object. Things must be worked up to a crisis and a settlement, if only because, as one of the three Delegates on the evening of the 31st is reported to have said, the Dutch Fleet was rumoured to be coming out, and the British Fleet must be prepared to meet it. That may have been a reason; but it is more likely that to Parker's mind it was clear that unless something came about, it would be difficult to keep the men steadfast to the cause, tuned up to the height of mutiny. However fervently they might declare their unalterable resolve not to be "appeased" until their grievances were met, fervour does not last unnourished. Added to these reasons, food and water were scarce; thus there was a physical as well as moral reason for the decision; and, indeed, Parker was to declare that the need for food was the only reason for the blockade. That certainly was the argument which appealed to the men. The London magistrate, Graham, whom we saw fruitlessly sniffing out sedition at Portsmouth, was to say:

> The want of beer and fresh beef prompted them to revenge, and that and nothing else induced them to interrupt the trade of the river. It was done on the spur of the occasion, and with a view of obtaining a supply of fresh provisions.[87]

That would seem to the men the common sense of it.

But whether Parker liked making this tremendous decision is another matter: it may have been forced on him. At all events the strain was beginning to tell, temperamentally nervous as he was; he felt himself in an increasingly false position, and dared not on the subject of the mutiny allow his spirits to fall below explosive heat. Watson, whose tender was detained until the 2nd, when he obtained a "release" for her, took pains to see as much of him as he could at this time, remembering his strange suicidal passenger of a month before, with the dark, sensitive face set with striking eyes, who had, moreover, given testimony in his favour when his vessel had been so roughly seized on the 29th. "I worked upon him," Watson was to confess,

> by every possible means; but whenever the subject [of the mutiny] was broached his brain took fire; he seemed intoxicated with a sense of his own consequence, and uttered nothing but incoherent nonsense,

which is, perhaps, not surprising. For, apparently, Parker received orders from the Delegates, orders which were hatched at what appears to have been the breeding-centre of the mutiny, the *Inflexible*, if we are to believe his "Dying Declaration." Watson, a little unfairly, egged him on to drink, "knowing his propensity that way. . . . In this state of inebriety, he exposed himself in an attempt before the volunteers, etc., to display his powers of oratory," [88] which proved ineffectual, since the recruits on the tender, after a little wavering, refused to come in with the mutineers.

But that he went about some of the business in a workman-like manner is vividly revealed by his handling of the *Hound* sloop on 2nd June. On that day the *Hound*, acting as a tender, arrived at the Nore with a hundred and eleven men to be transferred to the depot-ship. She was immediately boarded by some of the Delegates, Parker not being among them, and a violent altercation followed between them and the commander, Captain Wood. Parker had met Wood, who had been kind to him, before he was put on the tender at Leith, and when he came on board the *Hound*, said:

> Captain Wood, the differences in the fleet are of a very unpleasant nature. I feel myself, in some degree, under an obligation to you, therefore I would advise you to do nothing at present, but to suffer the *Hound* to proceed in the same manner as the rest of the ships; for I have no doubt but that, in the course of a day or two, the officers will resume their command.

Wood, who had driven some of the Delegates out of his ship by threatening them with death, saw fit to comply, since Parker told him that he "had the honour to represent the whole fleet," and interfered no more. But the seamen in the *Hound* were not at all inclined to join the mutiny, so Parker decided to moor her under the guns of the *Sandwich*. On the pilot objecting that the tide was not favourable, Parker, pointing significantly to the yard-rope that had been rove by one of the crew of the *Pylades* since he had come on board, remarked that if he did not choose to weigh at once, he could find means to make him. Upon that the pilot discovered that the tide would after all not be an impediment. But when the order was given to let the anchor go, it was found that the sloop was too near the *Sandwich*, whereupon Parker turned to the pilot, and told him, "You have committed one mistake, mind you don't commit another; if you do, I'll make beefsteak of you at the yard-arm." He appears momentarily as the commander who knew exactly what he was about, and would stand no nonsense. Once the sloop was moored between the flagship and the *Inflexible*, he harangued the men, and asked if they had any complaints against their officers, promising to send any obnoxious ones on shore: one man being insolent, he had him put in irons. The captain's letters were censored, a measure which could not have been of much use, since he was soon after sent ashore, by, he was told, the orders of Parker, whom he saw rowing about the Fleet to the usual musical accompaniment punctuated by cheering.[89]

While the mutineers were taking these measures, the Government in all its majesty and power behaved in a way as excited as Parker's, though since it did have the power, its actions were more effectual. The King's proclamation of pardon, dated 27th May,[90] had proved useless, not having been called upon to provide the happy finish to the Board's visit to Sheerness, for which it had been designed: another of the 31st, posted on the walls of Sheerness, and taken to the *Sandwich* in the Admiral's barge,[91] was a mere blustering fanfare calling upon every one to help in repressing the mutiny. It was discussed by the committee before promulgation—an exercise of authority which furiously annoyed the body of the seamen; but the temper thus aroused perhaps served the purposes of the Delegates by making the men still further resent the Government declaration, which, after all, was mere verbiage. "Sir," Parker wrote to Buckner on 3rd June:

I am commanded by the Committee of H.M.S. *Sandwich* to inform you that they have this day taken the opinion of the Delegates of the whole Fleet, who are universally of opinion, that the conduct of the administration has been highly improper in stopping the provisions by Government allowed to the seamen. And that the foolish proclamations which have been received are only fitted to exasperate the minds of a sett of Honest Men, who would never be more happy than in really serving their country.

I am sir,

Your humble servant,

RICHARD PARKER,

President.[92]

Hostilities between the Kingdom and the Floating Republic were not, however, confined to mutual blockade and an interchange of threatening notes, for besides the two Delegates they held fast, the authorities had seized some other seamen who had boldly ventured on shore. The mutineers did not indeed retaliate by kidnapping people from the shore, but the counter-measure they could and did take was to refuse officers permission to land, a permission which some had not unnaturally asked for, being tired of idly kicking their heels in ships where they were denied any authority or function. When their fellows were captured, the Delegates "finally determined that no officer whatever shall be permitted to go on shore, until the return of the people who are at present detained." They added, however, in a conciliatory tone of voice, as though to show there was no ill-feeling in the matter: "We are well convinced of the good conduct of our officers who are on board." [93]

By now Parliament was beginning to take a hand, urged to activity by a message from the King. On 1st June Pitt introduced a Bill "for the better prevention and punishment of attempts to seduce persons serving in the naval or military service from their duty and allegiance, and incite them to mutiny or disobedience." The penalties were mild, but two days later, when the Bill was being debated in committee, the phrasing was amended to "maliciously and advisedly inciting," and the punishment stiffened to that of death; for, as Pitt remarked, since the punishment for mutiny was hanging, it was illogical to have a lesser punishment for causing the crime. Pitt seemed to think that the sailors' lot was a perfectly happy one; they could have no possible ground for complaint. The sailors themselves, again, were fine fellows, chock-full of loyalty and other sterling virtues: it was clear that the root of the trouble was insidious Jacobin propaganda:

> The whole affair [he said] was of that colour and description which proved it not to be of native growth, and left no hesitation on the mind of any thinking man to determine whence it was imported.[94]

The House was docile; a few argued that the old provisions were enough to deal with the situation; Sheridan upbraided the administration for having by their ill-treatment brought the mutiny upon themselves, but agreed to the measure; the Bill was passed without a dissentient voice, was sent up to the Lords, and passed through all its stages that evening. The Act, intended to last a month or two, was stout enough to safeguard the loyalty of our forces till the year of grace 1934.

Another Bill, for restraining intercourse with rebellious seamen, was introduced immediately afterwards. This met with some opposition. Sir John Sinclair was of the opinion that in demanding this measure Pitt was not only drawing the sword but also throwing away the scabbard: to pass this Bill would virtually expatriate the British Navy. It was, indeed, a savage Bill, by which the Admiralty might declare any ship to be in a state of rebellion, after which any person remaining on board would be considered a felon and a pirate, while any person who aided, comforted, or encouraged them, was liable to the death penalty. Sir Francis Burdett declared that the Bill would drive the seamen to despair; their discontent was only part of that which pervaded the whole nation, and that the only remedy was for the King to dismiss his Ministers, and put an end to a corrupt system. In this he was supported by Charles Sturt, member for Bridport, who was the only man who had the courage actually to vote against the Bill. Following these two panic measures, another was shortly afterwards passed to prevent the administration of unlawful oaths, such as the seamen had sworn. It could have no immediate effect, but it is of interest since it was under this law that, in 1834, the Tolpuddle martyrs earned their uncomfortable fame.

If the legislative was thus busy, the executive authorities on their part were not idle. Sir Charles Grey was indefatigable, and was joined on 2nd June by Admiral, recently created Lord Keith, who came nominally as second-in-command to Buckner, but actually took over the reins from that somewhat ineffectual old gentleman. It was hoped, perhaps, that Keith's presence would have much the same healing effect as that of Howe at Spithead, for he had the reputation of being lucky, and was popular with the sailors; but since he had no communication with them till after the mutiny, this qualification was wasted. The business of fortifying strong points went on; a mortar battery was placed on the Isle of Grain, while furnaces glowing in every fort kept up a gratifying supply of red-hot balls. A little later the idea was brought forward of placing a boom across the Thames—there was already one across the harbour-mouth at Sheerness—but it was found the old boom once in use had been destroyed, and that it would take a fortnight to make another. A line of colliers was suggested as an alternative, but the notion was abandoned. Every possible step was taken to prevent the seamen having any communication with the land, especially as Buckner was convinced that men were sneaking across to Leigh and Faversham. Lines of soldiers watched the shore at likely landing-places; other lines were placed behind them in case any intrepid sailors should slip through; pickets of "peace officers" were stationed at all points of strategic importance between the east coast and London, while light cavalry exercised itself over the countryside in the eager hope of catching deserters.[95]

Stirring deeds were in prospect, and to help the military in repelling a horrible invasion, in which a handful of seamen without organisation or guns would subdue a whole nation (the seamen themselves had too keen a sense of realities, and perhaps too much sense of humour, quite apart from their loyalty, to dream of such an action), the civilian population roused itself in its lusty strength to do battle for its property. It may be that the blockade had been forced upon the Delegates, but at any rate it was a fatal error, for it antagonised the middle or trading classes of the community, classes which Joyce and his fellows had been careful to reassure. What happened in 1797 was to all intents and purposes precisely what occurred in 1926 during the general strike, when the food of London was threatened. Alarmed by the sailors, the merchants and shipowners met in a fluster at the Stock Exchange, where they expressed a noble anxiety to help the Government in its hunt for the "lurking traitors" who were seducing the seamen; never had their sense of security been so profoundly shocked, even when the Bank went off gold. In their enthusiasm they organised a public subscription to be scattered in gratuities to all seamen who would volunteer to fight their scandalous fellows, and they offered a reward of £100 for the conviction of those who had instigated the revolt. Alas for their hundred pounds: it was never claimed; the dastardly Jacobin who was at the root of all this mischief was never forthcoming. The snug City merchants could not conceive that horrible conditions could have produced the mutiny; they were as innocent of this thought as Pitt himself.

The more active members of the middle-classes were prepared to show their mettle in deeds: as in 1926 they offered themselves to save their country, and volunteered in their numbers, as though to prove that the heart of England beat true. As they flocked to the recruiting offices they were sent aboard the ships at Tilbury, and full of heroic determination were taken down to Long Reach to join Sir Erasmus Gower, who, flying his flag in the *Neptune*, was organising a naval force to battle against the rascally rebels. The Younger Brothers of Trinity House were told to record where they might be found, and to hold themselves in instant readiness for duty. Private shipowners, stimulated by these doings, patriotically offered the use of their ships; plenty of naval and marine officers volunteered, and many crews tendered their services in a body. The East India Company put its ships and men wholly at the disposal of the Government.[96] It was a glorious rallying to the flag; but to some it seemed a manifestation of "that misguided public spirit which animated the whole nation as one man against the erring but ill-treated sailors, who for endless years had defended their property, their lives, their liberties, all that made them what they were, under wrongs so crying, that one tithe of the seamen's real grievances would have driven"[97] them to vindictiveness and rebellion.

The desperately wicked men against whom these nobly patriotic measures were being taken, did not, however, present to the unprejudiced observer that depth of evil design which such measures presupposed. It is true that they did impound a store-ship or two and distribute the eatables, and extracted the fish from some passing smacks. They were hungry, and some of them went so far as to raid the Isles of Grain and Sheppey to ravish away sheep and cattle. They also carried out the blockade with complete efficiency, and soon over a hundred sail were huddled together at the mouth of the Thames, idle. This flotilla, moreover, was matched by another on the London side of Tilbury, consisting of ships of all sorts forbidden egress by the Admiralty for fear lest they should provide booty for the mutineers.

Jacobins, members of Corresponding Societies, where were they? Every ear was alert to catch the sound of them, and soon the listeners were given whispers to encourage their eagerness. Two sailors were found near Rochester bridge, who declared they were looking for "a gentleman in black" from whom they expected funds: tongues might even go so far as to suggest that this dark figure, never heard of in any other connection, was Whitbread, one of the leading figures of the Opposition, who certainly communicated with the men in the *Lancaster*.[98] Parker, again, mysteriously disappeared one night three or four miles from Sheerness on the Isle of Sheppey, and

> this excited so much alarm in the minds of the Delegates that a party was induced to go the next morning in search of him, but not finding him, and hearing that he had returned on board, they waited on shore till the evening and then seized the *Nancy* tender lying outside the garrison point. She was fired at from the Battery, but a fresh breeze from the land enabled them to get her away without damage, and proceed on board the *Sandwich*. The cause of this mysterious proceeding of Parker's was never publicly known.[99]

Was it not clear that he had gone to confer with some monster of sedition? But the suspicion could never be justified.

On their side, the sailors were determined to show how well affected they were, and on Sunday, 4th, Parker sent to Queenborough for Mr. Hatherall, the chaplain of the *Sandwich*, to ask him to hold a service on board, and to preach. Hatherall accepted: he was a courageous man, and was not going to shirk his duty in any way; he preached a thoroughly uncompromising sermon on Job xxvii, 5, "God forbid that I shall justify you: till I die, I will not remove mine integrity from me," an all too topical text which probably caused a certain perturbation among the Delegates, who did not subsequently invite his gentle ministrations.

The sermon, however, caused no revulsion of their humane feelings, for on that day the Delegates gave three days' leave to Captain Knight of the *Montague*, for the purpose of taking ashore his wife, who had been visiting him at Yarmouth, and had not had time to escape before the ship sailed for the Nore, so sudden had the departure been. The written permission shows how acutely the mutineers felt any suggestion of disloyalty to the Crown.

4th June 1797.

To Captain Knight.

SIR,

I am commanded to inform you by the Delegates of the Fleet assembled on board H.M.S. *Sandwich* that they feel for your situation, and on the undermentioned conditions you are permitted to accompany Mrs. Knight on shore. You are to return on board your respective ship in three days after your landing, and that you represent to Admiral Buckner that all the officers are detained as hostages for our absent Delegates, and you are to assure yourself that you are to be considered for three days on parol of honour, and that if which we will not doubt you should not return the breech of confidence would be resented as deemed necessary by the Delegates of the Fleet. You are further desired to inform on shore that every Delegate has sworn himself that he has no communication with any Jacobins or people of that description, which they have amply proved by having in their custody at this moment two vessels bound to our enemy's ports.

I remain, Sir,

With due respect,

Your humble servant,

RICHARD PARKER,

President.[100]

One would like to think that the contents of this note were communicated to those bold patriots the shipowners, who, not chary of accusing the seamen of comforting the King's enemies, were themselves trading with them.

It was a point on which the seamen not unnaturally felt justifiably bitter. They drew up a document for their fellow-countrymen, which a Delegate named Gregory took to an

American ship so that it might be printed and posted on the Royal Exchange. This manifesto, which was never printed, although Gregory had paid out three guineas to the American, concluded:

> We do not wish to adopt the plan of a neighbouring nation, however it may have been suggested; but we (will) sell our lives dearly to maintain what we have demanded. Nay, countrymen, more: We have already discovered the tricks of Government is supplying our enemies with different commodities, and a few days will probably lead to something more.

The whole appeal is extraordinarily dignified, though perhaps too tub-oratorical:

> COUNTRYMEN (it begins),
>
> It is to you particularly that we owe an explanation of our conduct. His Majesty's perverse ministers too well know our intentions, which are founded on the laws of humanity, honour, and national safety—long since trampled underfoot by those who ought to have been friends to us—the sole protectors of your laws and property. The public prints teem with falsehoods and misrepresentations to induce you to credit things as far from our design as the conduct of those at the helm of national affairs is from honesty or common decorum.

It then rises to a considerable height of theatrical eloquence:

> Shall we who have endured the toils of a tedious, disgraceful war, be the victims of tyranny and oppression which vile, gilded, pampered knaves, wallowing in the lap of luxury, choose to load us with? Shall we, who amid the rage of the tempest and the war of jarring elements, undaunted climb the unsteady cordage and totter on the topmast's dreadful height, suffer ourselves to be treated worse than the dregs of London Streets? Shall we, who in the battle's sanguinary rage, confound, terrify and subdue your proudest foe, guard your coasts from invasion, your children from slaughter, and your lands from pillage—be the footballs and shuttlecocks of a set of tyrants who derive from us alone their honours, their titles and their fortunes? No, the Age of Reason has at length revolved. Long have we been endeavouring to find ourselves men. We now find ourselves so. We will be treated as such. For, very far from us is the idea of subverting the government of our beloved country. We have the highest opinion of our

Most Gracious Sovereign, and we hope none of those measures have been taken to deprive us of the common rights of men have been instigated by him.

Then follows a passage to tell the people of England something of the life the seaman led:

You cannot, countrymen, form the most distant idea of the slavery under which we have for many years laboured. Rome had her Neros and Caligulas, but how many characters of their description might we not mention in the British Fleet—men without the least tincture of humanity, without the faintest spark of virtue, education or abilities, exercising the most wanton acts of cruelty over those whom dire misfortune or patriotic zeal may have placed in their power—basking in the sunshine of prosperity, whilst we (need we repeat who we are?) labour under every distress which the breast of inhumanity can suggest.

Then there comes a somewhat unfortunate trope:

The British Seaman has often with justice been compared to the Lion— gentle, generous and humane—no one would certainly wish to hurt such an animal.

But the writer soon recovers himself:

Hitherto we have laboured for our sovereign and you. We are now obliged to think for ourselves, for there are many (nay, most of us) in the Fleet who have been prisoners since the commencement of the War, without receiving a single farthing. Have we not a right to complain?

After which he expresses the determination of the men to hold out until their grievances are redressed, "but until that is comply'd with we are determined to stop all commerce and intercept all provisions, for our own subsistence."[101]

It is not necessary to suppose that the ideas of liberty, the reference to the Age of Reason, were due to the French Revolution—the American might have suggested them; and at any rate revolution was the last thing the sailors wanted. They seized the opportunity of the King's birthday to express their loyalty, a birthday which, though it fell on the 4th, was celebrated on the 5th, since the former day was a Sunday. Many of the ships were dressed with colours, the *Sandwich* flew the Royal Standard at the fore, and the Fleet fired the resounding salute which did such alarming damage to the old brick merlons of Sheerness fort. There might not have been the same eagerness to honour the Sovereign had the men known that he had written to Spencer a few days before that "the preventing of their getting fresh water will soon oblige them to submit." [102] At all events they felt it was imperative to make every gesture to show that their quarrel was not against either King or country, but simply against the administration. Perhaps it was for this reason that on that day they relaxed the blockade, merchant ships being allowed to pass, and only victualling ships being detained. [103] Whether the Delegates hoped by this move to soften the indignation of the traders, or whether it was simply that they did not know what to do with the ever-increasing mass of ships that cumbered the mouth of the Thames, it is hard to say. If the first was their intention, it was by now far too late: it is easier to declare a war than to put a stop to it. The probability is that they felt the blockade had served its purpose in showing the country what they could do if they were evilly inclined.

That the authorities were prepared to regard the state of affairs as a war was shown by an unpleasant incident which occurred on the 5th; it does not redound to the credit of the officers at Sheerness, and showed the sailors how little their loyal demonstrations availed them. On that day the Delegates collected some fifty or sixty of their sick—what they were likely to be suffering from we know from Surgeon Snipe's report—put them on board the *Nancy* tender, and sent them to be received on the hospital ship. Buckner, after consulting with Mosse and other captains, was inhuman enough to order the master of the *Nancy* to return the sick men to their respective ships. It was not a pretty action, and was not made better by the authorities giving "a bundle of proclamations to a confidential man of the *Sandwich*, with instructions to place them 'into the bosoms and pockets of the sick men,'" while the master of the *Nancy* was asked to try to thrust some in at the ports of the ships.[104] The effect of the proclamations, however, was dubious, if we are to gather anything from a paper addressed, "For the Lords Commissioners of the Board of Admiralty," dated a day or two later:

> Dam my eyes if I understand your lingo or long Proclimations but in short give us our Due at Once and no more at it, till we go in search of the Rascals the Eneymes of our Country.
>
> HENRY LONG.
On Board his Majesty's ship Champion.

NORE, *7th* (?) *June* 1797.[105]

The general feeling of the mutineers could not be expressed more neatly than that.

CHAPTER XVI

SIGNS OF WEAR AND TEAR

THE tension existing between the mutineers and the forces mobilised against them had now reached such a stage that it must have seemed that something was bound to happen. The knot had to be untied or cut, and that soon. In a sense, then, the events of the next two or three days are the most momentous in the history of the mutiny at the Nore.

On 6th June, Lord Northesk, Captain of the *Monmouth*, a post which he had enjoyed for a year, received a note couched somewhat in the terms of the following rough draft:

6th June.

To the Rt. Hon. the Earl of Northesk.

My Lord,

I am commanded by the Delegates of the Fleet to inform your Lordship that you are requested to repair on board the *Sandwich* to receive your instructions. A barge will attend your Lordship, and every mark of respect paid your Lordship could wish for.

We are etc: [106]

Northesk was a man not quite forty years old, robust, with "a manly open countenance," and very popular with his men, whom he had always treated lightly—indeed, according to Cunningham's martinet mind, a great deal too lightly, avoiding the use of the lash. He was known to have devoted hours together to the patient investigation of a charge before he would order punishment to be inflicted. Yet his solicitude for his men did not prevent him from being a good sailor, at least in Nelson's view, for he was third in command at Trafalgar, flying his flag on the *Britannia*: and, since he was to some extent in sympathy with the men, he raised no objection to their request. He was ushered on board the barge by the Delegates of his own ship, and as he approached the *Sandwich*, the band mustered on deck played "God Save the King."

When he went into the state cabin, accompanied by one officer, he was confronted by some sixty Delegates, with Parker sitting at the head of the table drafting a letter; but as soon as Parker saw he had arrived, he stopped writing, and gave the order for "God Save the King" to be played again.[107] The moment that muscles relaxed after this ceremony, some Delegate, too eager for the minute points of the law, fractiously demanded who the officer was that had come in with Northesk. It seemed as though there might be some check at the very outset. Northesk answered that he had brought the officer with him as secretary, since he had thought one would probably be needed. That seemed to cover the departure from the strict letter of the invitation, but the forms had to be complied with, and the authority of the committee vindicated. "Who knows him?" Parker asked: "say, Delegates of the *Monmouth*, what kind of man is he?" On the Delegates answering that he was a very good man, it was unanimously voted that he might remain.

The object of the invitation to Northesk was to ask him to take a petition to the King. The Delegates were particularly eager to proclaim their loyalty; nothing wounded them more deeply than to have their love for the Crown impugned. The word "rebel" applied to them cut them to the quick, and they had heard that they were being denounced as rebels, though no doubt the Royal Proclamation declaring them such, issued on that day, had not yet reached them. They read their petition over to Northesk, who told them that though he would be glad to present it for them, he could not give them any hope of its helping them at all; and that, since their demands were far too high, it could not possibly do them any good.[108] Nevertheless the Delegates held fast by their petition, and supplied

Northesk with a pass, respectfully, even courteously worded, though it could not be disguised that it was addressed by a superior authority to a lesser one. The postscript is pathetic in its eagerness to have the slur of treachery washed out.

> *Sandwich* at the Nore,
> 6 *June* 1797

To the Right Honble The Earl of Northesk.

MY LORD,

You are hereby required and directed to proceed to London with such papers as you are entrusted with and lay the same before our most gracious Sovereign King George the Third and to represent to our most gracious Sovereign that the seamen at the Nore have been grossly misrepresented to His Majesty, at the same time if our most gracious Sovereign does not order us to be redressed in fifty four hours after eight o'clock in the morning of June 7th 1797, such steps by the Fleet will be taken as will astonish their dear countrymen, and your Lordship is further requested to send us an account in the specified time by your pursur who is allowed to attend your Lordship.

> I am, my Lord,
> Your Lordship's humble servant,
> RICHARD PARKER,
> (*President*).

By Order of the Committee of Delegates of the Whole Fleet.

MY LORD,

I am further to acquaint your Lordship that an oath has been taken by the Delegates of the Fleet that they never had any communication with Jacobins or Traitors.

> RICHARD PARKER,
> *President*.[109]*

* This letter has always been referred to as insolent, though since it has never before been printed correctly, but always as follows, there is perhaps some excuse:

> *Sandwich*,
> *June* 6, 3 *p.m.*

To CAPTAIN LORD NORTHESK.

You are hereby authorised and ordered to wait upon the king, wherever he may be, with the resolutions of the committee of delegates, and are directed to return back, with an answer to the same, within fifty-four hours from the date hereof.

> R. PARKER,
> *President*.

It was all done with the best of intentions, and when Northesk set off with the message, the whole Fleet manned ship to cheer him, and grog was served on the *Sandwich*.[110] No doubt it was a mistake to make the letter also an ultimatum and a threat, but one can understand a certain irritation against the "dear countrymen."

The petition which Northesk bore to London with him was an appeal to the King over the heads of his ministers, and the only revolutionary thing about it is the implied contempt of democratic forms: the views as to the ministers were only such as were every day expressed in Parliament, and far more violently, by members of the Opposition.

To the King's Most Excellent Majesty.

MAY IT PLEASE YOUR MAJESTY,

We your Majesty's faithful and loyal subjects serving on Board Your Majesty's Ships and Vessels at the Nore, with the greatest humility beg leave to lay our Petition before you, and hope as you have always avowed yourself to be the Father of your People, that our Petitions will be attended to. We have already laid a state of our Grievance before Your Majesty's Board of Admiralty, which Grievances we have reasons to imagine, were never properly stated to you, as we are sorry to have reason to remark the conduct of your present Ministers seems to be directed to the ruin and overthrow of your Kingdoms, and as their Duty to its good and advantage, a particular instance of which is the Council they have given Your Majesty with regard to us in proclaiming us Rebels, traitors and Outlaws. This Council if we had not been men particularly attached to Your Majesty's sacred person and Government, moderate but firm in our demands, and resolved with our lives to oppose your enemies by land and sea, would before now have driven us to some acts of Outrage and Revenge that might have shaken the very foundations of this Kingdom. We here give you a list of our Grievances, which List is accompanied by a simple but true Statement of the reasons we have of demanding them, and after thus making our Wants known to Your Majesty, we cannot longer ascribe a non-compliance with those Wants to Ministry, with you it now rests to determine whether you will or will not get a Redress of our Suffering. Your majesty may depend that in Your Kingdom there is no more loyal and faithful Subject than we are, but at the same time we must assure Your Majesty till all those disgraceful Proclamations, which proscribe

Outlaws are contradicted, till we have all our Grievances redress'd and till we have the same supply from and communications as usual with the shore, we shall consider ourselves masters of Nore Shipping. We have already determined how to act, and should be extremely sorry we should be forced to repose in another country, which must evidently be the case if we are denounced as Outlaws in our own.

Your Majesty's Ministers seem to build their hopes on starving us into a compliance, but this is a wrong Idea. We have as much Provisions and Stores as will last Six Months. We were aware of their Intentions, and provided against them, but were it the reverse, and that we had but two days Provisions, we would sooner die in that state than give Up the least article of our Demands.

We shall trust to Your Majesty's prudence in chuseing such Councillors and Advisors in the present and other affairs as will have the goods of their Country in view, and not like the present Ministers its Destruction. And with respect to our own Grievances, we shall allow 54 hours from 8 o'clock on Wednesday June the 7th 1797 to know Your Majesty's final Answer. We shall likewise make known to our fellow-subjects on shore the particulars of the Address and Your Majesty's answer, so as to justify to them any Measure we may take in consequence of a Refusal.

With loyalty we remain,

Your Majesty's dutiful

Subjects, SEAMEN AT THE NORE.[111]

Northesk faithfully did his best for the seamen. He took the petition, which was perhaps not too tactfully worded, to Spencer, who carried him to Court, where the King was presented with the document. He was, naturally, unmoved by it; and even if his heart had been touched, he could have done nothing. His Government was committed to a definite course of action, and he could not be expected to throw over his ministers on the demand of a few thousand sailors. It is likely that Northesk pleaded hard for the seamen, since he had undertaken to be their emissary, however clearly he may have seen the futility of his journey. He did not go back to them; he had not been expected to, but it was Captain Knight of the *Montague*, returning from his parole, and not Northesk's purser, who took back a blank refusal from the throne, arriving at the Nore on the 7th.

There is evidence[112] to make it fairly clear that the grievances referred to in the petition were those presented to Buckner in the earlier days of the mutiny. What is chiefly significant about it, beyond the expressions of loyalty, and the appeal to the King as the father of his people, is the ominous suggestion that if the demands were not complied with, the seamen would "be forced to repose in another country." This was a counsel of despair, for, in spite of the brave statement about supplies in the petition, the Fleet was running short; otherwise there would have been no need for the sheep-raiding expeditions, or the seizure of store-ships, one of which, luckily for them, was a hoy containing three hundred sacks of flour.[113] More revealing still, is the request the *Director* sent to the *Montague*:

DR. BROTHERS,

   We would be exceedingly obliged to you to spare us the small quantity of 5 Ton of Water for our present use, as we are greatly in want of this useful Article.

Yours,

Commee. of the *Director*.[114]

and it is likely that the *Director* was not the only ship short of sustenance.

If, then, the sailors could get no help from shore, if accommodation with the authorities seemed unlikely—the answer to the petition would settle that one way or the other —the leaders would have somehow to wriggle out of the cleft fork in which they found themselves caught. It was either surrender, which at this stage would mean the death penalty, or escape. It was not so much a question of taking the Fleet over to the enemy, as of finding refuge somewhere. The how and the where seem to have been furiously debated; Parker himself, apparently, was against any such project, though the committee had captured, and retained under their hand on the *Sandwich*, more than twenty masters of vessels whom they meant to use as pilots.[115] On the *Swan*, one of the most fiercely determined ships, Rearden, the president of the committee, asked a pilot whether he would take them over to France or Ireland, and, further, if he could estimate the price the sloop would fetch if sold. George Shave, of the *Leopard*, informed his crew that if the petition was not answered, and that within the time limit, the Fleet would make for a foreign port, and anyone who objected would be "made an example of to the ship's company." A proposal to make for Bantry Bay was shown some favour, but a strong resistance was offered to any suggestion of taking the ship over to the French: better the West Indies, where there were "wood, wine, and water." On the *Champion* there was much discussion of a scheme of going to the Humber to take prizes and then sailing away for France: other ships were to repair to Cromarty Bay and the Shannon; others, again, were to go to some mysterious haven known as the "New Colony,"[116] but it is not clear where these Fortunate Isles are supposed to have spread their inviting shores. This place of dreams might even have been the island in which Bligh's mutineers had made for themselves so happy a paradise.

One of the most energetic of the Delegates in promoting schemes of escape, and of urging their necessity, was William Gregory, a man of thirty-one, who had joined at Montrose, and was rated as a member of the carpenter's crew of the *Sandwich*. It was he who had taken the still-born manifesto to the American pilot, and he seems to have been prominent at every juncture, a man of authority among the seamen, who had elected him President of the Committee of Internal Regulations. This indefatigable leader once more boarded an American ship to find out from the pilot if it would be possible to sail for America, that enticing land of freedom. He proposed that such seamen as did not want to go could be left behind in the *Sandwich*, which was not seaworthy. At the same time, he did not fail to point out forcibly what would happen to those seamen when they fell into the hands of a cruel and vindictive Government. He dashed everywhere trying to whip up fervour through fear, and to purge the Fleet of weaker elements. In the *Brilliant* he called the men together, gave them the gist of the King's pardon, and then said, "This can be altered in the course of a few hours. Should you go on shore, you are liable to be hung or shot. And any of you that has a mind to go on shore to your tyrannical country—you shall go on shore with a flag of truce." [117] Perhaps he really believed that the Government intended to play the sailors false, for a member of the Opposition had flung out the taunt in Parliament, and the accusation had been widely reported in the newspapers which the sailors somehow got hold of.[118]

It is doubtful whether the men of any ship would have consented to sail away from England; only the firebrand extremists such as Gregory seemed to wish it; but the notion of a movement was sufficiently discussed and popular enough to alarm Parker, who saw fit to issue an ukase, and take care that it was obeyed:

ORDER. *Sandwich.* 7 *June.*
   That no ship shall move from its place at the Nore till the expiration of 54 hours allowed Lord Northesk to bring an answer to their demands and that a boat from each ship shall keep a guard during the night to prevent such a separation.[119]

though it may be that the order was meant as well to prevent a break-away to Sheerness. In the meantime, steps were taken to keep up the spirits of the sailors, to the alarm of the local inhabitants. On that day watchers on land were sent into spasms of horror at seeing two figures hanging from the yard-arms of some of the distant ships, which figures were being fired at by the brutal mutineers, in an excess, apparently, of cruel rage. The news of a massacre of officers flared from house to house across the shocked town, while Brenton and other officers, peering from their cabins, were sure that their last hour had come.[120] But the figures were only stuffed effigies of the execrated "Billy Pitt" and Dundas, which some ingenious and happy mind had suggested might be used as pot-shots to keep the idle sailors entertained.

Whether or not the seamen seriously intended to bolt to other shores, the authorities took the petition's threat to do so very seriously. The ships must at all costs be prevented from moving, either out to sea or up-river. To make sure of the former, Trinity House arranged to have the buoys and beacon lights of the outward passage removed. As early as the 4th, the Trinity Yacht had begun work on the buoys of the South Channel, but since the matter now seemed urgent, a meeting of the Board on the 8th instructed Captain Bromfield, one of the Elder Brethren, to hire boats at Harwich to help in the destruction of the marks in the North Channel. The task was likely to be a tricky and dangerous one if the mutineers got wind of it, but somehow, whether by rapid work in the daytime, or under cover of darkness, Bromfield succeeded in doing away with all buoys and lights by the 9th. Since the work of lifting the buoys and their moorings with hand appliances would have taken far too long, the buoys were scuttled where they lay, and the beacons smashed. The Nore lightship, however, escaped. It was argued at Trinity House that its existence might help repentant ships to get out, and that on the other hand it would not be of much use to the Fleet if it wished to make for the open sea. Perhaps the fact that she was moored under the guns of the *Sandwich* lent conviction to the argument.[121] Whether through inattention, or because they were outwitted, the mutineers made no efforts to prevent these operations being carried out; and to make sure that they took no counter-measures, such as sinking small vessels on the sands, the *Ariadne* and two gunboats were sent to cruise about the neighbourhood of the Swin to scare them away. It was now impossible to move either in or out of the river, the former point being as important as the latter; indeed the Admiralty had hoped that they would have been in time to prevent the ships still remaining at Yarmouth from joining up at the Nore, but for this they were just too late:[122] they sailed safely in on the 6th. Notice was duly given to the world:

TRINITY HOUSE, LONDON,
June 8, 1797.

His Majesty having thought fit, by his order in council, to direct the buoys in the several channels to be removed, and the beacons to be cut down:

Notice is hereby given that the several buoys in the North, Nab, and Queen's Channels are removed, and the beacons cut down accordingly: and further notice will be given as soon as it is judged proper to replace the same.[123]

The order to replace them was not given until the 21st, and up to that time the estuary remained unnavigable.*

Hockless, Quarter Master in the *Sandwich*, one of the most violent of the Delegates, was furious at the destruction of the buoys, and swore that he would sail the Fleet out, marks or no marks: indeed the mutineers were so enraged against Trinity House that they promised to hang the first Elder Brother they could catch. This was somewhat unfortunate for Captain Calvert, one of that Brotherhood, for just at that time he was coming up the river from Broadstairs, returning from a little pleasure trip in his yacht, enjoying the summer season. With a disconcerting reversal of prospects, he was brought on board the *Sandwich*, and instantly taken to the ward-room to be tried for his life. The Delegates, however, so bloodthirsty in word, were charmed by

---

* When all was well again, Trinity House presented the Admiralty with a bill for £1260, 0s. 3d.

"the openness and manliness of his conversation and manner," and let him go on condition that he told them what the state of the public mind was. Calvert did tell them, unflinchingly. The whole country was against them, he said, and they would certainly be brought to "condign punishment." He was immediately ordered off the ship, but on the quarter-deck the kidnapped masters who were to pilot the Fleet out clutched him by the sleeve to ask advice. What should they do? They were threatened with hanging if they did not obey orders, and there were no marks. "If you do carry them out," Calvert said bluntly, "you will certainly be hanged," upon which the mutineers hustled the worthy Elder Brother down the gangway with a marked lack of politeness.[124]

To Pitt's fretted mind the removal of the sailing marks made an attack upon London almost certain. It was true that a force had been organised to meet a raid by the mutineers, but it was somewhat distressing to find that there were some five thousand men who ought to have been available, good seamen employed in easy jobs on shore—in the offices of the Revenue, Ordnance, East India Company, Waterman's Company, Press-gangs and Tenders, Victuallers and Bargemen to the Public Office and others—who, though liable to be impressed, refused to volunteer. They were not fighting men, they said, and had families to provide for.[125] In some consternation Pitt wrote to Spencer, on the evening of the 7th:

> In thinking over the circumstances respecting the ships at the Nore, I cannot help thinking it very probable that if the buoys being taken up prevent them going away, their next idea may be to force their passage up the river . . . probably if any attempt is made by the mutineers it will be on the first occasion that the tide serves after the term of fifty-four hours from this morning is expired.[126]

The vision of London cowering under the ravages of a horde of barbarians led by bloodthirsty Jacobins induced the Admiralty to order Sir Erasmus Gower, in his 84-gun ship, the *Neptune*, to prepare to attack the recalcitrant Fleet, supported by the volunteers eager for a tussle, who, valiant defenders of the City, were keyed up to a desperate fight against an invasion which was a figment of their fears.

On the morning of the 8th, Captain Knight went on board the *Montague*, and then to the other ships, carrying with him a bundle of bills and proclamations. The yards of all the ships were manned, cheers were given, and he was received with every dignity. On the *Sandwich* grog was again served as a mark of delighted respect.[127] He had returned the answer to the petition the night before; but now he brought news of the action the Government had taken, and copies of the King's proclamation of the 6th declaring the mutinous sailors to be rebels. The worsened position obviously called for some action on the part of the Delegates, who resolved that Parker should make a special tour of the Fleet in all pomp, to explain, to exhort and, possibly, to engineer some feasible plan. The future rested with themselves, since now they could look for no help from outside. The Government and the people were massed against them; Calvert had destroyed their last hope of public support; proclamations, perhaps spurious, had been sent them from the sailors at Spithead and Plymouth, expressing sadness at their behaviour, and adjuring them to return to duty;[128] while at Sheerness itself a demonstration against them had been staged. The loyal sailors of the *Espion*, *Clyde* and *Niger*, with those of the *Firm* floating gun-battery, which had escaped from the Fleet two or three days earlier, gathered together, about six hundred and fifty in all, and marched to Queenborough, while the band of the Norfolk Militia blared at their head. Further, they bore aloft their colours, and upon that of the *Niger* was blazoned in letters of gold beneath a crown, "Success, to a Good Cause."[129] Salvation, it was only too plain, could only come from within.

What could Parker do? He must himself have felt that his journey round the Fleet was a queer mixture of the loyal and the rebellious, with the Delegates using all their demagogic arts to exhort to stubborn resistance, while the bands incessantly blared out "God Save the King" and "Britons Strike Home"! The tirades and harangues on each ship seem to have been directed to explaining, or rather, ingeniously explaining away, the sense of the proclamation, which was now in everybody's hands, or, if it were not, could no longer be kept from common knowledge. When Appleyard, Quarter Gunner of the *Sandwich*, found Captain Wood of the *Hound* sloop reading out the proclamation to his men, he snatched the paper out of his hand, told the men that it was a mass of flummery, and, pointing to the clause excepting the ringleaders from pardon, declared that it would hang them all. Finding his audience the reverse of enthusiastic, this fiery Yorkshireman of twenty-two told them they were a packed of damned rascals who were led by the nose by their captain. His speech was not well received; and as he went off the ship, swearing he would have the *Sandwich* sink the sloop, one of the men shoved or struck him off a gun.[130]

Parker, nervous and volatile, was not the man for this tempestuous atmosphere. Even a stolid iron-nerved man would have found the position difficult. His attempts to arrive at any satisfactory end had failed dismally, and even if he privately believed that it would be better to submit, he was all the time forced from one irremediable step to another by his masters, the more extreme spirits who spread their fury from the *Inflexible*. Just as, apparently, the others did, when he read out the proclamation he glozed over the parts relating to pardon, and pointedly stressed those which declared the seamen traitors and rebels. On the *Ardent*, indeed, one of the officers broke in upon his reading to accuse him of selecting only such parts as suited him best, whereupon the men shouted out to the officer to read them the whole.

Parker had to allow it, remarking sourly "that the officers had too much to say,"[131] an observation which could not have added to the sailors' faith in their leaders.

In his extremity Parker was driven to adopt a ranting type of appeal; one catches the tone of a man who is not a born demagogue desperately striving to stir mob feelings. On the *Repulse* he declaimed:

> BRETHREN,
>
> I am obliged to you for your conduct. We have grievances which we wish to have redressed; we applied for the Lords of the Admiralty to come to the Nore, they only came to Sheerness, and we were not admitted to see them. Lord Spencer and his Aide de Camp only spoke to us through Admiral Buckner, which was no better than a speaking trumpet. We had sent Captain Knight to get our grievances redressed, but he returned without anything satisfactory. He brought news that we were all declared rebels to our country.
>
> Is there a rebel among you?

and when the men roared back "No!" he returned, "Then if we are not rebels to our country, our country are rebels to us."[132]

Sometimes he was even driven to try the effect of a personal appeal, little suited to a man of his wavering stamp, who, besides, had not been known to the men long enough to inspire their confidence. "Brothers," he said, to the men of the *Monmouth*:

> I have told you the contents of the King's proclamation, which ought to excite our indignation. It calls us *rebels*—are we so? (a cry from all sides, No! no!) Why, then, our countrymen are rebels to us in calling us so: [this part of the address must have been agreed upon beforehand] I say we are all honest men; I and my brother delegates are all united, and acting in the cause of humanity; and while life animates the heart of *Dick Parker*, he will be true to the cause.

Gregory supported him in commenting severely upon this aspect of the proclamation, and here perhaps the Delegates were on firm ground, for they, in common with all the men, were passionately eager not to be looked upon as rebels. They always declared that they would go to fight the enemy without a moment's hesitation; whatever their quarrel with authority, they were not traitors to their country. But the personal appeal was a mistake. Parker was no Duncan adored by his men, no Joyce who had earned their respect as an able leader. Besides, as a mere upstart, he had assumed a position which Joyce had never even hinted at, had usurped the position of Admiral of the Fleet, whether willingly or not, and this would naturally gall the sailors, filled with a strong sense of an ordained hierarchy. On the *Ardent* he even met with some personal sneers. Hotly rebutting a taunt that he had lined his own purse with the money collected for general purposes, he cried, "That is false; the fact is I owe my washerwoman eighteen pence, and have not even money to pay her"; upon which a jeering shout came from the crowd of men, "Why, then, you're a precious admiral indeed!"[133] There were enough ominous indications that any drastic concerted action would be difficult.

Nevertheless it was tried, for it seems to have been arranged that the Fleet, in spite of the removal of the buoys, should weigh anchor and set sail for the Texel, without, however, any precise object being set before the sailors. Moreover, though they might have faith in their leaders for the emergency of a strike, to follow them blindly as navigators was an altogether different adventure. The men of the *Ardent*, indeed, stated their firm resolve not to go to sea unless they had their captain on board. Yet, in spite of such considerations, on the morning of Friday, 9th, Parker made the signal for sailing; the fore-top sail of the *Sandwich* was loosed, and a gun was fired. A favourable wind was blowing fresh from the south-east; all the ships answered the signal, but strain his eyes as he might, Parker could see no sign of movement, no attempt made to unfurl sail, or even to clear hawse. If this is a clear proof that the seamen's only object was the redress of abuses, and not to injure their country, it was at the moment a conclusive sign that the confederacy was breaking up, that authority was challenged at the head, that, in short, the mutiny at the Nore had failed.

CHAPTER XVII

COLLAPSE

"THE Delegates," Duncan wrote to Spencer on the 8th, "seem strict disciplinarians, and if we was to adopt some of their regulations it would not be amiss." [134] Yet at about this time, sure symptom that all was not well, the Delegates awarded punishment not merely for drunkenness—the chief crime in the early days—but for failing to support the mutiny wholeheartedly. Most of the "criming" was now for "perjury," which meant faithlessness to the sweeping oath taken, or for speaking disrespectfully of the Delegates. If the charge was proved, the delinquent was subjected to ducking—an ordeal which could be very severe, the victim being weighted and plunged again and again into the sea until he was nearly drowned. Four seamen of the *Ardent* were severely flogged for disrespect. More significant still, an impulse towards wanton violence began to animate some of the seamen. Many officers were tarred and feathered, rowed through the Fleet, and then sent up the river to be dumped ignominiously at Gravesend. That the same uncomfortable disgrace befell the surgeon of one of the ships was, however, even at the time considered a piece of "wild justice," for he had been lying in his cabin for five weeks—drunk. On the *Monmouth*, a midshipman, the second master, and some other petty officers were tried for conspiracy, the midshipman being sentenced to two dozen lashes, the remainder to three. Since the second master was ill, he received only four lashes—but he had one side of his head shaved; a sergeant of marines was bereft of his hair besides receiving the lashes. All were put on shore after they had undergone their punishment. [135]

A good deal of furtive plotting must have gone on at

this time, a flitting of silent figures from deck to deck, a discreet knocking at officers' cabin doors, whispering of heads in close confabulation in dark corners of the orlop. The men were getting hungry, water was running ominously short. On the flagship herself the provisions were no more than a little biscuit and junk; her water was putrid, and so rigidly doled out that two sentries had to keep continual watch over it.[136] Nothing of good augury was happening to offset this state of doubt and discomfort, and it was morally impossible to sail away. Would it not, the sailors must have thought, be better to risk whatever punishment might be forthcoming if they surrendered now, than to wait till all pardon was withheld, and they were starved into submission?

On all the ships the officers were alert for a change of feeling; and at about three o'clock on the afternoon of the 9th, Lieutenant Robb, who was in charge of the *Leopard*, her captain having been sent on shore, decided that the change was marked enough for him to act. Seizing an opportunity when the Delegates were out of the ship, he gathered together in the ward-room the officers, petty officers and marines, with a few seamen he could rely on, and then and there primed, loaded, and manned the aftermost guns, which he ordered to be turned forward. Then, bursting open the ward-room door, thus unmasking his battery which now commanded the main deck, he and his party, well armed, flung themselves upon the surprised seamen, drove them together, and called upon them to surrender. In the immediate tumult which ensued all over the ship a small band led by an officer scuttled down to the lower deck, seized the foremost guns, which were pointed aft, and put them out of action by pouring vinegar into the vents; and at the same time a third detachment promptly swarmed aloft and loosened the topsails, which they sheeted home in no time. As soon as this was done, the officer who had disabled the lower-deck guns cut the cable, which he had rushed up from below to stand by, alert for the crucial moment. All was over in a flash; the struggle had been short and decisive, but not without damage: seven men were wounded, one of them, a midshipman, mortally—and the ship was making sail up-stream.[137]

Almost immediately the rest of the Fleet was alive to what was going on, and with hardly an interval the *Repulse* followed the example of the *Leopard*, there, too, the Delegates being conveniently out of the way. The other ships at once began to open fire on the escaping traitors. The *Leopard*, however, got away without harm, though when she ran into the left bank of the river near Leigh she was still within range of the Fleet, and was under a "smart fire" for some time. Luckily it was not long before she was floated off, and she made her way to the Lower Hope by nightfall, where Lieutenant Robb put eighteen of the leading mutineers in irons. The *Repulse* was not so lucky, for by the time she had got under way, counter-measures were being taken against the deserters. Parker at once had himself rowed from the *Sandwich* in a boat from the *Ardent*, and as he went was cheered by the men, himself crying back in answer that he "was going on board the *Director* to get a spring on her cable, and would send her and them [the *Repulse* and her crew] to the devil." It seemed as though he well might, since by this time the *Repulse* was aground, as her pilot had foreseen she would be; he had in vain told her loyal crew, impatient to get away, that the tide did not serve. Parker flew on board the *Director*, to find that her crew had already got a spring on her cable so as to bring her guns to bear on the stranded ship. But then, the guns laid, ready for destruction, a sense of his responsibility for life and death came acutely upon him. He ordered all hands to be called, and when his order was disregarded he shouted out as loud as he could, addressing anyone within reach of his voice, beseeching them to consider what a dreadful thing it would be for one brother to fire upon another. He begged for a boat in which to bear a flag of truce to the *Repulse*, an action which he was sure would save an effusion of blood: he did not mind, he declared, what happened to himself, even if he lost his life, so long as he could save so many others'.

But he was not in control of the Fleet; he was not even listened to: he was refused the boat and the flag of truce. He then asked that the *Director* should be taken alongside the heeling vessel, but he could hardly have hoped that any-one would pay him any attention. It is not certain whether up to that point the *Director* had fired at all, though other ships seem to have done so. But now, when the *Repulse* fired a gun from the larboard side of the quarter-deck, Parker's first impulsive emotion to send the deserting ship to hell was released. "They have returned fire," he yelled, and ordered the *Director* to shoot. That command at least was obeyed. He then had himself taken to the *Monmouth*, where his excitement seems to have made him frantic: if he could not lead the men where he wanted them to go, at least he would prove himself willing to lead them along the path of their own choice. Was he not their elected champion? He behaved frenziedly, and himself worked at the guns of the *Monmouth*: he thrust a bar into one of the muzzles as well as the cannon-ball, as if one missile would not be enough; and when a seaman tried to stop him from doing so, he hurled him back with a blow on the chest. All the unbalanced side of his nature came uppermost. According to the evidence of one of the sailors at his trial,

He ordered Vance [the mutineer captain] to get our stream cables up, and to bend to our stream anchor. Vance said he could not do it. " Why, damn it," replied the prisoner, " slip your bowers and go alongside the *Repulse*, and send her to hell where she belongs, and show her no quarter in the least." He then said . . . he would go on board one of the other ships belonging to the fleet, and despatch her after the *Leopard* to send the *Leopard* to hell likewise.

For over an hour and twenty minutes every ship in the Fleet which could bring her guns to bear on the "poor devoted *Repulse*" blazed away at her as she lay aground. Her men worked furiously to lighten her: "the water in the hold was started, the casks stove, and a strong party sent to the pumps." At last, as the tide rose, she floated, and as she did, Parker shook his fist at her and shouted, "Damn her, she's off!" It was not until all was over, and the ships had escaped, that he retired to the *Sandwich*.[138]

The sulphurous affair had been watched with intense anxiety from Sheerness, which was in a state of siege, cowering in expectation of the attack which the seamen's petition to the King had seemed to threaten.[139] The battering of the *Repulse* seemed terrible, but in actual fact she had not been very seriously damaged: the only casualty was to a lieutenant, whose leg was shot away. The hull was practically unscathed, though the rigging was very much cut about. It seems as though the mutineers had deliberately aimed high. This is certainly true of those in the *Agamemnon*, which had wished to follow the *Leopard*, but had been restrained by fear of the *Montague*, whose guns, they were asked to notice, were pointing into her. Brenton, who had as near as a touch shot one of the Delegates from the latter ship, but had just managed to control his foolhardy impulse, was actually aloft cutting loose the topsails, sure that the ship was deserting, when the crew decided after all not to slip the cable, but to fire guns at the *Repulse* in sign of adherence to the mutiny. It was all a feint, however, for they asked the officers to lay the guns, knowing they would be careful to aim wide of the mark.[140]

As soon as he had anchored, the commander of the *Leopard* sent an account to the Admiralty:

H.M.S. *Leopard* at the Lower Hope,
9 *June* 1797.

It is with the greatest pleasure I have to acquaint you for their Lordships' information of the arrival at this place of H.M.S. *Leopard* left under my command. You will be pleased to state to their Lordships that having good reason to suppose that the greater part of the crew deluded into a state of mutiny were willing to return to their allegiance and accept H.M.'s most gracious pardon, could their honest intentions be brought into action by a well concerted plan, I seized therefore on the opportunity which occurred this evening of the Delegates being out of the ship, and having previously armed the marines, petty officers and everybody in whom confidence and dependence could be placed, and being ably assisted and supported by the Lieutenants and other officers of the ship, the hands were turned up, and my intentions made known and insisted upon. A party held out and opposed us; I am sorry to say that in the scuffle seven men were wounded. The whole, however, were soon reduced to order. The cables were cut, and notwithstanding a continued fire from the neighbouring ships, we carried her in safety to this place. I am happy to add that our good example was soon followed by H.M.S. *Repulse,* which we have reason to suppose got safe into Sheerness harbour. But for further particulars I must refer their Lordships to Lieut. Ellis whom I have judged necessary to send express with this account.[141]

This reticent report of a daring action must have filled Spencer with joy. That two ships of prime importance, the first of fifty, the second of sixty-four guns, both of the Yarmouth squadron, had returned to duty in spite of dangerous opposition showed plainly enough that the mutiny was tottering. There would be no need to strike; he had only to wait.

Yet there was one man at least who was not of this opinion. Fretted by inaction, he proposed with his own hand to aim a thrust at the monster he considered as the head and fount of all the disgraceful trouble. This was Captain J. W. T. Dixon of the *Gorgon*, at Woolwich, a ship whose officers were so stern for duty that a few weeks later the crew mutinied and were eager to hang two of them.*[142]

* Dixon was immediately transferred to the *Raven* brig. Ad. 35/721.
Gorgon Pay Book.

Dixon made the incredible suggestion to Spencer, that if the First Lord could smuggle him aboard the *Sandwich*, he would take it upon himself to murder Parker! This infamous notion was on a far lower level ethically than anything the mutineers had put forward in their most distracted moments; but Dixon wrote that "he had so completely made up his mind to the result of the assassination, that his Lordship could be assured that he would be happy in performing that which appeared to him of such public advantage !" Spencer, scribbling notes for the answer to such a degrading proposal, replied with a biting irony which it is to be feared passed by the crazy mind of the recipient:

Private, 10*th June*.

Say that I give him great credit for his very spirited offer, but that I trust it will not be necessary to have recourse to so very desperate a measure on this occasion.[143]

Spencer, whatever his faults may have been, was after all a worthy child of the finest traditions both of family and of the service.

But if time was in favour of the authorities, it was clear to the Delegates that it was definitely against themselves. The Fleet was breaking up. That the store-ship *Serapis* should have slipped out of their clutches a few days earlier did not portend much, for she had not joined the mutiny, but had been captured and forced to adhere; that some merchant ships still held up by the blockade should have bettered the occasion of the fracas on the 9th to weigh anchor and slip through, was only to be expected; but that two of their main supports from the North Sea Fleet should have turned their coats was only too mournfully significant. And at about midnight of the 9th the *Ardent* also had stolen away to Sheerness, exchanging a few desultory shots with the *Monmouth*. Whatever was to be done must be done at once, and the only thing to do was to see if they could not at the eleventh hour get some sort of favourable terms in exchange for submission. Accordingly, on the 10th, Parker wrote to Captain Knight, whom the Delegates felt they could trust:

SIR,

I am commanded by the Delegates of the Fleet to inform you that you are authorised to proceed to London and to represent to our most Gracious Sovereign, that the Seamen of the Fleet at the Nore are determined on receiving his most Gracious pardon to return to their duty, with this proviso, that no officers sent from the ships be returned without the consent of the ship's company, and that they will trust to our most Gracious Sovereign for redressing our grievances in the way most agreeable to His Majesty.

I remain, Sir,

Your most humble servant,

RICHARD PARKER,

President.[144]

Knight was perfectly ready to undertake this new commission; it was no fun being on board ship, and no doubt he would be able to claim expenses from the Admiralty, as he had for his previous trip, to the tune of £11, 15s. But before leaving he was presented with a document:

SIR,

We the ships' company named in the margin [all the ships are named, including the *Sandwich*] take the liberty of laying our present grievances before you being resolved to invest you with full power to have our unhappy affairs settled being determined not to lay here any longer and have our enemies prejudice our beloved King and Country. We now being willing at any time to meet our enemies, and there is no doubt if ever we do fall in with an enemy to our loving King and Country there is no doubt but we will let them know that we are Englishmen and men which are true to our Country.

 (i) That His Majesty will be pleased to give an indemnification for all offences past signed by His Majesty.

 (ii) That all Wages and Bounty now due may be paid up as usual.

(iii) The *Montagu* to be repaired or docked unless the Dutch fleet are at sea.

(iv) That all the ships' company wherever they are with the officers now on board may be kept together and not separated.

We wish the officers that are offensive to us may be sent elsewhere to serve. We pray that all people of our ships that may be taken up on suspicion of being traitors may have the same indulgence granted as we have. We pray most sincerely that the Marines may have such encouragement as will satisfy them. That all men who may have deserted His Majesty's service prior to this date may be called in and pardoned.

The above delivered in presence of all the officers by the company of the *Montagu* requesting Captain Knight will speedily lay before His Most Gracious Majesty this humble request.

Dated on board the *Montagu*, the 10th of June 1797.

THE COMPANY OF THE *Montagu*.

To Captain John Knight.[145]

Probably they hoped that a new asseveration of loyalty would help them; but at all events they would put it on record, for what wounded them most throughout the whole "unhappy affair" was the stigma of treachery fastened upon them. Their new terms, obviously, were the least they could, not now demand, but beg for. They were again throwing themselves at their Sovereign's feet, giving up every claim, asking merely for pardon, and that they might not have once more set over them officers who no doubt would be only too ready to wreak a horrible revenge upon them. One might think that the monarch might be moved by this appeal if it reached him, which most likely it never did; and in any case he was hardly in a mood to listen to pleas for kindness, even to this last piteous appeal. The moment Knight arrived in London with his message, a Cabinet council was held, and in the evening an Admiralty Board sat to consider the subject.[146]

The events which took place inside the crumbling Fleet for the next two or three days were exciting enough: the mutiny was in dissolution, fierce arguments and struggles on every ship betrayed a mixture of panic and stubborn resolve. Buckner, intently on the watch, could see little and judge less; the fact that on the 10th all the ships temporarily struck their red flags and hoisted either the blue "signal of agreeableness" or white ones [147] merely indicated that the Fleet considered a truce to have been called for Knight to go on shore. On the other hand, the fact that trade was allowed to pass up the river unhindered was an encouraging sign. Buckner also gathered that the men of the *Hound* were trying to escape, and that thirty had been transferred to the *Sandwich*, where also violent dissensions amounting to "dreadful contests" were popularly reported to be taking place.[148] On the Sunday, for some unknown reason, the flags throughout the Fleet were flown at half mast.

The Admiralty was jubilant; things were shaping well, and Duncan had been reinforced not only by some ships from the Channel Fleet, and Admiral Makharoff's Russian squadron, but also by some of his own hitherto mutinous ships, such as the *Glatton*, which had never gone to the Nore. Convinced that some of the sailors would try to escape, they were on the look-out for deserters, and sent the following orders to Admiral Sir Thomas Pasley:

11 *June* 1797.

I am commanded by my Lords Commissioners of the Admiralty to signify their directions to you to repair to South End in Essex, where you will take the most effectual steps, in concert with the officer commanding H.M. military forces in that neighbourhood, for preventing the escape of any part of the crews of the said ships [*i.e.* at the Nore] which their Lordships have reason to think will be attempted, and to follow such further orders as they may judge it necessary to furnish you with. . . . It is only necessary for me to add, that in any communications which may take place, no encouragement is at any time to be given them that any proposition short of unconditional submission can be listened to by their Lordships.

E.N. [NEPEAN].[149]

The last sentence reflected the answer to the message carried by Knight, an answer which Buckner was ordered to convey to the crew of the *Montague*, in a letter which Nepean sent him on the same date by Knight, who returned to Sheerness that evening.

This reply was the final blow which shattered the organisation of the mutiny. So far as can be gathered, the Delegates now resolved to allow the officers to go on shore, to permit each ship to do as seemed best to it, and to let any further deserting ship go unmolested. But even now the matter hung in the balance. Thus on the morning of the 12th, although there were still twenty-two ships at the Nore, only two of them flew the red flag of defiance in the morning; but by three o'clock the number had been increased to eight, the remainder flying their proper colours. So it was reported that day by Sir Edward Knatchbull, with some command on shore, when he wrote to Mr. Speaker Addington (afterwards Lord Sidmouth) from the Headquarters at Faversham. At the same time he told the sad news that Pasley had had no luck, for only one runaway sailor had been captured. The worst feature of the situation for Knatchbull was that the revenue sailors (who were not fighting men, and had families to think of) showered such abuse on his troopers, that he could hardly keep them quiet under the fusillade of vituperation ! He had to see to it that the mate of the *Active* cutter was bound over to keep the peace, so deeply was the interference of soldiers in naval affairs resented.[150]

A note Knatchbull made in giving a list of the ships flying the red flag—" *Belliqueux* and *Director* moored on the bow of the *Sandwich* to sink her if occasion requires "—is significant of the rent state of the Fleet. Parker was evidently arguing for surrender, but those who opposed it were not going to allow the *Sandwich*, the centre of what remained of their organisation, to topple the whole structure down by going over to the enemy. Yet bit by bit, openly or furtively, the array of mutinous ships of war dwindled away. On the night of Monday-Tuesday the *Standard* slipped her cable and made up-river, whereupon her leading Delegate, Wallace, a man of some education, shot himself to escape his fate. She was followed by the *Agamemnon*, *Nassau*, *Vestal* and *Isis*, which, having springs on their cables, made their way out from the middle of the Fleet; and by one o'clock on the 13th all were anchored opposite Block House Fort near Gravesend. The *Montague*, *Lion* and *Director* were expected to follow.[151]

But the change over on these ships had not taken place without vigorous, and sometimes dangerous, opposition from those who were still loyal to the ideas for which the sailors had mutinied. A battle which must have been typical of many others bloodied the decks of the *Swan* sloop, once so hotly mutinous that she had been nicknamed "the little *Inflexible*" to show her honourable likeness to the big ship where the trouble was chiefly fomented. On Monday, the 12th, some of the Delegates went on board her to find out what the feelings of the men were, and mustered them, together with the master and the surgeon, so as to ask those who wished to adhere to "the Sailors' Cause" to go to the starboard side of the quarter-deck. To their horror, when the master and surgeon promptly moved over to the opposite side, they were followed by more than half the crew; whereupon the Delegates and their supporters immediately rushed below, collected weapons, and leaped back on deck to drive their weaker brethren into the boats, some being slightly wounded during the tussle.

The ejected part of the crew then made for the *Isis*, which had struck the red flag and was going up the Thames ; but when they climbed on board they found the officers and men furiously contesting the command of the ship. The men were victorious, and forced the officers with their small party to retreat to the poop, where they made another determined stand, to be eventually dislodged and compelled to slide down the stern-ladders into the boats. Even so they did not manage to get away, for they were fired upon, recaptured, and hauled on board, where some of them were put in irons. Many were wounded in this affray, and three— a midshipman, a gunner's mate, and an ordinary seaman— were killed. But the next day feeling had once again veered, perhaps because of the rumour that Sir Erasmus Gower was about to attack. The men resigned the ship into the hands of the captain, who was on board, and the *Isis*, as we have seen, meekly followed the surrendering flotilla to Gravesend.[152]

It was now transparently clear to every one that the mutiny was, to all purposes good or bad, at an end; and the most fiery leaders, accepting the fact, decided to make their escape. As early as the 11th a large boat-load of seamen, under full sail, had been chased by a revenue cutter, but had had the heels of her and got away.[153] Thus on the 12th the authorities sent a ship to cruise off the mouth of the Thames to capture any men who might try to escape by sea ; and on the 14th, hearing that Parker was on board a Danish vessel, or alternatively was intending to slip away with other ringleaders in the *Pylades*, the Duke of Portland, as Secretary of State, publicly offered a reward of £500 "to any person or persons who shall apprehend, or cause to be apprehended, the said Richard Parker." "Richard Parker," the office added under Portland's signature,

> is about thirty years of age; wears his own hair, which is black, untied, though not cropt; about five feet nine or ten inches high, has rather a prominent nose, dark eyes and complexion, and thin visage; is generally slovenly dressed in a plain blue half-worn coat, and a whitish or light-coloured waistcoat, and half-boots.[154]

Would he be caught? Had he escaped? It would be impossible to answer the question until the *Sandwich* came in.

But so far the *Sandwich* had not come in. Soon she would be almost alone, for ship after ship was leaving her to an ever more solitary ingloriousness. On the same day that the *Standard* and the other ships sailed up to Gravesend, the *Grampus* sent a message on shore asking her captain to resume command. Still the *Sandwich* did not move, though she sent a flag of truce to Sheerness begging Buckner to come on board, which he refused to do.[155] In the afternoon the *Champion* sailed in under the guns of the fort, and in the evening the redoubtable *Monmouth* bore down from the Nore. But she was so feared, so little faith was put in her good intention, that every preparation was made to subdue her by force. The guns of the fort were manned and primed, ready to open, while the *Ardent* drew up on the opposite side to be able to catch her between two fires. She had, however, come to surrender; yet it was with difficulty that the men of the *Repulse*, remembering the gruelling they had had on the night of their escape, could be restrained from going to take their revenge. Still the *Sandwich* did not come in, though under cover of darkness the *Brilliant* and some others joined the repentant ships snuggling close under the protecting fortress of Sheerness.[156]

But in the meanwhile what was happening to Richard Parker?

CHAPTER XVIII

THE END

THE ill-starred man exalted to the nominal leadership of a mass of people, with whom indeed he sympathised up to a point, but whose extreme elements he was forced to obey, found himself more and more a wisp tossed about on the surface of other people's tumultuous, uncertain and even conflicting passions. On the ships around him desperate action was being suggested by those who thought any fate preferable to surrender: better, some felt, to die under the guns of Gravesend than to submit, and were opposed by others, less forward perhaps in the mutiny, and therefore with less to fear, who advised quietly sailing into Sheerness. For a day or two a struggle of flags went on, sometimes the red predominating, sometimes the blue or white, while occasionally the Union colours were noticed by the watchers on either shore. Would Parker escape? they wondered. But he did not bolt, either because he was baffled in his attempts, or resigned to his fate: it is even possible that he thought he might be able to clear himself.

Even in the early days, as we have seen, the *Sandwich* was by no means solid in support of the mutiny; others besides Parker may have thought there was too much talk of hanging. Perhaps if the *Sandwich* had not been the flagship of the mutineers—as well as of the authorities—she might have yielded sooner than the 12th, on which day, so to speak, she began to surrender, for she released her officers, hitherto confined. The next day, however, the crew repented of this step and once more shut the officers up; but Parker himself let them out again on the 13th, though he forbade them to talk with the people. Then, on a suggestion of Parker's, while the committee-men were holding a conference in the ward-room, a number of petty officers went on shore with Lieutenant Mott to fetch further copies of the King's proclamation of pardon to all those—ringleaders excepted—who would give themselves up. Then Parker, mustering the crew, asked them whether they would prefer to continue under his orders, or return under the command of the officers. The men, sick of the whole business, and hungry as well, cried out almost unanimously, "To the officers," loudly incited by Black Jack Campbell, who, having been flogged under Parker's rule, saw no special benefit in it. Davis, however, the "much trusted" mutineer captain of the *Sandwich*, supported by one other, objected "The ships astern will fire on us"; but he was ignored. Some of the Delegates then attempted to hoist a boat to escape in, and were prevented by the rest of the crew, but Parker does not seem to have been among those who wished to run away. On the contrary, he led the three cheers which set the stamp of approval on the seamen's choice; and when Lieutenant Flatt demanded the keys of the magazine and small arms, he handed them over, saying, "I give up the charge of the ship to you."

The officers at once decided to run the vessel into Sheerness, but when they gave orders to cast off, Parker ran up to Flatt, crying, "If you offer to unmoor, the ships astern will fire on us." He was still in terror of the paramount *Inflexible*, whose attitude was threatening enough, as was that of the *Montague*. Flatt bluntly answered that he did not care a rap if they did fire, and ordered the fore-sails to be loosed. The deflated president, again unstable at a crisis, could not make up his mind as to how he should behave. First he asked Flatt to confine him; but when that officer told him he would order him to a cabin and put two sentinels over him, he refused to go, and insisted on helping to man the capstan. Once the ship was under weigh, Flatt consulted with Mott as to whether they should seize Parker on the

spot, or wait till they got to Sheerness. Agreeing on immediate action, they went up to him on the quarter-
deck. Mott caught hold of him by the collar, Parker
offering no resistance, and sent him to a lieutenant's
cabin, over which he set a guard of two trustworthy
men.[157]

It was now Tuesday evening, and the ship, owing to
weather conditions, could not make Sheerness that night;
it was not until three o'clock the next morning that she
drifted in to port, and then Flatt went to Parker's cabin to
put him in irons. At about half-past six the Admiral's boat,
commanded by the coxswain, and carrying a picket guard
of the West York Militia, rowed out to the ship, an action
which for some obscure reason was considered "pregnant
with danger," some doubt—though how there could have
been a doubt it is hard to see—still existing in the minds of
the authorities as to what the attitude of the *Sandwich* was.
The officers were in evidence waiting to receive the boat,
but otherwise the decks were almost deserted, and significantly silent. As soon as Parker heard the boat, which he
knew must be coming for him, he asked for a guard of four
seamen, for he was conscious that many of the sailors were
now incensed against him, and would hurt him if they could.
He was learning the bitter lesson that success alone, and not
good intentions, however clearly they may shine in action,
can earn the gratitude of human beings. No doubt he felt
the lesson acutely. After all, it was *his* neck that was in
danger, not theirs. "Remember," he was to write a few
days after,

> never to make yourself the busy body of the lower classes, for they are
> cowardly, selfish, and ungrateful; the least trifle will intimidate them, and
> him whom they have exalted one moment as their Demagogue, the next
> they will not scruple to exalt upon the gallows. I own it is with pain I
> make such a remark to you, but the truth demands it. I have experi-
> mentally proved it, and very soon am to be made the example of it.[158]

In this mood Parker was taken in charge by a party of eight or ten militiamen; his hands were tied together behind his back, and he was led very quietly to the waiting boat.

It was a curious freight that made swiftly for the expectant shore. In the forepart of the boat the militiamen sat with their loaded muskets held upright in their hands, and faced the stern in which sat, or rather lay, the now degraded president. He looked towards the bows; behind him was the coxswain with his knees upon his prisoner's shoulders so that the latter seemed to be lying back between his legs, while, seated, a lieutenant of the flagship held a drawn sword above his head. These elaborate precautions were unnecessary; the man was bound and unarmed, and had no hope, no intention, of evading his fate. A seething crowd, in which civilians mingled sparsely with soldiers, waited on the landing-place, agog to see him; and as he was led past the top of the stairs they burst into hoots and hisses. Parker, who had so far been as calm and dignified as physical circumstances would allow, was cruelly put out by this hostile demonstration. "Don't hoot me!" he begged. "It is not my fault. I will clear myself."

At the guard-house his pockets were searched, the officials' only reward being a cold diary of events (they had hoped for evidence of sedition), and he was then thrust into one of the cells under the chapel of the garrison, a place some ten feet square, provided with thick iron doors. It was known as the "Black Hole," since not the slightest ray of light could enter it. After a few hours he was taken to the Commissioner's house to be examined by magistrates; but they did no more than prove identity, and make out a warrant to have him incarcerated in Maidstone gaol. Thus at about midday he was set in a post-chaise between two stout constables of Sheerness, his elbows tied together at the back with a rope. An escort of some twenty men of the West Yorks, headed by a subaltern, took the humiliated but outwardly serene prisoner "very slowly" to his final lodging on the land.[159]

On the 15th, then, once the *Sandwich* had come in, only three ships—the *Inflexible*, *Montague* and *Belliqueux*—remained at the Great Nore,* but even they flew the Union instead of "the flag of contumacy." It was evident that they would have given in, but

> with a creditable consistency and courage, [they] remonstrated against the punishment of their delegates, and refused to surrender, until they were assured of a general pardon; for, they argued, the criminal intention was common to all, but in extent and degree, although the necessity of the case obliged them to select the best in energy and intellect to give unity to their purpose, and effect to their designs.[160]

Since this forgiveness was not forthcoming, some of the Delegates made up their minds to save their necks, as a few from other ships (notably, one suspects, the *Swan*) had already done. Three boat-loads of mutineers put off from the *Inflexible* and rowed to Faversham, where nearly twenty of them seized hold of a small ship called the *Good Intent*, sailed away for Calais, and landed there, honourably sending the boat back in charge of two boys.[161] It was reported that some of the men of the *Montague* also were able to get away, and found refuge in Holland.[162] Meanwhile at Sheerness, captains and subordinate officers went through the loyal vessels beating up for volunteers to man the gunboats, with which it was intended to attack the last refractory ships if they should not come in within the next two days.[163] But the following day, the 16th, these three ships finally surrendered. On Friday morning the *Montague* sent her committee-men on shore, and as each ship gave herself up the Delegates were seized and imprisoned. In some cases parties of soldiers were sent on board to prevent any further outbreak. The great mutiny was ended at last.

* According to Gill, Bligh's ship, the *Director*, was the last to come in; but the evidence is conflicting.

As soon as the *Sandwich* had been brought to anchor, Mosse, who had been absent from her for the last few days, went on board to resume command; and shortly afterwards Buckner's flag broke at the fore to the cheers of the seamen. While the prisons were gradually being filled to overflowing, till the *Eolus* hulk had to be requisitioned to house the surplus, every effort was made to bring things to normal; victualling was resumed without a hitch, and enquiries were pressed on. Lord Keith at once went on board the flagship to begin investigations, while two magistrates were sent down from London to help in the collection of evidence, and also to discover the secret causes of the trouble. They were to lay bare the link with Corresponding Societies and Jacobins. One of them was Aaron Graham of Hatton Garden. He was not at all pleased with this new commission, which he strongly suspected of being another wild goose chase. He had better things to do, and when the affair seemed to threaten his arrangements on the 16th, wrote to his office correspondent, King:

> I shall go into the country for a day or two (as my hay wants cutting) unless you forbid me by a note this evening. If you really want me don't mind my hay, but believe me always at moment's notice,
> Your faithful humble servant,
> A. GRAHAM.[164]

Alas for his hay; it went uncut, at least for the time being, for on that day he and Daniel Williams, magistrate at Lambeth, appeared at Sheerness, and it was they who went through Parker's preliminary examination.

The authorities rushed forward the trial of the chief fiend, as they thought him, and on the 19th issued the order for his court martial, appointing Admiral Sir Thomas Pasley to be President of the Court. Nepean, in a letter which does not read very pleasantly, egged him indecently on to convict the accused:

> You may prove almost anything you like against him, for he has been guilty of everything that's bad. Admiral Buckner will be a material evidence to state the proceedings which took place on his visit to the *Sandwich*, and which, indeed, of itself appears to be enough to dispose of a dozen scoundrels of Parker's description,

and it is to be feared that Nepean missed the rebuke neatly implied in a letter which Pasley wrote him after the trial:

> MY DEAR SIR,
>
>   The conviction of the villain Parker must have been so very dear to you at the Admiralty that the place and time of his execution might have been previously settled.[165]

At all events, the Court, with Pasley as President, and Mosse as prosecutor, sat on the 22nd in full pomp on board the *Neptune* in Long Reach.

The result was a foregone conclusion. As Parker wrote in his last missive: "I have reason to think the Civil Power would have acquitted me, but by the Articles of War my destruction was irremidiable [*sic*]"; but it is doubtful if even the most humane civil court could have pronounced a sentence less than that of death. For weeks Parker had been the ostensible head of a mutiny which had threatened the country's ruin, and during which many acts deserving of death, even under the civil code, had been committed. As anybody who has ever sat on a court martial knows, such tribunals are scrupulously fair, and this one was no exception. Not only was Parker allowed to call what witnesses he pleased, the Court even insisted on his bringing in Northesk and Knight to witness in favour of his character, and of his courteous behaviour to them: he was advised to withdraw a question damaging to him, even after the answer had been given; he was allowed extra time to prepare his defence.

Throughout his trial he faced his accusers collected and dignified, foreseeing the end, unfolding his defence in a speech which did not lack the eloquence of simplicity:

As I have been at sea from my youth, to the knowledge of one of the honourable members of this court, I hope nothing can be expected from me but plain facts. I cannot be expected to dress up my defence in that pompous language which a lawyer might have done could I have procured a lawyer's constant attendance.

In the first place I have to return thanks to this honourable Court for the great indulgence allowed me by giving me a sufficient time to defend myself against the heavy charges brought against me. Nothing but a consciousness of the integrity of my intentions, and a knowledge that I only entered into it after it had commenced, with a view to endeavouring to stop the fatal spirit I saw too predominant in the Fleet, could have supported me during the examination of so many witnesses against me. . . . I may be asked how I was the person pitched on. The answer is that the Delegates of the Fleet insisted, and as an individual, in the state the Fleet was in, it was impossible for me to refuse their commands, but I again solemnly declare that I knew nothing of the Mutiny until it broke out. . . . Conscious that I have prevented a number of evil consequences which would have insued, at the frequent hazard of my life, I can wait with calmness the decision of this honourable Court.[166]

He pleaded consistently that he had done all he could to prevent excesses; without him, and some of the other Delegates, he declared, there would have been a bloody descent upon the land: he had been compelled to act as the real instigators of the mutiny (the escaped men of the *Inflexible?*) had ordered him to act. No doubt he overstated his case when he said he had become president only to bring the mutiny to an end. Yet it is probable that he thought that with a moderate leader a solution similar to the one at Spithead might have been reached: that would indeed be to bring the mutiny to an end; but after the fruitless visit of the Board it was too late to resign. In any case the witnesses he called did not clear him of participating in the bombardment of the *Repulse*. Something of what he said was true; but even if all of it had been truth sworn and attested, his position at the head of the mutiny made his sentence indeed "irremidiable." On hearing it he remained perfectly composed, saying only to an astonished Court:

I have heard your sentence—I shall submit to it without a struggle—I feel thus because I am sensible of the rectitude of my intentions. Whatever offences may have been committed, I hope *my* life will be the *only* sacrifice. I trust it will be thought a sufficient atonement. Pardon, I beseech you, the other men; they will return with alacrity to their duty.

For the last time Parker preached moderation, and once more without result.

Pasley, not alone among members of the Court, wished him to be hung in chains as a more horrible example; and the King, whom Parker's wife, summoned in haste from Scotland, had uselessly petitioned on the 23rd, agreed with this grisly point of view:

The offence of which Richard Parker has been convicted [he wrote to Spencer on the 27th] is of so heinous and dangerous a nature that I can scarcely suppose there can be any legal objection, after confirming the sentence for his being hanged, to order his body to be hung in chains on the most conspicuous land in sight of the ships at the Nore. Earl Spencer has therefore very properly directed the legality of hanging the body in chains to be enquired into, and if it can be done is to order it to be effected.[167]

Whether it was found that the proceeding would be illegal, or that it was feared the step might provoke fresh murmurings among the sailors, or inspire a riot on land, the mutineers were spared the sight of their dead leader rotting in the wind.

At six o'clock on the morning of the 30th, Parker was awakened from a peaceful sleep on the *Sandwich*, where he had passed the night. After the barber had attended him, by his request, he dressed himself in a suit of mourning which he had been given by a friend, the waistcoat only being lacking; and having made a good breakfast, he drew up a will, leaving his wife the reversion of a small estate he said he was heir to. To those around him he declared himself deeply sorry that he had brought the country to the verge of calamity by fomenting the mutiny, but again insisted that he had had no connection whatever with any seditious persons, and once more maintained that but for him the ships would have been taken into enemy ports. He seems to have forgotten his own order to sail—which had been ignored.

At half-past eight he was told that the chaplain of the *Sandwich*, the stout-hearted Hatherall, was ready to pray with him on the quarter-deck, where he went at once, bareheaded. Just for an instant, when he arrived there, he lost his colour, but soon recovered, and bowed to the officers. Being given a chair, he sat down, and let his eye travel calmly over the marines under arms encircling the deck, beyond to the ships thronged with sailors paraded to see him die, and perhaps to the Isle of Grain, where a scaffolding had been put up so that the civilian populace should not be denied the pleasure of witnessing his end. After a few minutes he got up, told Hatherall he was ready, and asked him to read, besides the two psalms the chaplain had chosen, the 51st, which begins, "Have mercy upon me, O God, after thy great goodness; according to the multitude of thy mercies, do away mine offences." He recited each alternate verse in a clear, steady voice. While he was still praying, the nine o'clock half-hour warning gun was fired from the *Espion*, but he gave no sign of emotion on hearing it.

When the prayers were finished he asked if he might have a glass of white wine, which was immediately given him, upon which he drank "first to the salvation of my soul, and next to the forgiveness of all my enemies." The gesture was perhaps a trifle theatrical, but it is easier to die if you can act a part to yourself. He then asked Mosse if he would shake hands—a symbol of mutual forgiveness, or of human fellow-feeling—which the captain of the *Sandwich* did not refuse; and Parker's arms now being bound, a solemn procession moved from the quarter-deck to the forecastle. As he went up the scaffold he asked Mosse if he might be allowed to speak, adding hastily as he saw a look of hesitation on his captain's face, "I am not going, sir, to address the ship's company. I wish only to declare that I acknowledge the justice of the sentence under which I suffer, and I hope that my death may be deemed a sufficient atonement, and save the lives of others." He then asked for a minute in which to collect himself, saying after a moment, "I am ready." The halter was adjusted round his neck, and as soon as the cap was drawn over his face he walked firmly to the end of the scaffold, where, dropping the handkerchief, he thrust his hands swiftly into his coat pockets. As he jumped off, the bow-gun fired, and the reeve-rope catching him, he was swung slowly up to the yard-arm. He died almost at once. After hanging an hour, his body was brought down, a death mask was taken,* and he was carried to the graveyard on shore. His wife, who that morning had made desperate efforts to get to the *Sandwich*, came during the night to remove the body, which she had buried a few days later in the ground of St. Mary Matfellon, White-chapel.[168]

Parker's prayer that he might be the only man to suffer was disregarded. Courts sat for weeks, during which over four hundred men were tried, of whom fifty-nine were condemned to death, though only twenty-nine were actually executed, among them, of course, Gregory and Hockless. Nine were ordered to be flogged, while twenty-nine were condemned to various terms of imprisonment,[169] many of them finding their way to the Marshalsea and the Cold Baths Field Prison, Clerkenwell. Even among the prisons of those days, before Howard's reforms had gone very far, the latter had an unsavoury reputation. "It is stated that certain of the prisoners . . . obtained some paper, but as they had no other writing materials, they had to use skewers as pens, and tobacco juice or blood as ink, in order to inform

* Shown at the R.N. Exhibition at Chelsea in 1891.

their friends of their condition,"[170] and some years later Southey considered that it exceeded hell itself as a place of punishment. The site has since been occupied by the General Post Office, and tactfully renamed Mount Pleasant!

The rest of the sailors, apart from 180 who were imprisoned in the *Eagle* hulk at Chatham and were pardoned after the battle of Camperdown,[171] returned to their duty with that alacrity which Parker had foretold. On 23rd June Keith and Buckner had struck their flags, the former to go back to London on the way to a command in the Channel Fleet, the latter to sink into an obscure retirement. The pestilentially rotting *Sandwich* was broken up as being too foul for human habitation, and the rest of the Fleet put to sea, where on 11th October they exhibited their unimpaired fighting spirit by winning the glorious, bitterly contested victory of Camperdown. Seven of the mutinous ships took part in this battle, which is noted for its fury. The *Ardent* "lost her captain . . . as well as more than a third of her whole ship's company, [and] proved herself in the fight second to none, even without her captain."[172] She had more casualties than any other ship, the *Belliqueux* being third on the roll, while the *Director*, *Montague*, *Isis*, *Monmouth* and *Lancaster* also took part. The stain was washed out.

On 30th October the Fleet, gaily dressed, with all its flags and pennons streaming in the wind, was once more arrayed at the Nore, on this occasion impatiently awaiting its Sovereign. He was to review the ships, for he was eager to show his love for those men whom, not so very many weeks ago, he had wished to see ignobly starved into submission. The King embarked at Greenwich early in the morning, but unluckily it was so rough that his yacht could not get farther down the river than Gravesend. Although seriously incommoded, being, in fact, thrown out of bed by the violence of the waves, his first thought was for his sailors. "Do not consider my person," he begged Captain Trollope, whom he had just knighted, "but consider, if I cannot get to the Nore, the disappointment of those brave fellows, whom I long to thank for defending me, protecting my people, and preserving my country."[173] If he, or his ministers, had thought of the seamen in those terms a few weeks earlier, there need have been no hint of the alarming, blood-expiated, issueless, mutiny at the Nore.

CHAPTER XIX

CAUSES: LESSONS: RESULTS

1. Causes

THERE can be no doubt, to any fair mind, that the mutinies, especially that at Spithead, were thoroughly justified. "Doubtless," Marryat was to write, speaking of the Nore affair,

> there is a point at which endurance of oppression ceases to be a virtue, and rebellion can no longer be considered as a crime: but it is a dangerous and intricate problem, the solution of which had better not be attempted. It must, however, be acknowledged, that the seamen, on the occasion of the first mutiny, had just grounds of complaint, and that they did not proceed to acts of violence until repeated and humble remonstrance had been made in vain.[174]

It must be admitted that the men on whom the country relied for its safety, and who brought it a glory of which it was more than proud, were abominably treated. The general conditions of living were as bad as could be found to-day in the vilest slum: the food was disgusting, badly arranged from the point of view of health, and short weight at that; the drink, except for the rum, was nauseating. The system of impressment was bad enough in itself, but the whole scheme of the sailor's life was made infinitely worse by denying the men leave, even when it could have been easily granted. These things in themselves might have been enough to breed revolt; but the two issues which particularly rasped the men's feelings were the arrangements for pay and the tyranny of the officers.

It was not only that the pay was too small, being still that which had been considered adequate during the Commonwealth, when prices were very much lower, but that there were often years-long delays in getting it. Nelson, writing to Locker in 1783, told him:

> My time, ever since I arrived in town, has been taken up in attempting to get the wages due to my good fellows, for various ships they have served in the war. The disgust of the Seamen of the Navy is all owing to the infernal plan of turning them over from Ship to Ship, so that Men cannot be attached to their officers, or the officers care two-pence about them.

Again, writing to his wife in 1793:

> If Parliament does not grant something to this Fleet, our Jacks will grumble; for there is no prize-money to soften their hardships: all we get is honour and salt beef.

Finally, on 30th June 1797:

> I am entirely with the seamen in their first complaint. We are a neglected set, and when peace comes, are shamefully neglected.[175]

To Nelson, at any rate, the mutiny did not come altogether as a surprise.

The Articles of War, the code under which the seamen existed, had been laid down in 1747, and had been altered only to allow a punishment less than death for cowardice, negligence, etc.: as a consequence of the feeling aroused by the execution of Byng. It was a far fiercer code than that under Charles II, where a man would not be mercilessly flogged for drunkenness, but merely fined a day's pay; the earlier code was throughout correspondingly milder. The abuses as to pay, however, with the vicious system of tickets, date from 1665, and in the matter of food the sailors in Pepys's day were as unlucky as their descendants:

> Our beef and our pork is very scant,
> I'm sure of weight one half it want:
> Our bread is black, and maggots in it crawl,
> That's all the fresh meat we are fed withal,

a sea-poet sang, recording also of the purser that

> . . . he upon our bellies still is gaming.[176]

For pursers, it seems, were a race that bred true to type.

If the Articles of War contained the general formula upon which life at sea was based, it was the "Regulations and Instructions relating to H.M.'s Service at Sea" that determined the sailor's life, and the punishments he was to undergo. First issued in 1731, it was under the 13th edition of 1790 that the mutinies took place; and in both of these it was clearly laid down that no captain was to inflict more than twelve lashes upon the bare back with a cat of nine tails (according to "the Ancient Practice of the Sea" they declared in 1731) without a court martial. This regulation was little regarded at the period of the mutinies, terrible punishments being visited upon the men for the least offence. What the sailors objected to was not punishment as such, but the illegality of the monstrous penalties to which they were subjected, and the senseless brutality of many of their officers. When Collingwood exclaimed: "Mutiny, sir ! Mutiny in my ship! If it can have arrived at that, it must be my fault, and the fault of every one of my officers," he was making a statement based on long experience.

It is plain that in many respects the Regulations were totally disregarded by the officers. Writing to Spencer on 17th June 1797, Duncan declared:

> Many things should now be thought of as fixing the internal regulations of ships on one plan. Of late years every captain has taken upon him to establish rules for himself.[177]

In short, one can say that to our eyes the internal affairs of the Navy present a picture of culpable maladministration from top to bottom. It is only surprising that there was not a general mutiny earlier in the century. For since the reorganisation of the Navy in the seventeenth century, the standard of life of the people as a whole had improved considerably, but that of the Navy had stayed where it was. Men drafted into it, especially quota-men, whose standard was well above the lowest, were acutely conscious of this: and indeed the state of things was curious enough to have called forth suggestive comment:

> It may seem paradoxical to say—it is nevertheless true—that, however deplorable in themselves, there was much in these occurrences [the mutinies] of which all concerned might feel justly proud. . . . The conduct even of the mutinous seamen was far from being without excuse, and the demeanour of nearly all—especially in the Spithead fleet—was such that they had little reason to be ashamed of it. The men always expressed their readiness to go and fight the enemy if he came out of port. They earnestly repudiated the opinion that they were mutineers. . . . That they had real, great, and long unredressed grievances is beyond question. In the latter part of the eighteenth century the man-of-war's man was in many important respects worse off than his predecessor in the latter part of the sixteenth. . . . It is an uncomfortable reflection, but it forces itself on the student of naval history, that as parliamentary government developed, the Empire expanded, and the national wealth increased, so the lot of the sailor deteriorated . . . the seamen were paid with scandalous irregularity. . . . Men wounded in action were discharged from pay whilst still uncured. It was to be delivered from this atrocious spoliation, not to resist properly constituted authority, that the seamen mutinied.[178]

As a further comment, one may say that it is remarkable that the men should have fought with such valour for a country which maltreated them so callously.

The Government of the day was extremely anxious to put the trouble down to subversive foreign influence—it is a notion which seems to be attractive to Governments—instead of to its real cause. Some of the men were, no doubt, animated by political ideas, but how far it is difficult to say. There is enough evidence, carefully collected by Mr. Gill, to show that certain of the sailors were not only in communication with Corresponding Societies, but were actually members. It can be added that the mutineers of the *Leopard*, too, were overheard to murmur the words "Corresponding Society" with the suggestion that they had been "deluded."[179] There were, of course, libertarian and revolutionary ideas in the air; the American War of Independence, the French Revolution, the troubles in Ireland, not to mention such idealists as Thomas Paine in England, had spread them abroad: the notion had been born that men had rights. To say that many of the mutineers were imbued with a sense of such doctrines is one thing, but to say that these men had any effect on the course of events, or in any way directed the Delegates, is altogether another. Such individuals probably bore the same relation to the leaders as communists to-day bear towards the official Labour Party—that of an irritant impelling in the opposite direction. There can have been no connection with the French, otherwise Hoche and Wolfe Tone would have jumped at the golden opportunity; and we can safely put aside the wholly fantastic if delightful story told by Moreau de Jonnes in his *Aventures de Guerre*, written some fifty years after the mutinies by a man of whom no trace can be found in the French naval records.

Nevertheless, Pitt and the Government, with a touching fidelity to the idea of foreign influence, made every effort to discover Jacobin propaganda at the bottom of the murky business. Their attempts to discover it at Portsmouth proved futile, but they hoped for better luck at Sheerness, and sent down the trusty Graham, accompanied by Williams, to conduct a searching enquiry at that place. The story they told, as magistrates used to the disentangling of evidence, should carry enough weight to dispose of the idea that subversive doctrines inspired the behaviour of the men at the Nore. Their report is here given in full, except for an irrelevant paragraph at the beginning, and two others,* equally off the point, at the end:

* One of these is given later in this chapter.

Mr. Graham and Mr. Williams beg leave to assure his Grace [the Duke of Portland] that they have unremittingly endeavoured to trace if there was any connexion or correspondence carried on between the mutineers and any private person or any society on shore, and they think that they may with the greatest safety pronounce that no such connexion or correspondence ever did exist. They do not however mean to say that wicked and designing men have not been among the mutineers; on the contrary they have proof sufficient to found a belief upon that several whose mischievous dispositions would lead them to the farthest corner of the kingdom in hopes of continuing a disturbance once begun have been in company with the delegates on shore, and have also (some of them) visited the ships at the Nore, and by using inflammatory language endeavoured to spirit on the sailors to a continuance of the mutiny without however daring to offer anything like a plan for the disposal of the fleet or to do more than insinuate that they were belonging to clubs or societies whose members wished well to the cause, but from which societies Mr. Graham and Mr. Williams are persuaded that no such persons were ever regularly deputed. Neither do they believe that any club or society in the kingdom or any of those persons who may have found means of introducing themselves to the delegates have in the smallest degree been able to influence the proceedings of the mutineers, whose conduct from the beginning seems to have been of a wild and extravagant nature not reducible to any sort of form or order and therefore capable of no other mischief than was to be apprehended from a want of the fleet to serve against the enemy. In this state however they were unfortunately suffered to go on without interruption until they began to think themselves justifiable in what they were doing, and by stopping up the mouth of the Thames they were suspected of designs for which Mr. Graham and Mr. Williams can by no means give them credit. The want of beer and fresh beef prompted them to revenge, and that and nothing else induced them to interrupt the trade of the river. It was done on the spur of the occasion, and with a view to obtaining a supply of fresh provisions. Another thing, namely the systematic appearance with which the delegates and the sub-committees on board the different ships conducted the business of the mutiny may be supposed a good ground of suspecting that better informed men than sailors in general must have been employed in regulating it for them. This Mr. Graham and Mr. Williams at first were inclined to believe too; but in the course of their examinations of people belonging to the fleet they were perfectly convinced that without such a combination and with the assistance of the newspapers only (independent of the many cheap publications to be had upon the subjects relating to clubs and societies of all descriptions) and the advantage of so many good writers as must have been found among the quota-men, they were capable of conducting it themselves.[180]

Finally, it may be pointed out that the mutineers at the Nore at one time had London at their mercy. They were "in possession of thirty of the King's ships, and had effectually stopped the navigation of the river Thames and Medway, and might have starved the Capital, at all times ill-stored and supplied with food and fuel"; [181] yet they had done no more than rifle a few ships to fill their own stomachs. Had their policy been born of revolutionary ideas, they would certainly not have let slip such a decisive opportunity.

2. Lessons

There are two double lessons to be learnt from the affairs at Spithead and the Nore: how to conduct a mutiny, and how not to: how to deal with a mutiny, and how to exacerbate the sore.

One is compelled to admire the leaders at Spithead, however much one may deplore their action; and even if one does deplore it, one has to admit it was forced on them. They had made every effort to get their bitter wrongs redressed by the ordinary constitutional means, but their attempts had been ignored. When it came to deeds the Delegates proved themselves first-rate trade union leaders, better perhaps than have ever appeared since. First of all, their organisation was magnificent, worked up under conditions which made it exceedingly difficult to build it up at all. Secondly, they had thought out their demands, realising which were really soundly enough based to be supported by public opinion; further, though they were prepared to weaken on one or two minor points, they were never tempted by preliminary success to take the false step of improving on them: they knew when to cease to ask, as well as to begin. They were careful not to introduce any unnecessary irritation; they allowed no arrogant displays, and no wanton acts of ill-feeling; they took pains to show that they were concerned for the country's trade. Above all, they were careful to be sure of unanimity before they took the first step, and they never put anybody forward as being at their head. These men throughout have one's sympathy, and increasingly gain one's respect; their names deserve to be regarded with honour in the history of the betterment of the Englishman's lot.

It is difficult to feel in the same way about the people at the Nore. One's sympathy they have, but less of one's admiration and respect. It was, from the beginning, a muddle-headed affair. One can see no error in their action so long as it constituted a sympathetic strike in favour of their brethren at Spithead; but their behaviour after they knew that the mutiny there was settled, and very favourably, not only for the men concerned, but for themselves also, partakes of the wild and foolish. One may, indeed one does, feel very much for them: there were still many wrongs which they suffered, and which ought to have been redressed— the bullying of the officers (they had got rid of none of theirs), the maldistribution of prize-money, and so on. One may even grant there was just cause for another mutiny; their conduct of it is what provokes criticism. To begin with, there was hardly any preliminary organisation; it was enough, possibly, for a lightning sympathetic strike, but not for an independent one. Most of the leaders were not leaders at all, but pounced upon *ad hoc*, as Parker was, not so much to carry out a definite scheme as to represent a vague if strong emotional state. Leaders chosen in that way, without showing any ambition for the post (one of them even got drunk on purpose to be degraded) can never have enough authority, or the will to direct. Nor did the instigators make sure of having a majority in their favour, far less that the feeling was unanimous: they tried to impose unanimity by administering an oath, often under virtual compulsion. Nor did they know what they wanted. For some days they had on their hands a mutiny that had no definite purpose; they were forced, more or less, to invent an objective. They alienated what support they might have had from outside by displays of pomp, by electing a president, by tending to violence. Their most fatal error was the blockade, which terrified the whole country, and antagonised the middle classes, without whom nothing in this country has been done for centuries. And finally, towards the end, they began to show vindictiveness. Had Parker really been in command, he might have brought things to a better issue. But he was not in any true sense a leader; he was certainly an extremely brave man, but he was only an intelligent tool, asked in the end to do work for which he was in no way designed.

The Spithead affair, again, provides an object-lesson in the way a mutiny should be met, though, of course, the conditions which engendered it should never have existed. Nor, once Howe had handed over the petitions, should it have been allowed to occur. "I think Lord Howe's sending back the first petition was wrong," Nelson wrote.[182] But once it had started, the method of dealing with it was right. It was proper that the Board should go down to Portsmouth to probe into the matter in their own persons, and it would have been better still if Spencer and his colleagues had met the men face to face and had not attempted to haggle. But even so, thanks largely to the statesmanlike conduct of the Delegates, the negotiations went smoothly enough, while the idea of sending Howe to settle up the whole thing was one approaching genius, so rare is it to find common sense raised to that power. The Admiralty, it is true, made some remarkably tactless blunders, but that final promise to forget, to avoid retaliation, was both sensible and generous.

The way the Nore outbreak was treated offers a very different picture. Granted it was felt that enough had already been conceded the sailors, granted that the authorities ought to have shown no softness, there is no reason why they should not have attempted to display a certain degree of understanding. The system, if it can be so called, of ill-considered, brutal punishment had not been cleared up at Spithead, and the grievance as to prize-money was a just one. If the admission of a seaman to a place at every court martial smacked of the revolutionary, that would no doubt have been let slide if the Admiralty had shown a little easiness on the point of the desertions. But everything the Government did made matters worse. The blatant sending of troops to Sheerness was a crude act of provocation; the cutting off of supplies could only drive the men to illegal reprisals: the authorities seemed determined to incite the mutineers to extremes. The journey of the Board to Sheerness, with their minds hermetically sealed, was a cruel mockery. If only Spencer had consented to see the men, or at least hear what they had to say; if he had, in short, treated them as human beings, a peaceful settlement might easily have been arrived at. It was Howe in person, they should have realised, in body and voice, as representing the King, who had settled the earlier affair; but at the Nore there was no warmth, no humanity, to alleviate the hardness of official stone, the chill of an abstract system.

Even to-day the principle that personal contact is of the first importance is not universally acted upon, and in *The Times* of 1st August 1934, in the report of a debate, we read:

The situation at Invergordon in 1931 had many features in common with the naval mutiny of 1797, but in 1797 the Board of Admiralty faced the situation for which they were responsible. . . .

In these days of quick transport it would have been quite possible for the First Sea Lord, or other members of the Board or senior officers whom the Admiralty might delegate to represent them, to have flown to Invergordon and to have been there within a few hours. The Admiralty were entirely responsible for the situation which had arisen, and they alone had the power to investigate the men's grievance. He (Admiral Sir Roger Keyes) submitted that on the morning of the 16th Admiral Tomkinson had every right to expect the support and intervention of the Board of Admiralty. The action he had taken up to date made that intervention quite possible, and if the Board had taken bold and proper steps on the spot, this Service would be a happier service than it was to-day.

The fact that the mutiny at the Nore was not settled, as that at Spithead had been, but crushed and savagely punished, was almost certainly the reason why mutinies continued to break out sporadically for two or three years over the whole Fleet—at the Cape, in the East Indies, the West Indies, in the Channel Fleet itself, and especially at Cadiz: though sometimes, indeed, the men were goaded into it, as in the shocking case of the *Hermione* to which reference was made earlier in this book.

3. RESULTS

For although the mutiny at Spithead had at once bettered the sailors' lot with respect to pay and rations, the officers had not learnt the lesson that their men ought to be treated more like human beings and less like Turks, as the crew of the *Winchelsea* had it. The better officers, of course, had always known this—Admirals like Howe, Duncan, Nelson, and Collingwood; captains like Northesk and Knight; lieutenants like Beaver and Bover. But there were others more choleric, such as Admiral Gardner, Captain Cunningham, and especially Bligh, lieutenants such as Brenton, not to mention such madmen as Pigot and Dixon. They had not learnt that you cannot for long, or with good results for anybody, command men by terrorism: your swashbuckling martinet, your "On the knee!" type of officer, is more of a liability to the service than an asset. Even as late as 1806 a

Lieutenant Stephens, when at Bombay, ordered three men to be flogged—without the authority of a court martial—and

the punishment was inflicted with such horrible severity that they all three died in less than twenty-four hours after it was over. . . . It appeared that it was not uncommon for officers, of their own authority, and without any court-martial, to inflict very severe punishments ; and that they supposed this to be legal.[183]

The ministers of that day, engaged in compiling a new edition of the "Regulations," were quite aware that these things went on ; but knowing that they were already illegal, saw no point in framing a further Act of Parliament on the subject. They did not know what to do, for they felt that instructions sent to the Admiralty would fall into neglect, and the abuse would revive. Grey, afterwards Earl Grey of Liberal fame, at that time First Lord of the Admiralty, was a little uncomfortable about this question, but with the sensibility to criticism of a man in office agreed that to "draw public attention to the subject was very objectionable!"[184] Did he not remember that less than ten years before it had been considered most objectionable to draw public attention to the seamen's pay—with disastrous results ?

Whatever the faults of British democracy may be, it is certain that once the people are aroused to the knowledge that some cruelty or injustice is being perpetrated, they will not rest until the matter has been put right. Eternal vigilance over its governors is one of the vital necessities of democracy. The events of 1797 aroused the public. "There is perhaps no event in the annals of our history," Marryat wrote, in 1830, "which excited more alarm at the time of its occurrence, or has since been the subject of more general interest, than the mutiny at the Nore in the year 1797."[185] The people of England, terrified by the event, began to ask themselves why it was that the Navy, of which they were so proud, and which was their main safeguard, had mutinied in time of war, had laid them open to the attacks of their enemies, and even itself threatened them. Arden had not been wrong in referring to the situation as "the most awful crisis that these kingdoms ever saw." The enquiries the public made gave them a horrid glimpse of the life at sea, and roused opinion in the men's favour. It came to be seen that for nearly a hundred and fifty years the conditions in the Navy had not materially altered, although they had improved in every other walk of life—except perhaps where the factories were beginning to take their grisly toll. Nothing, in fact, had been done for the men who fought the country's battles and manned its fleets. It was not until the mutiny at Spithead wrung a few concessions from the Government that the eyes of the public were unsealed to what the seamen had to endure in the service of the nation.

Thus, it is universally agreed, the year 1797 opens a new era in the organisation of the Royal Navy, or at least marks a turning-point in its history. From that time, little by little, the sailor was to receive consideration and more humane treatment. Here it is possible to sketch only very briefly some of the reforms that took place in the succeeding seventy years or so. In 1806, A.B.'s received an increase of a shilling a week in their wages, and Ordinary Seamen, 6d., making the pay from 1st January 1807 up to the sum of £1, 13s. 6d. and £1, 5s. 6d. a month respectively; but it was not until 1825 that an Act was passed ensuring prompter payment. At this time certain monthly allowances were also granted. One can cite the establishment of sick-berth ratings in 1833; and in 1835 an Act which ruled that no person should be detained in the naval service against his will for more than five years. In the same year we find the establishment of a register of seamen, which seems to mark the fading out of the old system of impressment, which was never actually abolished by Act of Parliament. A year earlier, in 1834, an Order in Council laid down a more equitable distribution of prize-money, upon which even Brenton commented, "If it be just to do it now, it would have been equally so to have done it earlier."[186] * In 1836 libraries were provided in sea-going ships, and in 1853 the Continuous Service Act offered increased rates of pay and other advantages to men entering the service for ten years.

Corporal punishment came up for revision in due course. Flogging round the Fleet had died a natural death before the end of the eighteenth century, but ferocious punishments were still inflicted. By 1828 there was a marked improvement in this matter, once more due to outside pressure rather than to official initiative (to "draw public attention to the subject was very objectionable"), as was observed by a man who became Chief Clerk of the Admiralty:

> Much credit is unquestionably due to the able articles which have, from time to time, appeared upon this painful subject in the columns of *The Times* and other leading journals of the day.[187]

But it was not until 1860 that the Naval Discipline Act repealed the Articles of War, and with the Act of 1866 limited the number of lashes a man might receive to forty-eight. These were followed by the Admiralty Circular of 1871, which restricted the infliction of corporal punishment in peace-time; and, finally, 1879 saw the practical abolition of flogging. One may note, as a sign of the growing solicitude for seamen, that in 1857 there was founded a Savings Bank for Seamen and Marines.

* Brenton was afraid that since a captain now only got £1000 instead of £6000 for a prize, he would be reluctant to send neutrals into port for adjudication. He cannot have thought very highly of the keenness of his brother officers.

That sailors on attesting now take the Oath of Allegiance is largely due to the impression made on the authorities by the awed seriousness with which the sailors in the mutinies regarded the swearing of an oath. The Government of the day passed an Act prohibiting the taking of illegal oaths, but it was left to others to suggest that a better way would be to offer the sailors one that was unimpeachable.

I would also propose [Lord Keith wrote to Dundas] [188] that every seaman who shall voluntarily enter for His Majesty's Service and receive Bounty, should sign an Attestation something similar to that used in the Army, and that all Seamen in the course of Pay should be obliged to take and sign the Oath of Allegiance before they receive either Pay or Prize Money.

This I recommend upon the suggestion that many of the mutineers seem to feel the Impression of the illegal Oath they had taken to be true to those Mutineers' cause, but none had ever been tendered to them on the part of the King or His Majesty's Government, and this class of men are in general too ill informed to understand that all subjects owe Allegiance from their birth, but imagine that the serious circumstances of an Oath warrants a strict adherence to the object, altho' repugnant to every honest and justifiable consideration unless counteracted by equivalent obligations.

The same notion had occurred to the examining magistrates sent down to Sheerness:

Mr. Graham and Mr. Williams had various opportunities of remarking that the sailors in general had a very serious sense of the obligation imposed upon them by an oath (even when administered as in the case of the mutiny) and are therefore of opinion that the attesting of seamen as well as soldiers might be attended with beneficial effects,

they wrote in their report; and the sensible suggestion was ultimately acted upon.

It cannot be said, then, that Parker and his fellows suffered in vain, although at the moment their efforts seemed to have brought nothing but defeat and death. The mutiny at Spithead, though it had brought immediate benefit to the seamen, had not aroused much alarm in the public breast: the Government had settled it all for a trifling sum of money. But the fierceness of the outbreak at the Nore, to which the Yarmouth squadron had adhered; the length of time it lasted; the horror of the numerous executions; above all, the threat to London, had forced on every one's notice that there was something atrociously wrong with the way the sailors were treated. There is no smoke without fire. Men who live under decent, or only fairly decent, conditions do not revolt; and the fact that a revolt had taken place stirred up the men of good will among the public—and there are always many of them—to lend a willing ear to the tales told of the sailor's life. It was public feeling that gradually forced the politicians' hands: no amount of petitions from sailors, or even representations from Admirals like Howe and Duncan, captains such as Nelson and Pakenham, ever had the least effect on them.

Though the mutinies occurred nearly a hundred and forty years ago, the memory of them is not yet dead on the lower deck. The men are aware that the conditions before 1797 were abominably tyrannous and unjust, and they put this down to the "cynical apathy" of the Admiralty and Cabinet: the mutiny, in their view, "shook the complacency of authority." They feel that those responsible "shamefully betrayed" the lower deck, and the events of those days have left them profoundly hostile to the politician.

For over a hundred and thirty years this deep vein of distrust and suspicion has existed [a seaman wrote lately].[189] It has a far-reaching effect, inasmuch as the landsman has never been able to probe into the complex make-up of the British tar. There has always been a wide gulf, a strain of disguised hostility, which is but an expression of sturdy independence enjoyed by the seamen preserving their individuality. Respect and loyalty to the constitution has never wavered. . . .

I add, with due deliberation, that precisely the same spirit prevailed in

1914 as in the year 1797. Further, the rumblings of discontent heard about the years 1916-17 were largely due to bureaucracy taking the line it followed during the latter years preceding 1797.

Perhaps, after all, it is true that "History teaches, that history teaches mankind nothing."

APPENDIX I

List of the Delegates of the Fleet during the mutiny at Spithead, 1797. Compiled from the Muster Books of the various ships in the Public Record Office. A man's age is that at the time when he entered the ship, in most cases in 1796.

Surname.	Christian Name.	Ship.	Rating.	Age.	Birthplace.	Remarks.
Joyce.	Valentine.	Royal George.	Quarter Master's Mate.	25.	Jersey.	Continued Q.M.'s Mate after Mutiny.
Morrice.	John.	—	A.B.	32.	Aberdeen.	A.B. after Mutiny.
Richardson.	John.	Royal Sovereign.	A.B.	26.	Piltown.	—
Green.	Joseph.	—	A.B.	26.	York.	—
Harding.	Alexander.	London.	Gunner's Mate.	23.	Greenock.	Master's Mate, 1st Sept. 1797.
Riley.	William.	—	Quarter Master.	27.	Westminster.	Continued Q.M. after Mutiny.
Fleming.	John.	—	A.B.	25.	Glasgow.	Gunner's Mate, 1st Sept. 1797.
Huddlestone.	John.	Queen Charlotte.	Yeoman of Sheets.	34.	Holvach.	Formerly Q.M.'s Mate.
Glynn.	Patrick.	—	A.B.	34.	Dublin.	—
Duggan.	Patrick.	Glory.	Midshipman.	28.	Waterford.	Formerly Q.M.'s Mate.
Bethell.	John.	—	Midshipman.	33.	London.	Formerly Boatswain's Mate.
Adams.	Michael.	Duke.	Quarter Gunner.	33.	Rochester.	Formerly on H.M.S. Veteran.
Anderson.	William.	—	Quarter Master.	33.	Dublin.	Mid. till 9th Mar. 1797.
Allen.	Thomas.	Mars.	A.B.	29.	Hartley, Northumberland.	Promoted Q.M.'s Mate, 30th Sept. 1797.

Blythe.	James.	*Mars.*	A.B.	30.	Ashridge, Yorks.	Promoted Mid., 20th May 1797.
Screaton.	William.	*Marlborough.*	A.B.	27.	London.	A.B. till 1st Mar. 1796.
Vassie.	John.	—	Yeoman of Sheets.	27.	Lanark.	—
Berry.	Charles.	*Ramillies.*	Midshipman.	33.	London.	Promoted Q.M.'s Mate, 14th May 1797.
Clear.	George.	—	A.B.	25.	Angmering.	—
Wilson.	David.	*Robust.*	Yeoman of Sheets.	23.	Ipswich.	—
Scrivener.	John.	—	Yeoman of Sheets.	31.	N. Shields.	—
Porter.	William.	*Impétueux.*	Quarter Master.	25.	Suffolk.	—
Whitney.	John.	—	A.B.	24.	America.	—
Gallaway.	George.	*Defence.*	Midshipman.	28.	Coldstream.	—
Berwick.	James.	—	Quarter Master.	30.	Westbery, Wilts.	—
Turner.	Mark.	*Terrible.*	Midshipman.	37.	Harwich.	Serving as Mid. at least a year before the Mutiny.
Salkeld.	George.	—	Yeoman of Powder Room.	39.	Walsingham.	An old salt. Had been Y. of P.R. for four years. Made Gunner's Mate, 1st Jan. 1798.
Potts.	William.	*La Pompée.*	Quarter Master.	24.	Harthy.	—
Melvin.	James.	—	Quarter Master.	34.	Sunderland.	Q.M.'s Mate till 8th Mar. 1797.
Lawler.	Denis.	*Minotaur.*	Quarter Gunner.	34.	Kildare.	—
Crossland.	George.	—	A.B.	31.	Thorn.	—
Saunders.	John.	*Defiance.*	A.B.	33.	Pembrokeshire.	—
Husband.	John.	—	A.B.	27.	Whitby.	—

APPENDIX II

PETITION OF THE SEAMEN TO THE ADMIRALTY

To the Right Honourable the Lords Commissioners of the Admiralty.

My Lords,

We, the seamen of his majesty's navy, take the liberty of addressing your lordships in an humble petition, shewing the many hardships and oppressions we have laboured under for many years, and which, we hope, your lordships will redress as soon as possible. We flatter ourselves that your lordships, together with the nation in general, will acknowledge our worth and good services, both in the American war, as well as the present; for which good service your lordships petitioners do unanimously agree in opinion, that their worth to the nation, and laborious industry in defence of their country, deserve some better encouragement than that we meet with at present, or from any we have experienced. We, your petitioners, do not boast our good services, for any other purpose than that of putting you and the nation in mind of the respect due to us, nor do we ever intend to deviate from our former character; so far from any thing of that kind, or that an Englishmen or men should turn their coats, we likewise agree in opinion, that we should suffer double the hardships we have hitherto experienced, before we would wish the crown of England to be in the least imposed upon by that of any other power in the world; we therefore beg leave to inform your lordships of the grievances which we at present labour under.

We, your humble petitioners, relying that your lordships will take into early consideration the grievances of which we complain, and do not in the least doubt but your lordships will comply with our desires, which are every way reasonable.

The first grievance we have to complain of, is, that our wages are too low, and ought to be raised, that we might be the better able to support our wives and families in a manner comfortable, and whom we are in duty bound to support, as far as our wages will allow; which, we trust, will be looked into by your lordships and the honourable house of commons in parliament assembled.

We, your petitioners, beg that your lordships will take into consideration the grievances of which we complain, and now lay before you.

First, That our provisions be raised to the weight of sixteen ounces to the pound, and of a better quality; and that our measures may be the same as those used in the commercial trade of this country.

Secondly, That your petitioners request your honours will be pleased to observe, there should be no flour served while we are in harbour, in any port whatever, under the command of the British flag; and also, that there might be granted a sufficient quantity of vegetables, of such kind as may be the most plentiful in the ports to which we go; which we grievously complain and lay under the want of.

Thirdly, That your lordships will be pleased seriously to look into the state of the sick on board his majesty's ships, that they may be better attended to, and that they may have the use of such necessaries as are allowed for them in time of sickness; and that these necessaries be not on any account embezzled.

Fourthly, That your lordships will be so kind as to look into this affair, which is nowise unreasonable; and that we may be looked upon as a number of men standing in defence of our country; and that we may in somewise have grant and opportunity to taste the sweets of liberty on shore, when in any harbour, and when we have completed the duty of our ship, after our return from sea: And that no man may encroach upon his liberty, there shall be a boundary limited, and those trespassing any further, without a written order from the commanding officer, shall be punished according to the rules of the navy; which is a natural request, and congenial to the heart of man, and certainly to us, that you make the boast of being the guardians of the land.

Fifthly, That if any man is wounded in action, his pay may be continued till he is cured and discharged; and if any ship has any real grievances to complain of, we hope your lordships will readily redress them, as far as in your power, to prevent disturbances.

It is also unanimously agreed by the fleet, that, from this day, no grievances shall be received, in order to convince the nation at large, that we know when to cease to ask, as well as to begin, and that we ask nothing but what is moderate, and may be granted without detriment to the nation, or any injury to the service.

Given on board the *Queen Charlotte*, by the delegates of the fleet, the 18th day of April 1797.

> [Signed by the delegates named in Appendix I, with the exception of John Fleming, who had not yet been elected.]

From the *Annual Register*, 1797, State Papers, 380.

APPENDIX III

Fleming's letter. This is taken from Admiral E. G. Colpoys' (at the time of the mutiny Captain Griffith) "Letter to Sir T. Byam Martin," 1825. This letter of Fleming's offers certain difficulties. Why was he elected a delegate? The Muster Books show that neither of the Delegates of the *London* was killed in the affair of the 7th. One has to suppose that one of them was wounded badly enough to incapacitate him; yet Griffith himself says, "No delegate was shot." It is unlikely that either of them should have resigned, or have been asked to resign. It is curious also that this letter should not exist in the Admiralty archives where so many others do. For some inexplicable reason it fell into the hands of Captain Griffith of the *London*, and it was he who first printed it, twenty-eight years after the mutiny, when he was refuting certain statements made by Brenton about Admiral Sir John Colpoys. Further, the style seems peculiarly polished for that of an ordinary sailor, and with the exception of the wrong use of the word "unanimous" might be that of an educated man. Griffith adds, "It will be easily supposed that the merit of this man was duly appreciated on the termination of the troubles." The Muster Book shows that he remained an A.B. until 1st September 1797, when he received a small promotion to gunner's mate. However, here is the rest of the letter:—

To the Delegates of the Fleet.

You have, I presume, read the address of the ship's company, of which I am a member, to you, recommending me as their representative in future; they have further given me the most flattering proofs of their opinion of my abilities to act as a man and Christian ought to do. Under these circumstances, I flatter myself you will hear me with patience, as I am partly convinced your own sentiments, when compared with mine, will join me in saving a deserving character from ruin and destruction. I shall not dwell on the particulars of yesterday; they, I am confident, are still warm in your memories, but only recal [*sic*] your attention to the behaviour of our brother Valentine Joyce. His intrepidity in rescuing the unfortunate gentleman from the hands of an enraged multitude will, I am sure, make a deep impression on your minds, and will, I hope, influence you to act in a manner worthy the character of Christians and British seamen: thus much brethren, for preface. Permit me now . . . see text, p. 93 . . . You see, brethren, I act openly, and am determined to support it, as I will never form a part to do injustice to my country; and for the future, I shall

267

expect that whatever comes before us shall be only conducive to the much wanted and desirable end of restoring the fleet to the confidence of our injured country. Let these be your aims, and you may depend upon every support from me, and this ship's company. And be assured, that the life and character of Mr. Bover shall always remain inviolate in our hands; and we think any step taken to the contrary highly injurious to ourselves as brothers of your community. We expect your answer this night, and I beg leave to remain,

Yours most sincerely,

JOHN FLEMING.

Barrow, when he prints this latter in his Preface to his *Life of Anson*, adds: " Per desire of the *London's* ship's company."

It still remains a problem why Fleming should have written the letter at all if he had been elected a Delegate, and would meet the other Delegates at meetings of the committee.

APPENDIX IV

NOTES FOR THE LIFE OF RICHARD PARKER

(The Reference (S.) designates " Declaration of Richard Parker," printed in the *Spencer Papers*, II, 160-173.)

Born 16th April 1767 at Exeter. (S.)

Baptised 24th April. (Parish Register, St. Mary Major, Exeter.)

He was the son of Richard and Sarah Parker (Parish Register). Richard was a successful baker, and in 1787 retired on his fortune to an estate he possessed in a neighbouring parish in Exeter. (S.)

In 1775 he was placed under the tuition of " the Rev. Mr. Marshall, grammarian at Exeter," left him in 1779 to learn navigation from Osborne, keymaster at Topsham in Devonshire. (S.)

In 1782 he entered the *Mediator* as a volunteer and was rated as A.B. 10th April. (Ad. 34/509.) He himself says he was a midshipman; a first cousin of his was second lieutenant in the ship. The ship was paid off on 16th April 1783. (S.)

He followed the captain, Luttrell, into the *Ganges*, as a midshipman, and remained there till 4th September, when he " was discharged by order of Admiral Montague into H.M. Sloop *Bull-Dog* by application." (S.) The *Bull-Dog* went to the East African coast.

In 1784 he returned to England and was discharged sick to Haslar Hospital, 15th June. (Hutchinson, 274.) Parker left hospital the day before the *Bull-Dog* sailed. On the passage to Plymouth, where she was to call, he became worse, and was sent off to Plymouth Hospital, " I think on the 23rd of July." (S.)

After a partial recovery he was sent to the *Blenheim*. When on leave at Exeter he decided to join the merchant service, and obtained his discharge from the Royal Navy. (S.)

Till 1793 he served on various ships in the Mediterranean trade and in the India service. From 1787 till 1793 he sometimes served in the Navy. (S.) In 1791 he married Anne McHardy, daughter of a farmer at Braemar in Aberdeenshire. (Gill, 125, for date.)

In 1793 Captain Lucas of the *Sphynx* invited him to join the ship as master's mate, to do the duty of lieutenant, with the prospect of becoming lieutenant, since Sir Alexander Hood (afterwards Lord Bridport) " would have an eye to " his promotion. He began to work for the *Sphynx* in the way of getting men for her, but " a slight misfortune " prevented him from joining her.

He was then received on the *Assurance* as a supernumerary, till opportunity should arise to transfer him to the *Sphynx*. On the *Assurance* being ordered to sail, he asked to be transferred to the *Sandwich* to await the *Sphynx*, but was told he was too useful to the *Assurance*, and that he had been mustered as belonging to the ship and not as a supernumerary. When the *Sphynx* arrived in port, Parker was not allowed to communicate with her, and sailed in the *Assurance* in spite of a protest he sent to Admiral Dalrymple.

Being discontented on the *Assurance*, he came to be at odds with the lieutenant, Richards, who, over a question of the tidiness of some hammocks, goaded Parker into answering him back. When Richards told him to take up his own hammock, the following dialogue took place.

P. I am an officer in this ship.

R. Take it up directly, sir!

P. I am an officer in this ship and will not disgrace myself.

R. By God, sir, you shall take it up.

P. I will be damned if I do. (S.)

Richards applied to his captain:—

Sir,

Mr. Richard Parker, Midshipman, of H.M.S. *Assurance* under your command having on this day behaved himself in a contemptuous and disobedient manner to me, I have therefore to request you will be pleased to write for a Court Martial on said Richard Parker specifying the above charge, contempt, and disobedience of orders.

I am, sir,

John Richards.
(Ad. 1/5330.)

In 1797, on Nepean's request, Admiral Sir Peter Parker gave him some information about Richard Parker. He told him that Parker had been tried on board the *Royal William* on 12th December 1793, had been disrated, and ordered to serve on board such a ship as the Commander-in-Chief should think proper. It appears that the captain of the *Hebe* applied for him, and he was entered on board that ship on 24th December. From there he was sent to Haslar on 15th April 1794. His sick ticket is marked "rheumatism," and is enclosed with Sir Peter's letter. It describes Parker as A.B., aged 26 years, 5 ft. 8 ins. high, and dark complexion. He was discharged from hospital and came on board the *Royal William* on 15th May, but being very ill was returned again to Haslar on the following day. He remained there till 15th August, when he was re-entered on the *Royal William* as a supernumerary. On 26th November 1794 he was discharged "per order" (Ad. 1/1023.)

Parker and his wife remained in Exeter until the 15th April 1795, when they went to visit her parents at Braemar, and till 1797 they divided their time between Braemar and Exeter.

In 1797 he drew upon his brother-in-law for £23 in favour of John Duff of Edinburgh, which not being paid, he was arrested and put into Edinburgh gaol. After about three weeks he saw the regulating officer and accepted a £20 quota, with part of which he compounded with his creditor. (S.)

The rest we know. There is a consistent legend that when in Scotland he set up as a village schoolmaster.

When Anne Parker was interrogated before the Edinburgh magistrates on 20th June, she said that her husband was certainly at that time in a state of insanity: that he had formerly been deranged in his intellect, and that his discharge from the Navy bore out that that was the case. One of his sisters had been under confinement on that account for some time (*London Chronicle*). Brenton says (I, 297), " Having seen him on this occasion, and from the knowledge I had from my father, who was at that time regulating captain at Leith, and by whose order he was sent round to the Nore, I have no doubt that he was at times deranged. The burial register of St. Mary Matfellon, Whitechapel, has the following entry:—

" 4 July, 1797, Richard Parker, Sheerness, Kent, age 33 [*sic*]. Cause of death, execution. This was Parker, the President of the Mutinous Delegates on board the fleet at the Nore. He was hanged on board H.M.S. *Sandwich* on the 30th day of June" (Hutchinson, 279).

There is a tradition in the Spencer family that " Lord Spencer was so grieved at being obliged to sentence Richard Parker, that by way of compensation and some alleviation of her grief, he allowed his widow £1200 or £1400 a year as long as she lived" (*Spencer Papers*, II, 103-4).

Yet Parker's widow was forced to solicit charity. William IV at one time gave her £10 and at another £20. In 1836 the London magistrates provided for her in misery. A portion of the daily press also made an appeal for her. In 1840 she was seventy, blind, and friendless (Pelham, *Chronicles of Crime*, I, 358).

APPENDIX V

" The Dying Declaration of the late unfortunate Richard Parker, written two days previous to his execution, in a letter to a person who had known him from his earliest infancy." *

June 28*th*, 1797.

DEAR SIR,

In my awful situation I have great consolation to find that I still possess your esteem, and merit your commiseration. Heaven grant you may long outlive the painful recollection of my unfortunate fate. A little while and I must depart from this world, and for ever close my eyes upon its vanity, deceitfulness, and ingratitude. My passage through it has been short but checquered. My departure from it will be extremely boisterous, but I seriously assure you, upon my part, by no means unwilling.

The only comfortable reflection that I at present enjoy, is that I am to die a Martyr in the cause of Humanity. I know the multitude think hard things of me, but this gives me no uneasiness, for my conscience testifies that the part which I have acted among the seamen has been right, although not to be justified by prudence. The latter consideration is the only compunction which I feel under my doleful calamity. Yes, prudence urges *that I ought to have known mankind better*, than blindfold to have plunged into certain destruction. Long since I had learnt that the miseries under which the lower classes groan are imputable in a great measure to their ignorance, cowardice, and duplicity, and that nothing short of a miracle would ever afford them any relief. This experience, prudence too late teaches me should have been my guard against that fatal error which forfeits my life. However severe this reflection, still I preserve my fortitude, and am enabled to do this by considering that as a human being I stand subject to human passion, the noblest of which is a tender *sensibility at every species of human woe*. Thus influenced, how could I indifferently stand by, and behold some of the best of my fellow creatures cruelly treated by some of the very worst. I candidly confess I could not, and because I could not, fate consigns me to be a victim to the tenderest emotions of the human heart.

Upon the word of a dying man, I solemnly declare that I was not an original mover of the disturbances amongst those men, who have treated me so very ungratefully. Also, that I was elected by my Shipmates their Delegate without my knowledge, and in the same manner by the Delegates their

* Attached to the Official Copy of Parker's Court Martial in the Public Record Office (Ad. 1/5339). Never before printed.

President. I was compelled to accept those situations much against my inclinations by those who pushed me into them, and I did by no means attain them in the manner which has been scandalously reported by persons who are purposely prejudiced or ignorant of the matter. It is well known what authority the seamen had over their Delegates, and in what a ferocious manner the Delegates were frequently treated for not according with every wild scheme which the sailors proposed to carry into practice. I further declare that from the aggregate body originated every plan, and that during the time the Delegates held their perilous situations, they always acted pursuant to, and obeyed the instructions of their constituents. How I and my unfortunate colleagues have been rewarded for our fidelity in thus acting, those who have any sense of moral obligation will easily determine. The only instances in which the Delegates acted of themselves were in those of checking the violence and turpitude of their masters, and this God knows we had hard work to do, but considering all circumstances, those who know anything of sailors will readily allow that we preserved much better order than could reasonably have been expected upon such an occasion. For not according with the preposterous ideas of the seamen, I and many more must suffer Death. Had we been as decidedly violent as they were, we need not have died like dogs, for all the force which could have been mustered would not have availed, and necessity would have obliged a compliance to our demands. Owing to the Delegates moderation, they have been overcome, and for my own part I cheerfully forgive the vanquishers the bloody use they intend to make of their victory; perhaps it is policy in them to do it. From the first moment that I understood the kindness which the Delegates were to experience from their employers, I was prepared for the sacrifice, and may Heaven grant that I may be the last victim offered up in the cause of a treacherous and debased commonalty. Many will ask, however, how an insignificant man like myself could merit the confidence of the Multitude, so far as to induce them to thrust him forward upon such an occasion. If such enquirers will for a moment reflect that in a popular commotion any person who has the misfortune to be in repute for a trifling share of ability is liable to be forced into action though much against his will, their enquiry will easily be solved, and this was precisely my case. Others will say, how could a man of his information be so indiscreet? Tell such that Richard Parker in his last moments was pierced to the bottom of his soul with asking himself the same question. That he ingenuously owned he was indiscreet, but that it was, as he thought, from laudable motives.

At the pressing applications of my brother shipmates, I suffered humanity to surmount reason, and I hope my life is a sufficient atonement for my folly. I am the devoted scapegoat for the sins of many, and henceforth when the oppressed groan under the stripes of the oppressors, let my example deter any man from risking himself as the victim to ameliorate their wretchedness. Having said thus much of my concerns with the seamen, I shall now take the liberty to offer my friend some advice. It is the result of dear bought experience, and I hope he will profit by it. Remember, never to make yourself the busy body of the lower classes, for they are cowardly, selfish, and ungrateful; the least trifle will intimidate them, and him whom they have exalted one moment as their Demagogue, the next they will not scruple to exalt upon the gallows. I own it is with pain that I make such a remark to you, but truth demands it. I have experimentally proved it, and very soon am to be made the example of it. There is nothing new in my treatment; compare it with the treatment of most of the Advocates for the improvement of the conditions of the Multitude in all ages. Nay with reverence I write it, with the treatment of Jesus Christ Himself when on earth, and then declare whether or not my advice is to be regarded.

It is my opinion that if Government had not been too hasty the Portsmouth Mutiny would have been as readily overcome as that at Sheerness. A very trifling forbearance on their part would have occasioned the Portsmouth Delegates to have been delivered up like those at Sheerness, to have settled all the accounts. This is not mere supposition, but founded upon facts, though not generally known. The Mutineers have been accused of disloyalty, but it is a false accusation. They were only so to their ill-fated tools the Delegates. Both Army and Navy are in my opinion loyal, and setting aside the liberties which they have lately taken with their superiors, well attached to the ruling powers. The ignorant and the violent will call me a criminal, but when it is remembered what were the demands which I made for my unprincipled employers, I know the discreet part of mankind will acquit me of criminality. I have reason to think the Civil Power would have acquitted me, but by the Articles of War my destruction was irremidiable, and of this Government was well aware, or I should not have been tried by a Court Martial. By the Laws of War I acknowledge myself to be legally convicted, but by the Laws of Humanity, which should be the basis of all laws, I die illegally. My judges were respectable, but not totally disinterested, for one of the demands had for its tendency the abridgement of their emoluments in Prize Money.

Now my dear Friend, I take my leave of you, and may Providence amply return every kindness that I have received from your hands. Oh, pray for me, that in the last scene I may act my part like a man, and that when I am on the point of being offered up, that I may be inspired with a charity sufficient to forgive those for whom I am sacrificed. The moment my body is suspended the spectators will behold a wretch who is exposed as an example of his own frailty, and of the disgrace and dishonour of those men for whom I met so ignominious a death. Parting with life is no more than going to sleep, and God in His mercy grant I may sleep sweetly after my worldly toils, through the merits of my Lord and Saviour Jesus Christ. Amen.

Adieu, eternally adieu,

From your dying friend,

RICHARD PARKER.

APPENDIX VI

of H.M.'s Ships and Vessels concerned in the Mutiny at the Nore, 1797, with the numbers Court Martialled. Compiled from three lists bound up with the Rough Minutes of the Board of Admiralty, June 1797. (Ad. 3/137.)

's Name.	Number C-M.	Sentenced to Death.	Executed.	Flogged.	Imprisoned.	Pardoned.
dwich.	25	15	6	2	9	—
ntague.	16	9	4	—	6	4
rector.	12	—	—	—	—	12
exible.	41	—	—	—	—	41
nmouth.	51	11	6	4	4	29
liqueux.	3	—	—	—	—	2
ndard.	28	10	3	3	7	15
n.	46	—	—	—	—	46
ssau.	20	—	—	—	—	19
ulse.	6	—	—	—	—	4
ampus.	6	5	3	—	1	—
serpine.	7	—	—	—	—	7
lliant.	14	—	—	—	—	13
.	2	(*Note :* " Both have deserted.")	—	—	—	—
ampion.	22	—	—	—	—	22
net.	(General pardon for the whole of the crew.)			—	—	—
iphone.	11	—	—	—	—	11
lades.	8	—	—	—	—	8
an.	11	—	—	—	—	11
caster.	(General pardon for the whole of the crew.)			—	—	—
pector.	9	—	—	—	—	5
tal.	7	—	—	—	—	7
.	(Ordered to be tried at Portsmouth.)			—	—	42
pard.	41	9	7	—	2	32
amemnon.	13	—	—	—	—	13
ger.	13	—	—	—	—	12
Total	412	59	29	9	29	

ote.—The floggings ranged from 40 to 380 lashes, the latter being inflicted on a sea- of the *Monmouth*; the imprisonment from one to eight years. The number of ons are those given in an Admiralty document, dated 16 Dec. 1797, and would include e pardoned after the battle of Camperdown (Ad. 3/137). Thomas McCann, of the dwich, one of those sentenced to death, had his sentence commuted to transportation ife.

277

NOTES TO PART ONE

1. Spencer, II, 126.
2. A.R., 219.
3. Quotations from Ad. 1/5125.
4. Gill, 11 n.
5. Spencer, II, 105, 107.
6. Tunstall, 5.
7. Spencer, II, 108.
8. Hannay, II, 359.
9. Masefield, 123.
10. *Oglethorpe*, by F. H. Church, 1932, p. 29.
11. Gill, 10. Based on letter of Bridport to Nepean, 17th April. Ad. 1/107.
12. Letter from Lieut. Philip Beaver to Mrs. Gillies, 17/iv/1797, *Naval Misc.*, Vol. I (N.R.S. 20), p. 408.
13. Weyman Brown, Muster Book of the *Minotaur*. Ad. 36/12829.
14. Ad. 1/5125.
15. Ad. 1/5125.
16. Ad. 1/5125.
17. Ad. 1/5125.
18. Howe in Parliament, 3rd May. Quoted by Gill, 8.
19. Spencer to Bridport, 14th April 1797. Holograph. Ad. 3/136. This letter has not before been noticed.
20. "Review of *Spencer Papers*," *Edinburgh Review*, July 1925, by David Hannay. The remarks refer to the Pakenham letter, and Spencer's answer.
21. Petition to Parliament, 18th(?) April. Ad. 1/5125.
22. *Ibid.*
23. Ad. 1/1022.
24. *Account of the Mutinies at Spithead*, etc. This book, by Patton, was privately printed. The Admiralty copy has been consulted.
25. Gill, 17 n.
26. Ad. 1/107.
27. See p. 24. From Ad. 3/136.
28. Neale, 13. Brenton, I, 278.
29. Ad. 1/107.
30. "Meteorology," from *The Gentleman's Magazine*, 1797.
31. Gill, 17.
32. A.R., 221.
33. Ad. 1/5125. Neale, 13.
34. Gill, 22.
35. Quoted by Gill, 23.
36. Ad. 1/107.

37. Tunstall, 13.
38. Gill, 24, 25.
39. P.R.O. Index, 4829.
40. *The Times*, 12th May 1797.
41. Information from the Muster Books. See Appendix I.
42. Ad. 1/107.
43. Ad. 1/5125. Papers of the *Queen Charlotte*.
44. Patton, 5.
45. Ad. 1/5125. Papers of the *Queen Charlotte*.
46. Ad. 1/107.
47. Neale, 17.
48. Beaver to Mrs. Gillies, *Naval Misc.*, Vol. I, p. 142.
49. Gill, 26.
50. Hannay, *loc. cit.* Corbett, Introduction to *Spencer Papers*, II. Obituary notice in *Gentleman's Magazine*, Dec. 1834.
51. See Appendix II.
52. Neale, 5. The account mainly from Masefield.
53. Masefield, 152. It may be noted that lime-juice had been introduced in 1795, but its use was scanty.
54. A.R., State Papers, 382.
55. *Spencer Papers*, II, 116.
56. Gardner to Bridport, 16th April. Ad. 1/107.
57. *Joseph Farington Diary*, I, 223-4.
58. Spencer's Official Diary. Printed by Gill, 372.
59. Any account.
60. Neale, 35. Gill, 38 n. A.R., 224.
61. Ad. 1/5125. Not dated; but it seems plausible to place it here.
62. See Gill, 373.
63. *Spencer Papers*, II, 111.
64. *Ibid.*, 115. For an amusing account of Camelford see Tunstall, 221 *seq.*
65. 12th May.
66. *Correspondence* of E. Burke and W. Windham (Roxburghe Club), 1910, p. 236.
67. To Mrs. Gillies, *Naval Misc.*, Vol. I (N.R.S. 20), p. 410 *seq.*
68. *London Chronicle*. Letter from Portsmouth, 19th April.
69. Neale, 16.
70. Add. MSS., 35197, f. 109.
71. *Ibid.*, f. 115.
72. Quoted by Gill, 39.
73. A.R., State Papers, 384.
74. Collingwood, 58.
75. Ad. 1/5125.
76. Ad. 1/107.
77. *Naval History*, 1837, II, 65.

78. Masefield, 59.
79. Masefield, Chapter VI, *passim*.
80. At the end of the mutiny. Quoted by Gill, 278.
81. *Recollections*, by J. A. Gardner.
82. All three. Ad. 1/107.
83. Ad. 1/5125.
84. Ad. 1/107.
85. Gill, 41-44. Neale, 46-52.
86. *London Chronicle* of that date.
87. A.R., 229.
88. Gill, 374.
89. Quoted by Gill, 91.
90. Add. MSS., 35197, f. 112.
91. *London Chronicle*. Letter from Plymouth, 29th April. Letters from Portsmouth, 30th April and 2nd May
92. Hannay, II, 364.
93. Neale, 241, gives the whole.
94. Camperdown, 98 *seq*.
95. Neale, 54.
96. Camperdown, 101.
97. See Gill, 53.
98. Patton, 18.
99. Gill, 50.
100. Muster Book of the *Mars*.
101. Hannay, II, 366.
102. Gill, 55.
103. Ad. 1/107.
104. Gill, 56.
105. Gill, 94.
106. Quoted by Gill, 59.
107. Letter from Bover's sister to Sir John Barrow, printed in his *Life of Anson* (1839), Preface.
108. Colpoys to Lady Louisa Lennox. H.M.C. Bathurst, 713.
109. Whether of 1st May or of that day is not known.
110. Bover to his family, *Gentleman's Magazine*, July 1843, 32.
111. Accounts are confused. The one here is taken, as well as from the sources already quoted, from Hannay, Tunstall, and Neale; and especially from Colpoys' letter to Nepean of 8/v/97. See Ralfe, *Naval Biography*, III, 172-4.
112. Gardner, *Recollections*, 193. No date, but it must have been in the early morning of the 8th that this happened. Gardner quoted the men's letter from memory, and got the time wrong.
113. Ad. 1/107.
114. Gill, 67.
115. Printed by Gill, 70.

116. Neale, 65.
117. Ad. 1/107.
118. Ad. 1/107.
119. Ad. 1/107.
120. Ad. 1/107.
121. Patton, 16.
122. *London Chronicle*. Portsmouth Letter, 8th May.
123. Neale, 65.
124. *Gentleman's Magazine*, July 1843, 32.
125. Add. MSS., 35197.
126. Neale, 66-89.
127. Ralfe, *Naval Biography*, III, 177.
128. Preface to Barrow's *Life of Anson*.
129. *Correspondence* of Burke and Windham (Roxburghe Club), 1910, 244-5, 10th May 1797.
130. *Pitt and the Great War*, by Holland Rose, 313.
131. Add. MSS., 35197, f. 174.
132. *Buckingham Memoirs*, 380, 381, 9th and 11th May.
133. For Graham's letters and reports see Ad. 1/4172.
134. Neale, 120-1.
135. Barrow, chap. x, *passim*; and Gill, vii.
136. Howe to the Duke of Portland. Barrow, 342.
137. *London Chronicle*, 16th May.
138. Ad. 1/1022.
139. Admiral Young to Sir Hugh Seymour, 26/v/98, Barrow, 339.
140. *Gentleman's Magazine*, July 1843, 33.
141. Neale, 123.
142. Barrow, 337.
143. *London Chronicle*. Letter from Portsmouth, 14th May.
144. Quoted by Neale, 124. That place for the whole incident, which the critical reader can accept or not as he pleases.
145. Gill, 131.
146. Neale, 126, and *London Chronicle*, 15th May.
147. Gill, 80.
148. *London Chronicle*, 15th May. Gill, 81.
149. For the whole eight stanzas see Firth, *Naval Ballads and Songs* (Navy Records Society, 33), 280.
150. A.R., State Papers, 391.
151. Muster Books.
152. Gill, 132.

NOTES TO PART TWO

1. For references, and records of Parker's life, see Appendix IV.
2. Ad. 1/727.
3. Admiral Hotham's Papers, *Pages and Portraits from the Past*, by Mrs. Stirling, 1919.
4. Cunningham, 84.
5. Neale, 131.
6. Ad. 3/137. Papers of the *Champion*.
7. Mosse to Buckner. Ad. 1/727.
8. Cunningham, 4.
9. Ad. 1/727. Papers of the *Repulse*.
10. Parker at his trial. Neale, 268.
11. Ad. 1/727. Papers of the *Repulse*.
12. Cunningham, 13.
13. Ad. 3/137.
14. Ad. 1/727. Papers of the *Repulse*.
15. *Ibid*. Quoted by Gill, 389.
16. *Ibid*. Quoted by Gill, 387.
17. "Dying Declaration," see Appendix V.
18. Cunningham, 11.
19. Ad. 1/5486.
20. Ad. 3/137.
21. *Ibid*.
22. Gill, 109.
23. Mackaness, *Life of Bligh*, II, 37.
24. Ad. 1/1516. No. 323.
25. Cunningham, 19.
26. "Dying Declaration."
27. Camperdown, 113.
28. A.R., State Papers, 385.
29. Ad. 1/727.
30. Camperdown, 385.
31. A.R., State Papers, 387.
32. Ad. 3/137. Papers of the *Champion*.
33. Ad. 1/727.
34. Camperdown, 120.
35. "Dying Declaration."
36. Cunningham, 28-31.
37. Neale, 162.
38. Ad. 1/727.
39. *London Chronicle*, 25th and 30th May.
40. Ad. 3/137. Papers of the *Champion*.

41. Ad. 1/3685, and Gill, 112.
42. Grey to Dundas. Ad. 1/4172.
43. Ad. 1/727. Papers of the *Repulse*.
44. Gill, 150.
45. Schomberg, III, 33; and "Dying Declaration."
46. Cunningham, 20; but he misdates it.
47. Ad. 1/727. 24th May.
48. Cunningham, 32.
49. Gill, 148.
50. Spencer, II, 133.
51. Barrow's *Howe*, 345 and 347.
52. See A.R., Appendix, 388.
53. Spencer, II, 136.
54. Neale, 169.
55. Ad. 3/137. Letters of Spencer and Marsden to Nepean. Also Gill, 153. Parker's remarks are from A.R., Appendix, 143, and are suspect. Cunningham's account can be ignored.
56. Gill, 154.
57. Ad. 3/137. Spencer and Marsden to Nepean.
58. *London Chronicle*, 2nd June.
59. Camperdown, 127; and Ad. 3/137. Letters *cit.*
60. Ad. 3/137.
61. Ad. 1/4172. Grey to Dundas, 25th June. Allardyce's *Memoir of Keith*, 139. Keith to Spencer, 2nd June.
62. Cunningham, 39 *seq.*, and 132.
63. *London Chronicle*, 30th May.
64. Gill, 161.
65. Watson's evidence at Parker's trial.
66. Except where otherwise stated, the facts and quotations in this chapter are from Camperdown, chapter v.
67. Ad. 1/727. Papers of the *Repulse*.
68. Gill, 171.
69. Spencer, II, 134. Duncan to Spencer, 26th May.
70. Ad. 1/2017.
71. Lansdowne MSS., National Maritime Museum, Greenwich. By courtesy of the Trustees.
72. Brenton, I, 281.
73. Spencer, II, 137.
74. Brenton, I, 283.
75. Henry Carew, Lansdowne MSS.
76. Ad. 1/727. Papers of the *Repulse*.
77. Ad. 1/2017.
78. Henry Carew, Lansdowne MSS., and Ad. 1/1448, letter from Captain Alms to the Admiralty, 31st May.
79. Ad. 1/727. Papers of the *Repulse*.

80. Ad. 1/727. Quoted by Gill, 179.
81. Spencer, II, 172. Parker's Declaration: not "Dying Declaration."
82. Ad. 1/727.
83. *London Chronicle*, Saturday, 3rd June.
84. Henry Carew, Lansdowne MSS.
85. *London Chronicle*, 3rd June. Cunningham, 57.
86. Ad. 1/727.
87. Report, H.O., 42, Vol. 41.
88. Navy Records Society, Vol. 40, p. 295.
89. Neale, 272-5.
90. Printed by Neale, 187.
91. Printed by Neale, 194.
92. Ad. 1/727.
93. Neale, 199.
94. A.R., 242.
95. Gill, 198-9.
96. Gill, 201-2. Neale, 206. Cunningham, 105.
97. Neale, 200.
98. Gill, 350.
99. Cunningham, 95.
100. Ad. 1/5486.
101. Ad. 1/5486.
102. Spencer, II, 144.
103. Gill, 184.
104. Cunningham, 63.
105. Ad. 1/727.
106. Ad. 1/727.
107. Ad. 1/5486. Northesk's evidence at the trial.
108. Schomberg, III, 27; and A.R., Appendix, 145.
109. Ad. 1/5486. Produced at Parker's trial.
110. Ad. 51/1173. Mosse's log of the *Sandwich*.
111. Ad. 1/727. Papers of the *Repulse*.
112. See Gill, 218. Ad. 1/5125. Petitions.
113. *London Chronicle*, 4th June.
114. Gill, 221.
115. Report from Select Committee. See Bibliography.
116. Gill, 222-5.
117. Gill, 230.
118. Brenton, I, 297.
119. Ad. 3/137. Papers of the *Champion*.
120. Brenton, I, 285.
121. Trinity House Minutes.
122. Gill, 196.
123. Neale, 225.
124. Report from Select Committee. See Bibliography.

125. Keith MSS., National Maritime Museum. Keith to Dundas, 27th June. Another copy, Ad. 1/4172.
126. Spencer, II, 149.
127. Ad. 51/1173. Mosse's log.
128. These are printed by Neale, 207 and 211.
129. Cunningham, 65.
130. Gill, 231.
131. Cunningham, 73.
132. Henry Carew, Lansdowne MSS.
133. Neale, 227-8.
134. Spencer, II, 151.
135. Cunningham, 60. Schomberg, III. 24 n. Hannay, 377.
136. Neale, 232.
137. Brenton, I, 290.
138. It is impossible to say what Parker did exactly; the account given here is made up from evidence given at his trial. See Neale, 261-301 *passim*; also Brenton, 291.
139. *Granville Private Correspondence*, I, 152. Lady Sutherland to Lady Stafford, 10th June.
140. Brenton, I, 292.
141. Ad. 1/3092.
142. Gill, 391.
143. Spencer, II, 151.
144. Ad. 1/2017.
145. Ad. 1/2017.
146. *London Chronicle*, 13th June.
147. Ad. 3/137. Nepean to Buckner, 11th June.
148. *London Chronicle*. Letter from Chatham, 11th June.
149. Ad. 3/137.
150. Pellew's *Life of Lord Sidmouth*, 1847, I, 189.
151. *Spencer Papers*, II, 156.
152. Cunningham, 92-4.
153. Gill, 243.
154. Neale, 246.
155. *London Chronicle*. Letter of the 13th.
156. A.R., Appendix, 146.
157. Neale, 276-7.
158. "Dying Declaration." See Appendix V.
159. A.R., Appendix, 146-8. *European Magazine*, 1797, pp. 60-4.
160. Neale, 248.
161. Gill, 243.
162. Cunningham, 82.
163. A.R., Appendix, 149.
164. Report, H.O., 42, Vol. 41.
165. Both quoted by Gill, 248.

166. Ad. 1/5486. Account of Parker's trial.
167. Spencer, II, 159.
168. The account is taken from A.R., Appendix, 159.
169. See Appendix VI.
170. Patterson's *Sir Francis Burdett*, 1931, Vol. I, p. 66.
171. *European Magazine*, 1797, p. 355.
172. Camperdown, 220.
173. *Gentleman's Magazine*, 1797, II, 977.
174. *The King's Own*, 1830. Everyman edition, 1924, p. 1.
175. *Despatches and Letters*, I, 76, 12th July; I, 325, 11th Sept.; II, 402.
176. See *England in the Reign of Charles II*, by David Ogg, 1934, Vol. I, chapter vii.
177. Spencer, II, 157.
178. "Review of *Camperdown's Life of Duncan*," *Edinburgh Review*, July 1898.
179. Spencer, II, 156. Letter of Thomas Pearce.
180. H.O., 42, Vol. 41.
181. Keith to Dundas, *loc. cit.* Keith MSS.
182. *Despatches and Letters*, II, 409.
183. *Memoirs of Sir Samuel Romilly*, written by himself. Under date 1st April 1806.
184. *Ibid.*, 3rd April.
185. *Loc. cit.*
186. Brenton, I, 287.
187. Sir John Briggs, in *Naval Administrations, 1827-1892*, 1897, p. 68.
188. Ad. 1/4172, 27th June 1797.
189. Sidney Knock, in *Clear Lower Deck*, 1932, p. 148. See also pp. 14-21.

BIBLIOGRAPHY

MANUSCRIPT SOURCES

(i) Admiralty Documents in the Public Record Office:—

Muster Books of the various ships at Spithead, 1797: Ad. 36/11978; 11704; 11730; 11769; 11731; 11715; 12345; 12233; 11759; 11870; 14793; 12825; 14344; 13031; 12482; 12829; 11911; 11879; 11880; 12572; 12747; 12748.

Muster Book of the *Sandwich*: Ad. 36/11621; 11622.

Admirals' Despatches

Channel Fleet. Howe, Bridport. Ad. 1/107-110.
Portsmouth. Ad. 1/1021-6.
North Sea. Ad. 1/524.
Plymouth. Ad. 1/811-2.
Nore. Buckner. Ad. 1/727-8.
Downs. Peyton, etc. Ad. 1/668.

Captains' Letters

Lord Northesk, etc. Ad. 1/2226.
Captain Knight, etc. Ad. 1/2017.
Captain Mosse, etc. Ad. 1/2133-4.
Captain Bligh, etc. Ad. 1/1516.
Captain Ferris, etc. Ad. 1/1797.
Captain Raper, etc. Ad. 1/2400.
Captain Cunningham, etc. Ad. 1/1623.
Captain Neale, etc. Ad. 1/2226.
Captain Alms, etc. Ad. 1/1448.
Captain Hargood, etc. Ad. 1/1916.

Lieutenants' Letters

Lieutenant Robb, etc. Ad. 1/3092.

Captains' Logs

H.M.S. *Sandwich*. Ad. 51/1173.
H.M.S. *Inflexible*. Ad. 51/1202.

Solicitors' Letter

1797. Ad. 1/3685.

Secretary of State Letters

April-June 1797. Ad. 1/4172.

Nore Courts Martial

Reports. Ad. 1/5486.

Courts Martial

Reports. April-July 1797. Ad. 1/5339 and 5340.

Admiralty Board

Rough Minutes. Jan.-June 1797. Ad. 3/136-7.

Petitions to the Admiralty

1793-1797. Ad. 1/5125.

Pay Books

Ad. 35/721.

(ii) Home Office Papers, Public Record Office:—
    H.O., 42, Vol. 41.
(iii) British Museum Additional Manuscripts:—
    Add. MSS., 35197. Bridport Papers.
(iv) National Maritime Museum, Greenwich:—
    Keith MSS.
(v) Trinity House. Minutes.

PRINTED SOURCES

Allardyce, A., *Memoir of Lord Keith*, 1882.

Annual Register (Rivington's edition), 1797. (A.R.) (Not to be confused with Longmans'.)

Barrow, Sir John, *Life of Earl Howe*, 1838. *Life of Lord Anson*, 1839.

Bover, Peter, Letters, *Gentleman's Magazine*, 1843, II, 33-5.

Brenton, E. P., *Naval History of Great Britain*, 1837.

Burke, Edmund, *Correspondence of Burke and Windham*, edited J. P. Gilson. Roxburghe Club, 1910.

Burke, P., *Celebrated Naval and Military Trials*, 1876.

Callender, G., *Sea Kings of Britain: Keppel to Nelson*, 1934.

Camperdown, Earl of, *Life of Admiral Duncan*, 1898.

Clowes, Sir W. Laird, *The Royal Navy*, Vol. IV, 1899. "The French Share in the Mutiny at the Nore" (*Cornhill Magazine*, N.S., Vol. 13, 1902).

Colpoys, Admiral E. G., Letter to Vice-Admiral Sir T.-B. Martin, 1825.

Cunningham, Admiral Sir Charles, *Narrative of the Occurrences that took place during the Mutiny at the Nore*, 1829.

Field, Colonel C., "The Marines in the Great Naval Mutinies" (*Royal United Service Institute Journal*, 62, 117).

Gentleman's Magazine, 1797, 1843, II.

Gill, Conrad, *The Naval Mutinies of 1797*, 1913.

Granville, Earl, *Private Correspondence*, Vol. I, 1916.

Hannay, David, *Short History of the Royal Navy*, II, 1912.

Historical Manuscripts Commission (*H.M.C.*):—

> Bathurst MSS., 1923.
> Fortescue MSS., Vol. III, 1899.

Hutchinson, J. H., *The Press Gang*, 1913.

London Chronicle, 1797.

Mackaness, G., *Life of Admiral Bligh*, Vol. II, 1931.

Masefield, John, *Sea Life in Nelson's Time*, 1905.

Moreau de Jonnes, A., *Aventures de Guerre*, Second Edition, 1893. Translated by General Abdy, 1920.

Navy Records Society:—

> Vol. 20. *Naval Miscellany*, Vol. I, Lieut. Beaver's Letters.
> Vol. 31. J. A. Gardner, *Recollections*, 1906.
> Vol. 40. *Naval Miscellany*, Vol. II, Watson's letter to Admiral Digby.
> Vol. 48. Private Papers of Earl Spencer (*Spencer Papers*), Vol. II, 1914.

Neale, W. J., *History of the Mutiny at Spithead and the Nore*, 1842.

Parker, Richard (Anonymous Works):—

> *An Impartial Account of the Life of R. Parker.* London, 1797.
> *Trial, Life, and Anecdotes of R. Parker.* Manchester, 1797.
> *Whole Trial and Defence of R. Parker.* London, 1797.

Parliamentary History, Vol. 33, 1797.

Parliamentary Report. Report from the Committee of Secrecy, 15th March 1799. (Reprinted in *Reports from Committees of the H. of C.*, Vol. 10, pp. 789-826, 1803.)

> Report from the Select Committee on Foreign Trade. H. of C., 23rd July 1822.

Patton, Admiral Philip, *Account of the Mutinies at Spithead and St. Helens in 1797*, N.D.

Ralfe, J., *Naval Biography of Great Britain*, Vol. III, 1828.

Rose, J. Holland, *William Pitt and the Great War*, 1911.

Schomberg, I., *Naval Chronology*, Vol. III, 1802.

Stanhope, Earl, *Life of Pitt*, Vol. III, 1862.

Stirling, Mrs. A. M. W., *Pages from the Past* (Private Papers of Sir W. Hotham), Vol. I, 1919.

Tunstall, B., *Flights of Naval Genius*, 1930.

Windham, William, *Windham Papers*, ed. Lord Rosebery, Vol. II, 1913.

INDEX

Adams, Michael, Delegate of the *Duke*, 262

Admiralty, Lords Commissioners of, petitions and letters to, 17, 28, 30–31; at Portsmouth, 42–51; supposed plot to kidnap, 52; attend Cabinet meeting, 67; seamen's mistrust of, 77–79, 205; regard outbreak at the Nore as of little consequence, 137; requested to visit Sheerness, 141; demands of seamen at the Nore to, 141–146; refuse to visit Sheerness, 149; visit Sheerness, 154–159; stop provisions at the Nore, 162; seamen's petition to, 265–266; suggest that Duncan should attack the Nore Fleet, 177; letter of a seaman to, 201; mentioned, 8–12, 23, 27

Allen, Thomas, Delegate of the *Mars*, 262

Anderson, William, Delegate of the *Duke*, 35, 262

Appleyard, Delegate at the Nore, 214

Arden, Lord, 7, 42, 155

Articles of War, 46, 62, 81, 138, 143, 246–247

Bank of England, 5

Bantry Bay, 4, 208

Bardo, a seaman, 165–167

Bear and Ragged Staff (Inn or Tavern at Portsmouth), 28

Beaver, Lieutenant Philip, 53, 65

Bedford, Captain, 38

Bedford, Duke of, 6, 75–76

Bell, Surgeon, 65

Berry, Charles, Delegate of the *Ramillies*, 263

Berwick, James, Delegate of the *Defence*, 263

Bethell, John, Delegate of the *Glory*, 262

Blake, John, 150

Bligh, Captain William, letter to the Admiralty, 138–139; Admiralty instructions to, 161; at Yarmouth, 176–177; mentioned, 8, 170

Blythe, James, Delegate of the *Mars*, 262

Books, supplied to R.N., 15 *n*

Bover, Lieutenant Peter, and mutiny on the *London*, 83–97, 112, 268

Braemar, 271

Brenton, Lieutenant, 179–180

Brest, 4, 39, 76, 80

Bridport, Admiral Lord, letter to Spencer, 29–30; letter to Nepean, 30–31; appeals to seamen, 34; negotiations at Portsmouth, 41–51; reads royal proclamation, 67; letter to Admiralty, 81; Spencer's letters to, 95, 98; Pitt's letter to, 99; his reply to Pitt, 99; sails with Channel Fleet, 118; mentioned, 4, 7, 22, 75, 77, 79, 90, 115, 269

Bristol, 4

Bromfield, Captain, of the Trinity House, removes buoys, 210

Brown, Weyman, 20, 279

Brutality in the Navy, 8–10, 59–66, 110, 130, 247

Buckner, Vice-Admiral Charles, negotiations with Nore mutineers, 140–146, 148, 151–152, 155–159, 197, 207; Parker's letter to, 191; mentioned, 127,